To Dakar

21 DAYS ACROSS NORTH AFRICA BY MOTORCYCLE

and Back

LAWRENCE HACKING

with Wil De Clercq

ECW Press

Published by ECW Press
2120 Queen Street East, Suite 200, Toronto, Ontario, Canada M4E 1E2
416.694.3348 / info@ecwpress.com

LIBRARY AND ARCHIVES CANADA CATALOGUING IN PUBLICATION

Hacking, Lawrence
To Dakar and back / Lawrence Hacking with Wil De Clercq.

ISBN 978-1-55022-808-3

1. Hacking, Lawrence—Travel. 2. Paris-Dakar Rally. 3. Motorcycle
racing—Africa. 4. Motorcycle racing—Europe. I. De Clercq, Wil
II. Title.

GV1034.82.P37H33 2008   796.7'5092   C2007-904145-0

The publication of *To Dakar and Back* has been generously supported by
the Canada Council for the Arts which last year invested $20.1 million in
writing and publishing throughout Canada, by the Ontario Arts Council, by
the Government of Ontario through Ontario Book Publishing Tax Credit,
by the OMDC Book Fund, an initiative of the Ontario Media Development
Corporation, and by the Government of Canada through the Book
Publishing Industry Development Program (BPIDP).

Canada Council   Conseil des Arts   Canadä   ONTARIO ARTS COUNCIL
for the Arts   du Canada   CONSEIL DES ARTS DE L'ONTARIO

Developing editor: Michael Holmes
Cover and text design: Tania Craan
Typesetting: Gail Nina
Cover and spine photo: Maindru
Second printing by Transcontinental

PRINTED AND BOUND IN CANADA

ECW PRESS
ecwpress.com

Table of Contents

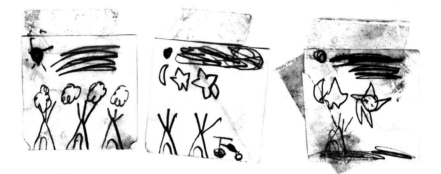

For Mia, with her drawings

Acknowledgments

Any attempt at the Dakar takes an incredible amount of support — it's impossible to do it on your own. I would like to acknowledge the many family members, friends and companies that backed my effort to get to the starting line: you all helped me over that first hurdle. Since 2001 I have been involved in many other significant projects, and through thick and thin my friends have stood beside me. You know who you are, and I thank all of you sincerely.

My wife, Françoise, has the greatest spirit of anyone I know. Without her I can't imagine what path my life would have taken. I know it wouldn't be nearly as enjoyable, interesting or exciting. Thanks to her this book became possible.

Without Wil De Clercq *To Dakar and Back* would still be pages of notes sitting in a filing box beside my desk. He took that material and applied his craft. Thank you, Wil, for accurately conveying the message.

Thanks to the good people at ECW Press for believing.

Foreword

I awoke in a daze, listless and disoriented. Harsh sunlight streamed through the tent's walls, nearly blinding my eyes. It seemed like I had dreamt the whole night that I was struggling through the desert on my bike, on foot, and even on camelback. I'd had very little sleep and I didn't want to get up. I could have used a blast of smelling salts to shake me out of my stupor but I knew I had to persevere and tackle the next stage. It was not a good frame of mind to be in to take on 535 kilometres of African desert. Everyone was in agreement that Stage 13, of which 513 clicks was competitive, would be one of the toughest ever seen in a Dakar. But "toughest," like "worse," is a relative term. I didn't want to think that anything could be tougher than what I had just endured.

The route we were to follow looped from Tidjika and back. It was the second of the marathon legs, in which no assistance from chase trucks was permitted. Not that that meant much to the privateers who had no team infrastructure to assist them in the first place. Once the special kicked off, we would have to navigate our way through a pass over a cliff, run along the base of the cliff, and climb back up on the plateau through the infamous Nega Pass. In between, everything the desert has to offer would have to be dealt with, including rutted and fast-winding tracks, and steep, soft dunes. Yeah, okay, this probably would be tougher than anything else I had to tackle so far. It wasn't an inviting prospect. I dragged myself out of my sleeping bag, got suited up, a challenge in itself, and quickly ate breakfast. Feeling like some kind of automaton, I crawled onto my motorcycle and rode out of the bivouac on the same road southwest of the airport to where Stage 12 had ended the night before. The timing tent served as the start line for the special. It was only a three-kilometre jaunt from the bivouac to the start and I was wishing it was a lot longer: I needed some time to thoroughly wake up so I could concentrate on riding. I felt I was too rushed and too tired to ride with a strong enough focus to guide the Honda through the hazards I would face. Something didn't feel right. Maybe I got dressed too quickly and didn't take the time to make sure everything was fitting right. Or some clothing was bunched up, or my toolbag was loose and hanging too low. Whatever the case, I was receiving warning signs that I should have heeded. Perhaps I should have taken the time to settle down and take a different attitude towards the day. I didn't dare admit to myself that I wanted to throw in the towel. Fortunately, I couldn't give myself the right excuse to do so. There was a carrot in front of me: the end of the rally at Dakar.

Only a few riders were gathered around the start area, which I thought was rather strange because there should have been quite a few more. I didn't have much time to dwell on it as I was directed straight up to leave. I was a few minutes late for my designated departure. It was hot and the sun hung high in a cloudless blue sky. The course followed a rocky road set by a bulldozer blade through the flat black rocks and sand. I rode fast but had trouble focusing on the terrain and corners. As usual, with the weight of the full fuel tanks, the bike was unwieldy and it was a struggle to stay on two wheels. Everything was exacerbated and exaggerated by fatigue. I had a bad feeling this wasn't going to be my best day. All my internal alarms were sounding, warning me to slow down or risk making a costly mistake. A little farther along, the trail wound past a dry riverbed that meandered in between short palm trees. Prior to this point I knew I was making some mistakes that played on my mental strength. I was riding like an absolute beginner, making errors from which I barely recovered. Then it happened: just 22 kilometres out on the course I missed a corner and slid across some rocks like an out-of-control railway car. The bike hit the ground hard. So did I! This was too absurd to comprehend. This was an error a rookie would make, not an experienced rider. I slowly got back on my feet and if I could have kicked myself I would have. I ached all over but fortunately I wasn't seriously injured. My eyelids weighed a ton: I could hardly keep my eyes open. I laboured to pick up my bike, which had never seemed so heavy before. From what I could see, other than a few more dents and scrapes, it had sustained no major damage. This could have been much worse. Being too tired to focus has cost many a rider his racing career or worse, his life. Maybe thirteen was bad luck after all; or maybe, considering I wasn't hurt and the bike was still intact, thirteen was good luck. . . .

This book is about a unique and incredible experience: my participation in the world-renowned Paris-Dakar Rally. It is an undertaking few people ever have the opportunity to experience or, in most cases, would even want to. I took part in this monster rally in 2001, when I was forty-six years old. My means of travel was a motorcycle. Despite tackling this marathon race at such a relatively advanced age, I not only finished the event, I had the honour of being the first Canadian to do so. Paris-Dakar is without question the most arduous and notorious rally on the planet. It is considered one of the world's top five adventures, in the same league as climbing Mount Everest. The 2001 edition traversed two countries in Europe and four in Africa, with a total distance of nearly 10,000 kilometres. To put that into perspective, consider taking a motorcycle trip from Toronto to Vancouver and back again, most of it off-road through some of the most brutal terrain imaginable. Then, when you get back to Toronto, you've actually got about 500 kilometres more to go, enough to travel on to Quebec City.

The Paris to Dakar Rally is not only intriguing; if its vortex grabs you it is all-encompassing. According to the organizers, the Dakar is based on two essential values, courage and endurance. These are played out in a grandiose setting: the Sahara, the most beautiful and mythical of all deserts. The effects of the rally before, during and after are like a tattoo imprinted on one's mind. It can never be erased and becomes the standard everything else is measured against. For better or worse, the Dakar alters the life of all who fall under its spell. This unique rally offers the individual an opportunity to get to know and understand him- or herself on a level only such epic undertakings are capable of providing.

The Dakar is in a continuous flux: it is something intangible yet very real. Paris-Dakar offers a combination of moments that grind their way into the psyches of all who take part in it. Not just the motorcyclists, racecar and truck drivers, but the event's staff, volunteers, sponsors, and accompanying journalists. More than 1,500 people were involved in Paris-Dakar 2001. The inhabitants of the areas the rally passes through are also affected. For many, especially in Africa, the rally is the highlight of an otherwise routine and uneventful year. For the millions of people who follow the race on television from the comfort of their homes, Paris-Dakar is pure entertainment, the ultimate reality show. For the companies that sponsor the event, race teams, or individuals, Paris-Dakar provides unprecedented exposure. No matter how you roll the dice, Paris-Dakar is a gruelling enterprise. It is three weeks of blood, sweat and tears — hell and paradise on earth all rolled into one. The Dakar Rally encompasses many complex levels. These boil down to a lowest common denominator: a stage from which its participants can shout to the world, "This is who I am. This is how I accept a challenge. This is how I perform under extreme stress and impossible conditions." While Paris-Dakar is many things to many people, it is first and foremost an extravagant motorsport circus that challenges its participations to the nth degree. It is about the basic tenets of life: respect, appreciation, sincerity, compassion and fair play. While self-importance, image, deceit, and avarice do filter into the Dakar — as they do into all areas of existence — for most of the rallyists, dignity and common sense prevail.

From a business point of view Paris-Dakar is a marketing juggernaut that not only pushes the dream of good old-fashioned adventure, it sells everything from cars to motorcycles, headache remedies, toiletries, soft drinks, alcoholic beverages, gasoline, oil, televisions and computers. Every imaginable product has been plugged into the massive and far-reaching marketing power of Paris-Dakar. Last but not least, Paris-Dakar is a paradox of cultures: on the one side we find excess at its most extreme; on the other, a simple centuries-old lifestyle. En route from glitzy Paris to fabled Dakar the rally swallows up and spits out casualties — competitors and otherwise — for the entire world to see. Perhaps what is most captivating about the Paris-Dakar Rally is the human drama that defines it: men and women from all walks of life mixing it up with corporately supported motorsport professionals. Although no two Paris-Dakars are exactly alike, one thing they all have in common is that they are fraught with excitement, danger and the unexpected.

In June of 2000 I met Hubert Auriol, the director of the Paris-Dakar Rally and former winner of the event in both the two- and four-wheeled classes. He gave me a bemused look and asked me how old I was. I knew exactly what Auriol was thinking. Motorcycling, whether competitive or recreational, is all about experience. If you feel you know everything there is to know, you're courting disaster. When all was said and done Paris-Dakar reconfirmed exactly who I thought I was and what I was capable of doing. It also reconfirmed the notion that one can never do enough research and planning.

Lawrence Hacking
Georgetown, ON
September 2007

Chapter 1

The rally
to end all rallies

▬ ▬ ▬ ▬ ▬ ▬ ▬ ▬ ▬ ▬ ▬

On January 14, 1977, Jean-Michel Sine, the organizer of the Abidjan to Nice Rally, found a solitary Thierry Sabine perched on a rock in the vast Libyan Sahara Desert, one of the most remote places on earth. Sabine, who was taking part in the rally, had become disoriented near the border that separates Niger from Libya, spending three days and two nights alone in the formidable Sahara. The young Frenchman had been unable to find his bearings; his only hope was that somebody would come across him in this desolate place. He also had had plenty of time to think about the things he would do once rescued. Whether Sabine knew then where this intimate meeting with the sands of the desert was to lead, and what influence he was about to have on the world, especially the world of motorsport, is pure speculation. Here, in the shadow of the massive Emi Fazzan Mountain, Sabine conceived a dream that would make history, an idea that would become the Paris-Dakar Rally. In his mind, Paris-Dakar would be the rally to end all rallies. He would turn the topography of Northern Africa into the adventure of a lifetime for anyone brave or crazy enough to attempt it. The brave and the crazy answered Sabine's call as if the rally he had envisioned was something they had been waiting for all their lives. A total of 170 entrants signed up for what was billed as the ultimate adventure; 90 of them were motorcyclists. The competitors who tackled the inaugural Paris-Dakar in 1979 faced adversity like nothing they had ever encountered. They spoke of civilizations so removed from modernity it was like stepping back hundreds of years in time. They recounted tales that ran the gamut of extremes and dangerous predicaments only a rally like the Dakar could produce. Less than half finished the rally. The Frenchman Cyril Neveu won the event aboard a Yamaha. Neveu, who would go on to victory four more times, received strong competition from a Honda-mounted Philippe Vassard. Vassard would try the rally again but never succeeded at winning it.

In France, the larger-than-life profile projected by the Paris-Dakar Rally became a sensation and a matter of national pride overnight. Although it would take time to capture the imagination of people worldwide, Paris-Dakar gradually became one of the most anticipated motorsport events of the year. Since 1979, it has attracted more than 3,000 adventurers from all walks of life. The men and women who have taken up the Dakar challenge have at least one thing in common: a desire to measure themselves against like-minded individuals and the desolate sands of the Sahara. The rally has attracted participants from the international community of motorsport luminaries, the lofty ranks of European nobility and celebrity, captains of industry and commerce and common everyday people. French rock crooner Johnny Hallyday, Princess Caroline of Monaco — daughter of the late Grace Kelly — and French World Cup Champion skier Luc Alphand, to name a few, have all participated. One celebrity who caused quite a stir in the Dakar was former British Prime Minister Margaret Thatcher's son, Mark. The would-be rallyist got lost in the desert for several days while competing in the 1982 edition. He was eventually spotted by a search plane and rescued.

Over the years, Paris-Dakar created a new breed of hero, men and women who rank with the bravest of the brave. Figures like Hubert Auriol, Cyril Neveu, Rene Metge, JoJo Groine, Jan De Groot, Jacky Ickx, Jutta Kleinschmidt, Jean-Louis Schlesser, Fabrizio Meoni, Giovanni Sala, Cyril Déspres,

Bruno Saby, Pierre Lartigue, Hiroshi Masuoka, Edi Orioli and Stephane Peterhansel have become household names after their participation in the Dakar.

The adventure and the human drama that unfolds during the first two to three weeks each January is both unimaginable and unparalleled. Although essentially a race, Paris-Dakar is much more than a competition to see who finishes first. While the thrill of victory is clear, the agony of defeat is much less defined — just finishing is itself a victory. For the lion's share of participants simply reaching Dakar is the goal. The non-finishers — often as many as half the entrants — add to the reputation Paris-Dakar holds as the world's toughest motorsport competition. Every participant leaves Africa with the story of a lifetime. In the final analysis even completing the challenge matters little. Each time a participant returns home from the desert the notoriety of the rally is further enhanced. The immensity of the Sahara grows larger; the distances become greater; the heat seems more unbearable; and the ruggedness of the terrain that much more difficult. Tales of danger, blinding sandstorms, endless vistas of dunes, incredible hardship, perseverance, tenacity, ingenuity, triumph and tragedy have greatly contributed to the aura and mystique of the rally.

Paris-Dakar takes no prisoners. Many participants have been severely injured and no less than thirty-four people have lost their lives. Only a few days into the Dakar's inaugural running the first death was recorded. Patrick Dodin succumbed to a fractured skull, after crashing near Agadez. Included on the list of fatalities are a number of unfortunate locals — it is a great sadness these individuals didn't make the bargain associated with the danger the fast-moving rally vehicles represent. Even Sabine would see his life cut short by the rally he created. Perhaps it was inevitable that the father of Paris-Dakar would come to a dramatic end. It is hard to imagine the passionate adventurer ending his days with his feet up in front of a television. In 1986, nine years to the day after he had been found in the desert by Jean-Michel Sine, Sabine perished in a helicopter crash during a blinding nighttime sandstorm in the Sahelian

Desert near Gourma-Rharous. With Sabine was popular French singer Daniel Balavoine, who was on a humanitarian mission to oversee the installation of water pumps in Malien villages. The three other victims included French journalist Nathaly Odent, radio technician Jean-Paul Le Fur and the Swiss pilot, Francois-Xavier Bagnoud. The tragedy made international headlines and shocked everyone in the rally. Without its creator, the continuity of Paris-Dakar was in jeopardy. But the remaining organizers and participants grouped together and decided the event needed to continue. Everyone agreed it would have been what Thierry wanted. From that day forward the rally has persevered to overcome every hardship and obstacle.

* * *

In its infancy, the Dakar evolved rapidly. Africa's strange customs and people drew the curiosity of many, and soon a burgeoning entry list and accompanying entourage saw more than a thousand people make the trek from Paris. One year to the next the rally grew more professional in organization, higher in profile and of greater importance to sponsors and publicity seekers. The media frenzy that has enveloped the Dakar from its early days has played a key role in the success it has enjoyed and the direction it has taken. Without the intensity of the media attention the rally would be entirely different, and perhaps not even exist at all. Journalists and photographers are an integral part of Paris-Dakar. The intrigue and human drama generated would be lost if the immediate and extensive media coverage was taken out of the equation. Conversely, the window the media coverage has opened on Africa has brought wondrous landscapes and unusual cultures into living rooms worldwide. Millions of people who normally wouldn't be aware of such things have been introduced to African traditions, tribal customs and village life courtesy of Paris-Dakar. Even with amenities improving each year, conditions in Africa are a stark contrast to life in the West. They offer the rally's participants and followers an experience far removed from anything they are accustomed to in Western society.

When Thierry Sabine decided to organize the ultimate off-road adventure, the reason or reasons why were never questioned. There was no ulterior motive, no hidden agenda. It seemed like the thing to do during the era in which it was conceived. Madness, and Paris-Dakar can certainly be viewed as a form of madness, invites no explanations. Sabine's motive was simple and upfront: to take as many people as possible into the desert to experience the immensity of the sand. If a reason for a Paris to Dakar Rally has to be given, basic human nature needs to be brought into the discussion. Humans have an innate desire to compete, to test themselves and to push the limits of what it is to be human. We tend to gravitate to challenges that allow one's true character to reveal itself. In this modern era of carefully orchestrated endeavours, even those considered extreme, an opportunity like Paris-Dakar has become so infrequently available that the rally remains one of the few genuine adventures left to be experienced. It is also human nature to want to observe others in action, especially under extremely arduous conditions. The challenge of the Dakar Rally is like no other. The sheer scale of the desert makes a single human feel like a tiny part of an immense picture. Yet this same single human can also face the desert, overcome the odds and emerge a victor. As the history of the rally has proven, the rewards are there for those who accept the challenge. Lives are changed forever, even for those who don't finish. For the few who do, the rewards are as sweet as they get, and have nothing to do with money. For those who have conquered the Dakar, the deep-seated sense of contentment wanes ever so slowly . . . perhaps never. Wilfried Thesiger, author of *Arabian Sands*, summed it all up like this: "No man can live in the desert and emerge unchanged. He will carry, however faint, the imprint of the desert, the brand which marks the nomad."

The Sahara covers nearly one third of the African continent. In Arabic, *sahara* simply means desert. The Sahara is equal in size to the continental United States — or about twice the size of Europe. Surprising to some is the fact that only about one quarter of the desert is covered by dunes. The majority of this vast dry ocean is composed of rock, gravel or a combination of both. Sedimentary rock makes up a great deal of the desert surface. Sandstone, granite and limestone are most common. Soaring mountain ranges composed of crystalline rock jut from gravel valley floors. In prehistoric times, the Sahara was a lush, vibrant landscape, home to many species of mammals and reptiles. Early man hunted giraffe, leopard and other wild beasts here to eke out a meagre existence. Evidence of this is marked by ancient cave drawings found throughout the desert's expanse. Studying the geology of the region, one can recognize how the earth was formed through volcanic activity and water and wind erosion. The surface of the desert is key to the Dakar Rally. This surface and its ever-changing conditions can pummel machinery into submission and bring even the staunchest competitor to tears. The Sahara presents one of the most formidable climates on earth. Temperatures can exceed 49° C (120° F) and drop well below freezing at night. Rainfall is rare. When it does rain, it can cause flooding of catastrophic proportions. Yet the Sahara, despite its harshness, is anything but an uninhabited wasteland. It is literally teeming with flora and fauna. Millions of people are dispersed over its expanse. Nomadic tribes, existing as they have for centuries, sustaining life on camel or goat's milk or by hunting, call the Sahara home. Tribes such as the Tuareg, Targui, Moors, Nemadi, the "Meat Eaters" of Mauritania and the Teda of Chad occupy this corner of the world.

Insects, reptiles and mammals make their home amongst the rocks, sand, thorny shrubs and trees. Vegetation is largely made up of tufts of long-bladed "camel grass," either Aristida or Jerboa. Low acacia trees, with their tiny green leaves, offer food for camels from above, goats from below, and a bit of shade for herdsmen. Strange-looking, vine-like plants that flourish in sand, Saharan Colocynth, act as ground cover and produce wild melons. These melons can break off from the vine and are then pushed and cajoled by the wind for great distances. Birds occupy the airspace immediately above the desert floor; many species migrate from Europe's northern climate and back each year. Palm groves spring up in oases where villages are located, near the essential source of water. Wells as deep as 300 feet provide the lifeblood for its inhabitants. Date palms produce a rich fruit that is widely traded among the nomadic tribes as a form of currency as well as food. The baobab — the tree of a thousand years — symbolizes the African Sahelian plain. The baobab is leafless for nine months of the year and can grow up to 25 metres (82 ft) tall. The villagers use the tree's bark to fashion rope and its leaves for food or as the basis of a soothing tea. Farther south, well below the Tropic of Cancer, towering deciduous trees provide a ceiling for a sparse savannah. Beneath the canopy, crude irrigation systems allow the earth to be cultivated, although the soil itself is far from rich in nutrients.

* * *

Michelin map No. 953 is the bible of the Paris-Dakar Rally. Detailed in many ways, this map shows much of northwest Africa, where the rally has, for the most part, taken place over the past twenty-six years. The map isn't like the travel maps that represent North America, Europe or other highly travelled areas. Map No. 953 is laced with small symbols, including ones that indicate "good water" locations at prescribed depths, usually between 10 and 30 metres (32-98 ft). Seasonal camel routes across the Tenere Desert are also shown, as are areas where the road may be covered in sand or where the numbered cairns from previous expeditions may no longer be visible. In the lower part of the quadrant, from 8° to 12° east longitude and 20° to 24° north latitude, just below the Tropic of Cancer, a small black triangle indicates the final resting place of Thierry Sabine, the man who gave the world Paris-Dakar. This corner of the Tenere du Tafassasset is hallowed ground for followers of the Dakar. The epitaph engraved on the plaque is simple: *For those who go a challenge — for those who stay (home) a dream.*

Chapter 2

Becoming an off-road racer

From an early age I was attracted to racing and speed. I spent a lot of time riding my bike pretending it was a motorcycle. My fantasy world involved riding a powerful Triumph 500 around town, twisting the throttle, leaning hard into corners and powering out. Playing cards, held in place by a clothespin on the forks so they would rattle against the spokes, provided a roaring exhaust noise.

I was born Lawrence Robert Hacking in Peterborough, Ontario on September 25, 1954, to a father who was a mechanical engineer and mother who was a devoted homemaker. I believe it was my destiny to end up living the life of an adventurer who relies on his own wits as he moves from one challenge to another. My formal education is rather limited. I learned much of what I know in the school of hard knocks. Given that my father Robert was a professional engineer, it's no surprise that my adventures would involve machines. Dad was employed by Atomic Energy of Canada and worked on the country's nuclear energy programs. During the early 1960s we lived in Deep River, Ontario. Dad was part of a team that developed the CANDU reactor, a successful, safe, nuclear power producer that was sold around the world. The initial development of this reactor was done at Chalk River in the 1950s, at a research facility that drew scientists from far and wide to test theories and break new ground in nuclear energy. Dad instilled in me many fundamental values very early on. One thing he taught me was to always do things the right way.

My mother, Alexandra, descends from hardy pioneer stock. Her parents immigrated from Romania in the early 1900s and settled in the formidable landscape of northwestern Manitoba. At the age of fifteen, in 1905, my grandfather George Burla came across the Atlantic by ship with his father. Sadly, Canadian Immigration turned my great grandfather back for having a sty in his eye. Although Grandpa was prepared to return to Romania, too, he was encouraged by his selfless father to stay behind and make his future in the New World. Grandpa took up the challenge and made his way to the Assissippi Valley near Russell, Manitoba. Here, he hewed a log cabin out of trees and built it on the 160 acres the government had granted him. He sired nine children and built a farming/cattle ranch empire that spread across most of the land in his immediate area. The majority of his children married and settled on one of his farms nearby. Some of these grandchildren still live and work that land to this day. I spent many happy summers in the Asessippi Valley, helping with the haying during the scorching months of July and August, and playing with my many cousins when time allowed. From Mom I got my grandparents' drive and determination, and a firm belief in myself.

Like many boys of my generation, I loved building things with my Meccano set. I constantly played around with it, almost to the point of obsession. In addition to building structures for which there were directions, I built ones devised from plans of my own. When Dad introduced me to the fascinating world of Meccano, he told me to hide the nuts and make the assembly look cleaner by placing the bolts so the head is what you see, not the nut. Not a huge revelation, but a small lesson I still hold close: do it right and make it look right. Dad always wanted me to take my time and work meticulously. This is something he imparted not just verbally but by example. Dad did most of his personal mechanical maintenance himself. He was constantly cleaning and repairing the engines of cars and other machinery. He built his own wooden boats and was forever formulating and designing various devices or developing new concepts. In his world there was no room for error or sloppiness; everything was calculated by slide rule. Dad would examine a problem and come up with a viable solution. It was a fertile environment for a boy with a curious and active mind. Without a doubt, I got the motivation to see things through to their conclusion and an analytical train of thought from my father. His mechanical prowess rubbed off as well. As I got older I spent hours poring over Canadian Tire catalogues and magazines like *Popular Science* and *Mechanics Illustrated.* I wanted to send away for plans to build minibikes, hovercrafts and whatever else was advertised in the small classifieds section. I graduated from my Meccano set to building bigger things, like soapbox cars. I remember it feeling like Christmas whenever I came across a good set of wheels; it was like an artist finding a blank canvas. Wheels were at a premium and hard to find. Decent wheels meant top speed and better control of the soapbox. Coasting down a big hill without brakes or brakes that dragged on the ground required all the steering control available. If you had speed you had the world by the tail. Most of my friends were happy with wobbly wheels they plundered haphazardly from their sisters' baby buggies. My wheels had to be perfectly aligned, perfectly matching pairs. I was usually left to my own devices to complete the constant projects I had under construction. In addition to fabricating soapbox racers, I wanted a snowmobile so bad I decided to build my own using Dad's electric jigsaw. I cut and hammered away for weeks until the boxy sled, which had curtain rods for ski runners, saw daylight. It looked the part but didn't work too well. These projects, silly as they now may seem, were background to my life in the world of motorcycling.

* * *

Although Mom and Dad were a conventional couple by most accounts, they also had adventurous spirits. In the mid-1960s, Atomic Energy Canada Limited (AECL) ran a project in

Rajasthan, India, and Dad applied for a position. The thought of going to India fired up my imagination and I couldn't wait to go. A general excitement hung over our household as we awaited Dad's posting to come through. Finally, in 1967, my family, which also included my brother Mark and sisters Judy and Jennifer, packed up many of our belongings, gave away or sold the rest and flew to India. We landed in Bombay in stifling heat, choking pollution and a stench that made me gag. After staying at a luxurious hotel in Bombay for a few days, we made our way to Rajasthan, located in a remote area of the north-western part of the subcontinent. Life in India was a far cry from what I was accustomed to. It was my first "real" adventure. India is incredibly rich in history, steeped in tradition, culture and beauty. The people are magical, serene, peaceful and deeply religious. I made many good friends of all creeds and colours. I attended a one-room school where a Canadian teacher, paid for by AECL, held court. All lessons were taught in English to a small group of children whose fathers were employed by the company. I also picked up enough Hindi from the servant we employed to carry on conversations with my Indian friends. The months passed quickly as I hungrily discovered my new world. I reached high-school age eighteen months after we arrived in India, but the AECL school provided classes to grade eight only. Thus, the only option was for me to return to Canada and live with my Aunt Lena and Uncle Pete on their farm in Manitoba. I flew from New Delhi to London to Toronto, and finally to Winnipeg, where I was met by my cousin John at the airport. From Winnipeg we drove the four hours to the farm, in the middle of the prairie hinterland. Although the journey was a daunting one for a thirteen-year-old, it was in keeping with my thirst for adventure and travel.

Life on the prairies was good. I went to a local high school and had plenty of projects to work on. Around this time, I bought my first motorcycle with the money my parents had given me for emergencies. It took me only a few weeks of deliberation to invest the money in something it wasn't really intended for, but I felt I was old enough to make the decision for myself. I rode the bike, a little Honda 50, every chance I got. The sense of freedom and independence it inspired made me feel larger than life.

* * *

When I first heard about the Paris-Dakar Rally in 1980, I was in Europe trying to become an international motocross rider. My interest in Paris-Dakar was sparked not only by the scope of the rally but by the two fascinating Frenchmen who first brought it to my attention. They conveyed the story of *la grande aventure* with such conviction, passion and desire it was hard not to get seduced by their tales. Furthermore, their demeanour was most intriguing and, without question, not at all what I was used to. One of them was Serge Bacou, a large, dark-haired fellow with chiselled features and a strong purposeful manner. I remember Serge during that fateful summer of 1980 as if it were yesterday. Meeting Serge would profoundly affect my life, albeit not until two decades later. I ran into Serge on the outskirts of Thouars, France, at a modest workshop owned by Patrick Barigault, the other Frenchman who made me take notice of the rally. Serge was busy preparing a custom-made swing arm for his Yamaha xt500 in preparation for the second edition of Paris-Dakar. I distinctly remember Serge animatedly describing the rally, leaving me with the impression the event was very important, and not just to the motorsports community. At the time Serge was a well-known and respected motocross rider who had competed at the Grand Prix level for many years, most notably on Bultaco motorcycles. He was at Patrick's fabrication shop because in those days, Barigault was considered one of the best custom-frame builders in France. The shop was a simple galvanized metal building fully equipped with all the tools necessary to design and build an off-road motorcycle frame from a handful of chrome-moly tubes. Patrick's amazing skill at brazing and fabricating allowed him to build motorcycles from scratch, something I had never seen done before. Patrick, as Serge described him, was an artisan. Knowing Patrick gave me access to someone with unequalled information and skills.

More importantly, he was someone who had a very clear picture of what he wanted to do, and did it regardless of the odds. Patrick was one of the first of many people I have had the pleasure of meeting over the years who were visionaries, people who live their lives the way they want to without caving to social pressures. Back then, I didn't in the remotest sense entertain the thought of entering such an unconventional-sounding rally as the Dakar, but it was firmly imbedded in my mind by the charismatic Serge and Patrick.

In 1980, for a greenhorn like myself to follow the International Motocross circuit in Europe was pretty farfetched. Only a few pro riders, like Canadian national motocross champions Bill McLean, Stan Currington and Al Logue had attempted it, with varying degrees of success. An article I had read in the magazine *Popular Cycling* convinced me that I should, and could pursue such an adventure. The article was a profile of Roger Harvey, a prominent British motocrosser who commanded much respect in the motorsport community. Harvey had been competing in the 125cc World Motocross Championship on a shoestring budget. He simply loaded up his van, crossed the English Channel and went racing. Harvey had embarked on his GP tour with no huge sponsors and no factory support, just grit and desire. Years later, when I worked for Yamaha Motor Europe, Harvey was running Mitsui Yamaha U.K.'s motocross team and I had the pleasure of telling him the story of how he inspired me to cross the Atlantic and follow in his motocross bootsteps. He was both amused and honoured.

Peter Adams was the other factor in my heading off to Europe. Peter was, and still is, a good friend. We first met at Ontario regional amateur motocross races in 1973. When I look back at the directions we took in life, it's easy to see we both got a lot from racing dirt bikes. Peter knew what he wanted and how to achieve it. He was a hard worker, a diehard competitor and a level-headed guy. He took his racing seriously and was able to secure sponsorship from local bike shops and aftermarket distributors. I, on the other hand, bounced around with no clear direction. I had little in the way of long-term plans, and never really took racing seriously. It was just something fun to do. My desire to be a professional racer was there but the commitment to follow that path wasn't.

During the winter of '79–'80, Peter finished university and went to work on an Alberta oil rig to fund his trip to Europe. Meanwhile, I spent the winter in Mississauga, Ontario. I had some money set aside from a house I had sold in Winnipeg. I made reservations for us to fly to England in early April. I chose the U.K. as our first destination because I had a friend in London, and we were welcome to hang out there for a while. Other than the decision that Peter was going to race and I was going to be his mechanic, we had no specific game plan before our departure and hadn't confirmed anything with anybody. We just showed up in England — land of my paternal ancestors — and were going to let destiny rule our lives. All we brought with us were some basic supplies, like tools, duct tape, air filter oil, Pete's riding gear and a *Federation International Motocycliste Annuaire*. The *FIM Annuaire* listed events, dates and locations of motocross races, and we'd checked off those we were thinking of entering. After shopping around, we bought a used VW van in London. It had some camping equipment inside and seemed to run fine. From the U.K. we crossed the English Channel by ferry and landed in Ostende, Belgium. From there we headed to the Netherlands, where Peter had a friend in Sneek, a medium-sized city in the country's northern province of Friesland. We only had some Canadian Automobile Association (CAA) maps of Europe, which had so little detail it was a miracle we actually found the place. We spent a few days in Sneek and we travelled around a little, taking in the sights. Peter's friend Petra had some connections in the motorcycle industry and she helped us out by calling the Kawasaki distributor near Frankfurt, Germany. She arranged a meeting with them and we drove down to Frankfurt to see if we could somehow get a bike from the distributor. It was cold that time of year, and the people at Kawasaki took pity on us, allowing us to sleep in their office for the remaining few nights we were there. To our delight, the accommodating Germans resolved things and we soon took possession of a new KX420 from a motorcycle dealer by the name of Krauter. We finally had a race bike. The dealership, which specialized in Kawasaki motorcycles, was an impressive affair in the Black Forest.

We had heard that the international motocross races in France paid start money to foreign riders. France, needless to say, was our first motocross destination. It was time to start flipping through the *Annuaire*. Canadian motocrossers were a rare sight in Europe, and a bit of a curiosity, so we figured it would be a shoo-in to pick up some easy money. Using our CAA maps, we set out due west and crossed the border into France, the fifth country we'd visited in just a few weeks' time. We pulled into Thouars on Saturday afternoon and had no problem finding the racetrack. It was almost surreal. Thousands of spectators milled about; there were huge transporters and famous riders we had only read about in magazines. This was nothing like the laid-back motocross we were accustomed to in Canada. For a couple of kids from Ontario, this was like motocross heaven. The entry list, in addition to some of France's top motocross stars, included a number of renowned Grand Prix riders. To our pleasant surprise we discovered we weren't the only Canucks in Thouars. Alberta's Stan Currington — 1979 500cc Canadian National Motocross Champion — was there to test his mettle against the Euros. Jim Pomeroy, the first American to win a Grand Prix motocross, was also entered in the event.

We soon started meeting people who would play a key role in the many unusual directions my life would eventually take. While I performed the duties of mechanic, Peter got to race in one of the biggest and most highly touted international motocross events France had to offer. "We're doing it! We're really doing it!" said an excited Peter, slapping me on the back for emphasis. Not surprisingly, Peter wasn't able to provide much competition, considering the illustrious roster of stars he was racing. Still, he received his start money and that made us feel like a couple of real pros. We were in the big leagues. After the event was over, we sat around with Currington, who gave us some valuable racing tips. As current Canadian champion, and with a season of European racing behind him, he was competitive enough to be able to battle the front-runners. At the end of the day, the Edmonton native had won some good prize money. We were impressed. Later that evening, we had dinner with Stan. Graciously, he paid the bill.

One of the people we crossed paths with in Thouars was Janine Gauthier, a local motocross enthusiast. Like many others we met at our first big-time European motocross, she was extremely hospitable and asked if she could help. Janine is the one who introduced me to Patrick Barigault. She also introduced us to the Pommier family, who lived in a very small village south of Thouars. Their home became our home away from home that season. We'd return from a race, park in their front yard and begin prepping the bike for the following weekend. The Pommiers operated a small machine shop business out of a building attached to their house. This, of course, was a bonus. The Kawasaki motocross bike needed a lot of work after most races, so the Pommier's hospitality routinely saved us from disaster. Peter, who is a pretty fair machinist himself, was allowed to use the shop's equipment any time it was free. To liberate space inside the van, one of the first things we made was a bumper rack for the bike. When the rear suspension links failed, or the frame cracked, or the muffler needed repacking, we fabricated what was necessary to get it race ready. A bit of ingenuity was called for when the bike's rear shock let go early in the season. The seal blew and leaked oil. The shock was not rebuildable and a new one would have severely cramped our financial resources. We decided to use a hacksaw and cut the shock body in half. We found a seal that matched the shaft diameter, epoxied it in place, and welded the body back together, praying we didn't melt the new seal.

At the following race the weld leaked, however, so I found a local to weld the shock some more. We gave it a shot of weld and then dunked it into a pail of cold water to cool off the seal. Next, we filled the shock with hydraulic oil and pumped some pressure into the reservoir with a bicycle pump. That rebuilt shock lasted a long time and we didn't miss a single event. This was just one of the many ways we managed to race for a season in Europe on a minimal budget. It instilled a never-say-die attitude in me and taught me to reach deep when the going got tough, something that has saved my skin on many occasions.

That summer we roamed like nomads from race to race. Each weekend took us to a different venue and a new escapade. Many foreign riders spent time between races at the same campground at Connere, near Le Mans. One of the attractions at Connere was that mail could be sent *Poste Restante*, meaning the postmaster held letters and packages until they were picked up. There was a convenient practice track nearby, which we often visited so Peter could improve his style and I could test the bike after repairs. From time to time a great number of riders would be out training and testing and something new could always be learned. We also went running to improve our fitness, often with other riders. It was a chance to share information and gather all kinds of good advice. The social life at Connere was incredibly international. People from all over the world came and went. We played volleyball and trained. Among the foreign riders who frequented Connere were a number of Swedes. I soon discovered that the Swedish took racing very seriously. They showed up with hulking Mercedes vans that were equipped with living quarters and separate bike storage. One thing I learned early on, however, was that it didn't matter what truck you showed up in, or how fancy the graphics were on your bike. What counted was getting down to business and giving it your all, something an Australian named Geoff Ballard exemplified. Like Serge Bacou and Patrick Barigault, Ballard left a lasting impression on me, yet another person who helped shape my future. Geoff took his sport very seriously and was an exceptionally good rider. He was also a free-spirited innovator with a keen business mind. Over the years, he became a legend in off-road riding. Geoff was working the same series of races we were and also happened to be travelling in a VW van. He trained hard, rode like the wind, and stuck to the principles ingrained in him by his father and grandfather. Geoff often shared his learned wisdom with me: simple lessons in calculating risk and playing the percentages.

Towards the end of the season we ventured off our usual path and headed north to attend a motocross event in Sweden. Although there was a bit of an intimidation factor, to Peter's delight he was able to race with the likes of Hakan Carlqvist, Ove Lundell and numerous other world motocross championship contenders. In Sweden, our racing season came to a somewhat disappointing end, when the tired Kawasaki frame finally could take no more abuse. The bike had proven to have a reliable engine, but it was mated to a chassis that was untested and completely unreliable. Peter repaired the frame before dropping it off at Krauter for resale. Our European motocross adventure was over. I was happy to be returning home but also sad to leave. It had been a fantastic experience and I'd already made plans to return the following year. That entire six-month motocross tour of Europe had been an incredible voyage of discovery for me. It seemed now that anything was possible.

* * *

That fall, back in Canada, some other significant events happened in my life. I crashed my bike and dislocated my right shoulder. It was a wakeup call for how easily one can get hurt racing motorcycles. It was a painful but valuable lesson. After that I was able to keep injuries to a bare minimum — and fortunately none that were of a serious nature. Shortly after wrecking my shoulder, I took a job with Yamaha Motor Canada. I was hired on a three-month contract basis to set up their display at motorcycle shows in major Canadian cities. This job opened up doors for me in the motorcycle industry, basically setting a course that would guide my life from that point on. I spent part of December 1980, and January, February and March of 1981, travelling from coast to coast, unloading trucks, setting up displays, tearing them down and reloading the trucks for the next show. I met motorcycle people nationwide. We all had something in common . . . a great passion for what we were doing.

I had spent many summers during the '70s working with my cousins John and Gordie on their farm in Manitoba. Toiling on the great Canadian Prairies taught me one of the most important lessons I have ever learned: work hard, bite the bullet, and never complain. My cousins didn't let up from morning till night, slogging out long hours doing a myriad of farm chores. Both of them thought big. They had the biggest spread of land; they built the biggest haystack in the area; the biggest herd of cows; and they did more work than anyone I'd ever seen. I took this attitude with me when doing the motorcycle shows for Yamaha. I'm a quick study and easily learned the necessary skills to do a bang-up job, paying careful attention to the details, big and small. To my delight, I was rehired for four consecutive show seasons. Right after my fourth contract expired, I was invited to apply for a full-time position at Yamaha Motor Canada's head office in North York, Ontario. I went for an interview and, against the better judgment of the company's Human Resources manager, was hired to work in the marketing department organizing Yamaha's racing programme, which I would run from 1984 until 1988. I was now firmly grounded in the motorcycle industry and engaged with its various racing disciplines. My hobby had become my job.

During the winter of 1981 I banked as much money as possible so I could set out for Europe again. This time it was to race motocross on my own, not act as a mechanic. I bought a new Yamaha YZ465 and had it shipped to Germany. I also bought a used Ford Transit van, set it up for camping and hauling the bike, and hit the road for France and beyond. The rough and tumble routine of racing and doing everything on my own was less fun than the previous year, however. My results were mediocre and I felt like I was a long way from home.

While the Paris-Dakar Rally was still a distant dream for me, I had become interested in taking dirt bike racing beyond the neatly structured agenda of motocross. I was thinking more and more about enduro racing. Geoff Ballard had a part in building the foundation that led me to take on the International Six Days Enduro (ISDE). The ISDE, considered one of the toughest of all motorcycle competitions, has a history dating back to 1913 and takes place annually in a different country. Ballard had ridden the Six Days and had some good finishes. When he talked about the ISDE, it was obvious it was his *raison d'etre.* "Enduro racing is the ultimate racing experience," he told me. "It really separates the men from the boys. Anybody can race around a track for half an hour or so, but not everybody can race all day long and do it day after day like in the Six Days." The ISDE format is unique in motorcycle racing because only the rider is allowed to perform work on the bike. Stringent rules dictate that few parts can be changed and the race's tight time schedule must be adhered to regardless of conditions. Rain or shine the Six Days goes on, through, over and around mountains, forests, valleys, swamps, rocks and whatever else lies in your path. The Six Days soon became an obsession of mine.

My first ISDE was in 1985, in the Pyrenees Mountains of northern Spain. It was a rugged event and very satisfying to complete. To meet this challenge I ran nearly every day, rode constantly and prepared my Yamaha IT200 to near perfection. I remember practising tire changes over and over to get the time down to under five minutes per wheel. Every day of the race, the time allotted for maintenance is limited and the more you can get done in a small amount of time, the better. Finishing my first ISDE in Spain was immensely satisfying, but many lessons were yet to be learned.

I returned to Europe to ride the ISDE the following year, this time in Italy. It proved to be a humbling experience, and took the wind out of my sails for a while. I realized afterwards I took the Italian ISDE far too seriously, and had set my expectations much too high. Instead of a Yamaha IT200 I had prepared a Yamaha YZ125. That was my first mistake and one I would not repeat in subsequent races. I spent a lot of money putting special parts on the bike. It had all new plastics, lights, a speedometer, muffler and Renthal handlebars. I fitted an Ohlins rear shock and had special fork springs and fork caps that would eliminate built-up air pressure. To give my pride and joy an extra touch I had all the aluminum parts polished. It was a sharp-looking, well-prepared bike, but it wasn't suited for enduro work. Even though it was fitted with a brass flywheel weight, the motor lacked the torque necessary for climbing the steep hills in and around Bergamo, Italy. The Italian Six Days didn't go as planned. I wasn't in a good frame of mind and was perhaps too cocky going in. I crashed a couple of times, quite hard, and hurt my wrists and an ankle. This reduced the enjoyment of the race. The fiasco did teach me some valuable lessons, however. I should have been riding more loosely, had more fun, and done my homework better.

I didn't ride the Six Days again until 1990 in Sweden. It rained four of the six days and it was cold. I struggled with a poor front tire choice, lack of preparation, and a low fitness level. Despite these liabilities I did finish the event. The most basic lesson I took in was to never, ever, give up. I didn't throw in the towel even when quitting seemed like the prudent thing to do. I got angry, gritted my teeth and stuck with it. I found out just how deep I could dig to reach a goal. And I was becoming more analytical about what I was doing. These are things that would serve me well a decade later when I tackled Paris-Dakar.

During this period I was living in Amsterdam, employed by Yamaha Motor Europe NV. I had moved to The Netherlands in the fall of 1988 and remained with Yamaha until 1990. I was involved with their world championship motocross team and organized press launches and other special events. It was a heady time. I worked with renowned motocross and off-road stars while gaining valuable insights into the international side of the motorcycle and motorsport industry. Among many others, I attended meetings concerning Yamaha's factory Dakar effort, which further endeared me to the thought of taking part in it someday. My first taste of desert riding in North Africa was a direct result of my stint with Yamaha: I helped organize their Spirit of Adventure Tour in 1990 and the press launch of the XTZ 750 Super Tenere in 1989, both in Egypt. For the XTZ launch I had the honour of hobnobbing and riding with Yamaha factory pilots Stephane Peterhansel, Franco Pico and Jean-Claude Olivier, all of them Paris-Dakar heavyweights. Although it was an exciting and often glamorous time, the extensive travelling and living out of a suitcase had me thinking of returning to Canada and feeling like I had a home again. Then, while in France on business in the summer of 1990, I met my future wife Françoise. She was reason enough to postpone going home. I hadn't been in a serious relationship for some time and the feelings we had for each other had all the earmarks of something serious. I went to Dijon early in 1991 to be with Françoise. I became established in the country to a certain degree, and started learning French. We ended up moving to Metz and then, later, to Thionville where Françoise, a dentist by profession, opened her first practice.

While living in France, I bought a Honda xr250 and made a point of learning the sport of enduro riding "European style." The Euros have a different approach to enduro competition and my learning curve was sharp. I rode some excellent events in France and trained reasonably hard to prepare for the isde, which was held in Czechoslovakia that year. I rode a bone stock Honda xr250. I liked the bike. It was fun to ride and brought with it an underdog factor. After learning the Euro technique of pacing oneself on the trail or liaison sections, and changing pace to fly in the shorter timed special tests, I felt confident and truly enjoyed the isde challenge. I was well prepared for the Czech isde, relaxed, and I had a lot of fun doing it. It was my best isde finish; the silver medal I took home was cherished for a long time. Experience was now playing a bigger part in what I could accomplish. The European strategy of out-thinking one's opponent had started to sink in. Rather than charging headlong into the fray, I learned to be patient and methodical. I looked at a problem, analyzed the options and made sound decisions. I was much more confident and didn't second-guess myself as much. My powers of observation were becoming more finely tuned. Noticing the difference between something done well and something done poorly, especially in off-road motorcycling, is critical to improving on your results. Patience is very important. Energy management is crucial. Thinking longer term than your adversaries gives you an advantage. Having contact with as many knowledgeable people as possible and sharing points of view is also key. I like to think of it as cooperative competitiveness.

* * *

The 1990s proved to be full of changes and growth. After doing the 1990 ISDE in Sweden and the '91 edition in Czechoslovakia, I ventured all the way to Australia in 1992. That year, the ISDE was held in Cessnock, New South Wales. When the opportunity presented itself, I couldn't resist. My brother Mark and I flew to Sydney with the CR250. I had disassembled the bike and actually carried it in my luggage. We put it back together on the outskirts of the city in a shop, which belonged to an old friend, Pelle Granquist. A few days before the event, Pelle loaded us into his van and took us up to Cessnock. The setting was entirely different from the ISDE venues of Europe. The outback "bull dust" there is a deep, fine powder, and the varied terrain is an excellent test for man and machine. In some ways I struggled at the Aussie Six Days, but I found it an incredible experience in others. I felt I rode well, but was not strong physically because I was suffering from a bout of stomach flu. I still managed to finish with a silver medal but I had hoped for a stronger result. Gold had once again eluded me. Still, it was nothing to complain about, and I had added one more successful ISDE to my resume.

Meanwhile, back in France, my career had pretty well stalled. Racing was fun, but I needed a bigger challenge. Although I liked living in France, by 1994, the year Françoise and I were married, it had become evident the country offered only limited opportunities for me. Françoise agreed that returning to Canada was the only solution. We started making plans for our slow return to my home country. For Françoise, this wasn't a problem: all she would have to do was apply for her Canadian dentistry certificate. She began making preparations to write the necessary exams that would qualify her to practise in

Canada. The entire process of becoming a certified Canadian dentist would prove to be a tedious and expensive affair, however. For a number of years, our lives rotated between France and Canada. In 1994, I went back to Ontario and bought a house in Acton, a town within an hour's drive of Toronto that has easy access to Pearson International Airport. That year, I rode "hare scrambles" events in Ontario and even dabbled in speedway racing on a borrowed Jawa 500 alcohol-burning, brakeless speedway bike. In May 1995, our daughter Mia was born in France so I spent most of my time there. For a few years I did consulting work. In the summer of 1997, I agreed to work for Canadian Kawasaki. My main job was to organize their dealer meeting, which was held in Calgary late that year. I also did a stint with the organization that runs the Canadian Superbike Championship series. Another project was for Turbo Press, publisher of *Cycle Canada* magazine, organizing events for the annual Sportbike Rally in Parry Sound, Ontario.

By 1999, Françoise and Mia were ready to move permanently to Canada. I had found the ideal location for Françoise to establish a dental practice in Georgetown, also a short drive from Toronto. Starting in July 1999, most of my time was spent converting a house we bought in a developing area on the outskirts of town into a dental office. By December, Françoise was ready to launch her practice and I was ready to resume my life in the world of motorcycles. Like everyone else, we celebrated the dawning of the new millennium and looked forward to our new life in Georgetown. I was also glued to the Internet and my television set, watching Paris-Dakar 2000 unfold. It was then I decided I would not be among the viewers of the 23rd edition — I would be one of the competitors.

Chapter 3

Preparing for the Dakar

‒ ‒ ‒ ‒ ‒ ‒ ‒ ‒ ‒ ‒ ‒ ‒ ‒ ‒ ‒ ‒ ‒ ‒

Paris-Dakar is no ride in the park. The first thing you need to ask yourself when planning on taking part in a monumental twenty-one-day rally is: am I physically up to the task? 27 Although I try to stay in good physical shape all year round, I decided to dramatically step up my training programme the day I knew for certain I was going to do the Dakar. It is far easier to spread the physical suffering over a long period of preparation rather than pack all the suffering into the short three-week period of the event. That's a recipe for disaster. I prefer working out at home, but getting ready for an attack on the Dakar required some professional guidance. At the beginning of April 2000, I joined a fitness club. I went to the club religiously right up until a few days before I headed to Europe in December. I knew I had to toughen up for the punishment the Dakar would dish out. I focused my resistance training — at least one hour per session — on strengthening muscle groups without bulking up. To ensure my cardio level was up to the task of handling a bike for hours on end, I ran seven kilometres every other day. I closely monitored my heart rate and recovery period, making sure I got plenty of rest in between training sessions.

To keep my bike-handling abilities sharp, whenever possible, I rode the stock Honda xr650r practice bike I had purchased for that purpose. I was planning on doing the rally with the same model, albeit modified to suit the race. Although some roadwork was included, I usually stuck to the riding trails available in southern Ontario. For a more gruelling workout I went to MotoPark, a motocross facility in Chatsworth, Ontario, which had been the venue for a number of world championship motocross GPs back in the 1980s. To minimize the risk of getting hurt, I chose not to ride competitively in the months leading up to the Dakar. Like most competitors, once I put on my race face I like to be in the thick of things, and that involves taking risks one normally wouldn't consider when trail riding or practicing for an event. As my departure date drew near, I felt myself become stronger. Unless I had the misfortune of injuring myself, I knew my body wouldn't quit on me, no matter how taxing the rally proved to be.

Eating properly, of course, is equally important and should accompany any exercise programme one chooses to pursue. I've never been one to follow a strict dietary regimen, however. I just make sure I eat wisely, and that excludes junk and fast foods. I'm basically a meat, potatoes and vegetables kind of guy. I also like pasta — lots of carbohydrates. Whenever possible, I go for fresh, organically grown produce. When it comes to meat, I try to purchase it from a store that specializes in naturally raised animals. Fish is also on my weekly menu. Other than the odd beer, I avoid alcohol, caffeine and soft drinks. I don't like anything that alters my consciousness or biorhythm. Spring water is my drink of choice. During the months leading up to the Dakar, I consumed up to five litres of water a day so my system would get used to absorbing such quantities. For breakfast, I usually eat granola, bananas and apples, sometimes with yoghurt. Lunch may consist of whole wheat bread with tuna. Dinner usually includes a salad. I'm the kind of person who doesn't eat a big meal: I usually spread my food intake out as required throughout the day. When I'm burning a lot of calories, I have regular snacks that may include fruit, nuts or energy bars. After a workout, I drink a protein milkshake. Ultimately, I don't think any one diet is the right diet; it's an individual choice. If you pay attention to your body, it tells you what it needs to perform most efficiently.

It would have been nice only to have to worry about the physical preparation for Paris-Dakar, but as a privateer, I was faced with the daunting task of handling the logistics side of the event, too. And that includes putting together a budget. The $14,000 entry fee and $750 FIM licence fee is only the beginning. Factor in a well-prepared motorcycle, travel and shipping expenses, supplies, and time away from making a living and you're looking at close to $50,000 CDN. This does not include the bike and parts from Honda, and products received from motorcycle industry aftermarket companies which included Kimpex, Sinisalo, Arai Helmets, Scott Goggles, EVS, the numerous companies that sold products at cost, and the people who performed all kinds of work free of charge. In racing terms, $50,000 is a shoestring budget. Factory teams spend more than that on their motorcycles. Through various sponsors, I put together enough funding to support my race. Françoise and I supplied the rest.

In motorsports, a privateer is a private competitor, meaning he or she isn't on someone's payroll and has no official team infrastructure to coddle and assist, before, during or after an event. You have to do everything yourself, and there's no passing the buck if you fail. Privateers, who can be broken down into semi-pros and amateurs, represent about 80% of the Dakar entries. For the most part they are the unsung heroes of Paris-Dakar, the rally's essence. I was by that time also familiar with the logistics of entering major events, but those paled in comparison to what I was up against preparing for a rally that spanned twenty-one days and over 10,000 kilometres. I soon discovered it was something akin to a full-time job. Still, it was a job I enjoyed, because every task I completed put me one step closer to being on the start line in Paris on January 1, 2001. Taking care of all the pre-event details means you have to be totally committed. If you aren't, you're destined to fall apart during the race. Any endeavour, large or small, calls for meticulous preparation — without it, the desired outcome is reduced to a crapshoot. A successful Dakar privateer, in addition to being an accomplished car driver or motorcycle rider, needs to be an astute business person as well. Marketing skills are very important. So is being a good technician and planner, having a vision and being able to think long-term. Knowing proper fitness and training techniques is a big help. Being flexible, having the ability to roll with the punches, also comes in handy. Last but not least is experience. All the knowledge in the world, without practical experience, is like a door without a key.

The first thing I did in my preparation for the rally was research the event and its history. I wanted to know as much as possible about previous rallies, the highs and lows, the facts and the stats. This called for a lot of data gathering, mostly from the Internet. The more I learned, the more pumped I got. I also spoke with actual competitors about their Dakar experience, trying to learn as much as I could from their triumphs and mistakes. These were not the factory-supported riders, but the privateers. I started by contacting fellow Canadian Mike Markoff, who had attempted the rally years earlier. Although he didn't make it to Dakar, he had no regrets and spoke of the rally with the passion of a true adventurer. One of my main concerns was to find out why the lion's share of rallyists fails to finish. It might seem obvious, but considering the high annual dropout rate, I suspected it was poor preparation — whether it was physical, mechanical, or psychological — that made most competitors come up short.

At the top of the list was running out of fuel. Making a costly mistake and crashing were also common problems. A close third was *tombe en panne de morale,* running out of fortitude, a mental throwing in of the towel. Mechanical failure, of course, was another prime reason for not making the finish line. Anticipation, I would learn, is the key to staying ahead of the Paris-Dakar game. Being aware of time and the frantic pace of the rally is paramount. The rhythm of Dakar is very rapid; there is very little time available to waste. Time-consuming mistakes, though inevitable and necessarily factored into the cadence of the rally, were to be avoided at all cost.

After careful deliberation, I decided the 2001 Honda XR650R would be my best choice. Still, it wasn't an easy decision, considering the wide range of motorcycles available. Although I had built up a close relationship with Yamaha over the years, and would no doubt have received support from them had I asked, Yamaha didn't produce a hybrid like the XR650R. The bike they previously had won Dakar with, the XTZ 750 Super Tenere, was now antiquated and the company had not kept pace developing a successor to this excellent machine. As much as I like Yamaha motorcycles, I came to the conclusion my chances of finishing the Dakar would be best met by going with Honda. Honda's reputation for quality bikes, especially one with the XR650R's profile, is known throughout the motorcycling world. I could rest assured the bike was built to exacting specifications, well tested and proven under extreme conditions. In 1999, when the XR650 made its rally competition debut, it won the Nevada 2000, the Tecate/San Felipe 250, and the prestigious Baja 1000. Very few bikes can claim these kinds of results in their first year of competition. It was impressive to say the least.

The bike's early successes aside, a huge issue in deciding to go with the XR was the fact that it came equipped with a traditional kick starter. While watching the 2000 Paris-Dakar unfold, I noticed that at one point, Nani Roma, who was leading the event, had to be push started by two of his mechanics. The electric starter on his KTM, which had no kick start backup, had failed. I knew that if something like that happened to me, there would be no mechanics there to push start me. I wanted a bike that could be kick started. Despite this drawback, some forty-five riders would show up for the '01 Dakar with KTMs, including the riders from the official KTM factory team.

Another reason I chose Honda was support. Honda Motor Corporation has a large infrastructure in Canada. They are approachable and receptive to helping privateers such as myself, albeit via an authorized dealer and not officially through the head office. I knew that if I was successful, Honda would celebrate that success and, perhaps, if I decided to make another Dakar attempt, would support a second effort more fully. For the most part, I was right. The 650 would prove extremely reliable and the mainstay of my eventual success. Second, Honda Canada made sure they capitalized on my being the first Canadian to finish the rally. They put out a special XR brochure and displayed the bike at various shows and events. For me, this was of far more value than monetary support, because positive publicity can generate far more significant rewards long term.

The process of acquiring the XR650, spare parts and technical support was relatively straightforward. Three people were instrumental in getting this package to me: Honda Canada's Don Zaharia and Warren Milner, and Machine Racing's John Nelson, co-owner of a large motorcycle dealership near Newmarket, Ontario. I knew all three quite well through the motorcycle business, which, of course, made the process of obtaining the bike easier. Nelson is an icon in the Canadian motocross and off-road scene and someone who is passionate about racing. At the time, Zaharia was national sales manager at Honda Canada while Milner worked in marketing. I knew John and Don not only as industry colleagues, but as guys I had competed against in the past — John in enduros and hare scrambles, Don in ice racing. They had racing blood in their veins, and the prospect of getting involved in my Dakar effort appealed to them both.

Once I had the bike sponsorship lined up, my next task was to find out what needed to be done to turn the XR into a desert rally machine. Ideally, the Honda would be ready each morning to be taken off-road all day long, propped on its stand at night, untouched, and ridden again the following day. But that's in a perfect world. In a punishing race like the Dakar, mechanical hiccups must definitely be expected. No motor-driven vehicle, two-wheel or four, will take its pilot from point A to B in a rally like Paris-Dakar without some kind of mechanical problem arising. To expect anything else would be naïve. No matter how good the vehicle, or the amount of prep work and maintenance, something will go wrong. It's Murphy's Law of Racing.

Some modifications were obvious, others required a bit of

research. Though running out of fuel was a big problem, there was a fairly easy solution: make sure the bike could carry enough gasoline. It was a simple matter of finding the largest fuel tank available for the XR. I considered the options, which included plastic, carbon fibre and aluminum. I decided on an aluminum construction because it was durable and easy to repair. If I fell and the tank was dented, it could still hold fuel. At least as long as it wasn't split open. I made sure epoxy putty was on my list of things to take along, just in case I had to repair leaks. With the marvels of GPS (Global Positioning System) navigation available to Dakar rallyists, it was pretty rare for anyone to really get lost anymore. GPS has reduced the skill needed to navigate in the desert, and the challenge that goes along with it. It also cuts down the amount of fuel you need to carry. The route everyone takes is more direct, with very few added kilometres resulting from wrong turns. I figured that, even in a worst-case scenario, a forty-litre tank with a fifteen-litre rear reserve would carry enough fuel to get to the next stage.

The XR650 was so new, very little was already available that could help me make the bike "desert rally ready." I had to turn to France to find the hardware that would transform the Honda into a true desert machine. In early summer, Françoise, Mia and I went to see her family in Thionville for a holiday. I used much of my free time to chase down information on what I needed and where to get it. I went straight to Thierry Millet, the owner/operator of Accelere Motos, a motorcycle dealership in nearby Metz. Thierry was an old Dakar hand and a privateer. He had entered the rally on at least four occasions and finished twice. If anybody could steer me in the right direction, he could. Thierry, a straightforward type of guy who doesn't mince words, offered me the straight goods on the event from his perspective. He provided insightful information on how to approach and ride the Dakar as a privateer. What was really important to me was the fact he agreed the XR650R was a wise choice to tackle the rally. "If I entered the event again, the 650 is what I would do it with," he said. "Just make sure you make the necessary modifications and I'm sure it won't let you down."

In Aix-en-Provence, I found a company called Durendal that advertised rally kits for XRS. I felt like I had struck the motherlode. In typical French style the people at Durendal provided some great advice and were able to construct most of the parts I needed. These included a chrome-moly rear subframe, which was much stronger than the stock aluminum one, an emergency water tank, a *balise* or emergency locator beacon mount, front navigation mounts, and a massive skid plate with toolbox. I also got a long, sweeping down pipe with open muffler to allow the rear fuel tank to be mounted on the opposite side of the stock air box. Retaining the stock air filter set-up was the simplest and most reliable way to keep things in order. Fabricating an air filter system would be a complex task. I chose ease of maintenance. I would carry a number of pre-oiled stock filter elements and, if necessary, change them frequently.

From my own experience, and from talking with people like Thierry Millet, I knew only one rule of thumb applied when

preparing the XR650R for Dakar — the KISS theory: Keep It Simple Stupid. The bike's motor had to be easy to work on, and its electrical system needed to be uncomplicated and reliable. The rest had to be easy to repair if I crashed the bike. And the law of averages almost certainly guaranteed at least one fall — big or small. The XR definitely fit the bill when it came to being repair friendly. This is important, as one can't predict the amount of time there will be available to fix things at the end of each day. It could be hours, or no time at all. Because night riding is common in the Dakar, the lighting set-up had to be powerful. The better you see in the dark, the less surprises jump out at you. I opted to replace the XR's enduro-style (halogen) headlight with a Baja Designs HID (High Intensity Discharge) light. Because of the long liaison and special stages the Dakar is renowned for — up to 800 kilometres — the bike had to be comfortable to ward off fatigue. It needed to be suited to all-day riding for three consecutive weeks, so a custom seat was called for: I wanted it taller, wider and shorter than the original.

The front suspension had to be the best. I wouldn't have time during the rally to adjust it for the various terrains it would have to handle. I decided I would replace the stock 46mm conventional leading axle fork with an Ohlins inverted-style fork. This fork was designed to fit on a Honda CR250 motocross bike. I opted for the heaviest springs available for the forks. To complement the package, I went for an Ohlins rear shock to replace the original. It too was fitted with a heavier spring. It was ordered from the Ohlins distributor, Steen Hansen's, as an XR650 rally shock, and came with modified damping settings. These modifications were designed to make the XR handle better, be more comfortable, and more reliable. I knew the front wheel would take a lot of punishment, so I opted to replace it with special wheels, ordered through White Brothers in California. They were works of art, consisting of machined aluminium Talon hubs made in the U.K., heavy-duty stainless steel spokes, and Excel Takasago rims. The hubs and rims were brilliant gold anodised. The only weak point in the equation were the aluminium spoke nipples. I was assured by White Brothers, however, that they were the strongest available.

Within six months of getting the ball rolling, Honda Canada had shipped my XR650R to Machine Racing. One hazy morning in September, I received a call from John Nelson to tell me it had arrived. "Hey Lawrence, your bike's here. Come and get it. It's taking up room," Nelson barked in his endearing off-the-wall way. I wasted no time hitching up the trailer to my car and driving the 75 clicks or so to Machine Racing. When I got there, John was in a meeting with Chuck Mesley, a top-ten Canadian motocross pro at the time who raced for the dealership's team. One of John's employees directed me to the XR, which I proceeded to push onto the trailer, making sure it was securely fastened down. Just as I was ready to leave, John came over to see me off.

"You're the man, Lawrence. I guess you're all set. Well, have fun dude," he said.

"Definitely John. Definitely. Sure you don't want to hang in?" I bounced back.

"I wish," he said and shook my hand. "See ya later. Let me know if there's anything else I can do."

I jumped into my car and happily headed home with my new pride and joy. A few days later, the list of spare parts I had requested, including chains, chain sprockets, levers, throttle parts, gaskets, chain rubbing blocks and spare hardware, was delivered directly from Honda Canada to my home. Additional parts like foot pegs and foot-peg mounts, and electrical parts such as an ignition coil and CDI box, I would borrow from the XR650 I had bought as a practice bike.

As soon as I had the bike in my possession, I started the job of getting it prepared for the Dakar. In September, my Durendal parts had arrived in Canada. It was like Christmas in the middle of summer, and things really started taking shape. Dakar was no longer a dream; it was taking on substance. The more I could visualize the bike transformed, the more excited I became. Doing all this work on the bike also allowed me to become more familiar and intimate with it. The XR was no longer just a motorcycle; it was becoming a friend of sorts.

The massive main fuel tank I had ordered arrived in October. It came through a German company called African Queens, but it was actually made in Italy. The chunky behemoth was a work of art. It held close to the desired fifty-five litres in two separate compartments. I was pleasantly surprised when I opened the boxes and found the handcrafted seat I had ordered nestled in the packing material. It was exactly what I had in mind, made of thick, soft foam. I contacted Factory FX and had them send me an XR650 seat cover, which I had modified at a local upholstery shop. The result was one of the most comfortable seats I would ever use and it would contribute greatly to my being less fatigued over the duration of the rally.

Upon examination, I discovered that the front fuel tank was designed to use a vacuum-operated fuel pump to deliver the gas into the carburetor. I knew this wasn't a viable option. A carburetor designed to accept fuel under the very low pressure of gravity feed wouldn't handle having fuel pumped into it without serious consequences. I took the tank to Bill Kidd Rad, a custom radiator shop in London, Ontario. I had them install a small, milk carton–like aluminium reservoir inside the tank in the location just above the carburetor. Fittings and mounts allowed the use of the stock fuel tap near the original location. The tank had a tube welded in place to allow the tap to be turned on or off with a specially made key. The set-up was simple, clean and reliable.

Nearly all of the fitting of these parts was done close to my home at a small machine shop in Ballinafad. Two friends of mine, John Biersteker and Lou Costello, operate the shop aptly named Abbot and Costello Machine. Like the famous comedic duo, John and Lou do things mostly for the fun of it. Unlike the bumbling comedians, renowned for their screw-ups, Biersteker and Costello do anything but. Their "nothing is impossible" attitude made them the perfect candidates for helping me prep the XR for action. They never winced at or dismissed any of my farfetched ideas, and really contributed to making my Dakar race happen.

Finally, close to the end of November, the XR650R was ready, transformed from a stock enduro bike into a mean rally machine. I was itching to take it for a ride but an early snowfall put a damper on that idea. Other than babying it for less than half a kilometre on the street in front of my house, the bike was going to be shipped to France without any kind of testing. By this point I was convinced it would hold out all the way to Dakar. Nothing had been left to chance. Only the best after-market and custom parts had been used to complement an already great bike. I was satisfied that I had done everything possible to ensure my XR could not be improved upon. About the only thing that would prevent me from reaching my goal would be a debilitating accident. Crashing hard and damaging a bike is really not an option when trying to finish Paris-Dakar as a privateer. I knew I couldn't have a big wreck and still be able to finish. Even one heavy fall can make life so miserable you want to quit right then and there, if you're still physically able to compete. What often happens in a situation like that is you subconsciously do something to seal your fate so you won't have to continue. A serious crash has the ability to put the fear of God in you; you don't want to tempt fate too often.

Only one item remained on my to-do list before heading back to France; draw up my will. Because of the hazards in racing motorcycles, this is something I should have done years earlier. Not returning home from an event isn't something you like to think about. Still, off-road racing is risky under the most ideal conditions, never mind a rally designed to create conditions that are anything but ideal. Even the most careful and experienced rider can't take all the risk out of the equation. Some rallies are forgiving — Paris-Dakar isn't one of them. The immense distances and ever-changing circumstances breed danger. The varied and treacherous terrain offers a never-ending range of ways to hurt or kill oneself. The dozens of serious injuries and fatalities associated with the Dakar are testimony enough. One thing is certain: the Dakar would be a very risky enterprise. Managing and calculating risk needed to remain front and centre at all times. Hoping for the best is not the ideal way to approach a challenge like the Dakar. But after all the preliminaries have been diligently taken care of, hoping for the best is all that remains.

Satisfied that everything possible had been done, I got the bike ready to be shipped. For this purpose I had ordered a sturdy wooden crate from AirShip Packing and Crating, a company that specializes in building custom crates. I took the bike and spare parts to their shop in Mississauga and crated it myself, making doubly sure everything was securely fastened. I had the AirShip people load the crate onto my tired Toyota truck and drove over to the cargo terminal at nearby Pearson International. Once the crate was out of my hands, all I could do was pray it would arrive undamaged. I felt like a parent watching his young child leave on a bus trip to another city, unable to accompany him, entrusting him to the driver.

ChaPTeR 4

Heading for
the City of Lights

▬ ▬ ▬ ▬ ▬ ▬ ▬ ▬ ▬ ▬ ▬ ▬ ▬

On December 15, 2000, I departed for France accompanied by Mia. We flew from Toronto to Luxembourg, rather than Paris, because it was just a short hop across the border to where Mia's grandparents lived. Françoise, who had patients to look after, was scheduled to join us just before Christmas. The rally that would define my life and career was just fifteen days away. I felt on top of the world. My dream of participating in Paris-Dakar was on the verge of becoming reality. I had spent nine solid months preparing for this event, and I knew I was as ready as I would ever be. I had the bike to do it with and I was in peak physical condition. I was ready to devour the monster. My in-laws, Guy and Monique Prioretti, met us at the airport in Luxembourg City. After fussing over Mia, whom they hadn't seen for some time, we drove the short drive to their home in Thionville, France. I spent the next few days getting the Honda and spare parts through customs in Luxembourg. Jean-Luc "Darry" Sagnou, a close friend whom I've known since the early 1980s, drove me in an Iveco van to the cargo warehouse at the Luxembourg airport to pick up the massive wooden crate containing the bike and spare parts, and a separate box containing the spare engine.

I was anxious to get back to Thionville and check on the

bike. The crate looked none the worse for wear, so I knew the freight people had handled it with care. When we got back to Thionville we headed directly to the home of my brother-in-law, Jean-Michel, where we unloaded everything into his garage. With help from Darry and Jean-Michel, I proceeded to remove the XR650 from its crate. My rally machine was greeted with "oohs" and "ahs" from my helpers. To my relief, it appeared to have arrived in pristine condition. After a cursory inspection I poured some gasoline into its massive fuel tank and placed my foot on the kick start lever. All it took was one kick and the bike's powerful motor sparked to life. It was music to my ears. Jean-Michel and Darry gave me a thumbs-up. My father-in-law dropped by to have a look at the bike and, like Jean-Michel and Darry, was bowled over by what he saw.

"She's a beauty. What a machine. If she performs as good as she looks you'll be just fine," Guy said. He and Jean-Michel were convinced I would do the family proud.

I knew I had a lot to live up to. Considering I had been unable to really ride the brand new bike back in Canada, I couldn't wait to take it on the road to see how it handled. I also wanted to put some easy break-in kilometres on the engine. As expected, the XR ran like a charm and proved to be a real show-stopper. Everyone I passed was instantly drawn to the big red and silver machine.

The rest of my time in Thionville was spent doing chores like picking up the special Michelin desert tires and Bib mousse inner tubes I had ordered from the local Euromaster shop in Thionville. I took these and the bike's spare wheels to Thierry Millet's Honda dealership in Metz to have them mounted. Thierry was pleased I had taken his advice to get the Michelins and the inner tubes. When I mentioned the modifications I had made to the bike — many of which he'd recommended — he beamed.

"I wish I was going with you," he said. "No, actually, I wish I was riding your bike. I would accept bets that it would take me all the way to Dakar."

While I was taking care of business matters, Mia was

having the time of her life with her loving grandparents. Like any grandparent with a young granddaughter, they treated her like a princess. She hardly seemed to miss me when I wasn't around. Just before Christmas, Françoise closed her office for the holidays and joined us in Thionville. It was a happy reunion, and we had a wonderful time celebrating the holiday season with family and friends. Conversations often found their way to the subject of Paris-Dakar. Although everyone knew I had raced major events like the ISDE, the Dakar seemed to elevate me to a whole different status in their eyes. In France, I discovered, this rally is a major item and the buzz leading up to it is quite intense, including lots of media attention. Shortly after Boxing Day, I packed everything into the Iveco van Darry had been kind enough to lend me and left for Paris. Françoise was scheduled to join me there a few days before New Year's Eve. In my life as an off-road racer I have set off to many venues, near and far, but nothing compared to the feelings that welled up inside me that day when I was heading for the City of Lights.

The winter weather in Paris was a far contrast from what I had left behind in frigid Canada. The air was fresh and crisp. A high-pressure zone had parked itself over central France for a number of days prior to the actual start of the rally. Conditions were near perfect. After checking into the hotel flat I had reserved, I proceeded to lug everything, from bike to spare parts and riding gear, into the unit's living room. I had received prior permission from the building manager, who was only too happy to oblige a Paris-Dakar competitor. I'd heard enough horror stories of bikes and equipment being stolen from parked trucks and vans. I wasn't going to risk the same thing happening to me. To have my Dakar end before it even started because my bike was stolen would have been too much to bear. In the days leading up to the event, I walked around town to get a bit of exercise and attended a briefing at the fancy Hotel Meridien Montparnasse by the Thierry Sabine Organization (TSO), the rally's organizing body. On the 29th, I drove to Chateau de Vincennes at Parc Floral on the outskirts of Paris.

This is where TSO had set up headquarters to process the multitude of competitors and their vehicles. In total, 142 motorcyclists, 118 car drivers, and thirty-five truck drivers were slated to start Paris-Dakar 2001. In addition to the competitors' racing machines, forty-six assistance vehicles accompanied the entourage. I wasn't due to register until the following day, but I wanted to check things out and orient myself for what I knew would be an involved procedure. I walked around Parc Florale taking everything in with hungry eyes. People from around the globe descended on the large building and parking lot that housed the hundred or so TSO volunteers who made this juggernaut happen. The ambience at Parc Florale was jovial and relaxed. It appeared more like a family reunion than the preliminaries to a race event. The French seem to have a knack to turn any event, large or small, into a celebration, and this was no exception. In keeping with the spirit of the Dakar the whole affair was open to the public, free of charge, no less.

After a few hours taking everything in, I decided to make one last stop. Although I had been told I would not be able to claim my privateer's storage trunk until the day I was processed, I went to the depot from which they were issued. I had heard from some of the old Dakar hands that not all info supplied by the organization was 100% reliable or accurate. They looked at the entire Dakar as a grey area, open to interpretation. It was wise to take everything with a grain of salt. I approached two of the volunteers manning the depot and asked if I could pick up my trunk a day early. "Sure, that's no problem, but how do I know you're in the rally," one of them queried. I showed him my pre-entry forms and it was as simple as that. I became the recipient of a trunk and he and his buddy became the recipients of a Canadian flag pin. "Hey, don't forget not to make it too heavy. There's a 50-kilo weight limit," the other guy advised as I walked away with the trunk.

When I got back to the hotel, I was happy to discover Françoise had arrived from Thionville. She had come prepared with some groceries and cooked us an excellent meal in the flat's kitchenette. When we were finished eating we set to work packing the trunk, which was actually a surplus French military footlocker. All privateers received one and were allowed to keep them when the rally was over. I tried to maximize the space, measuring 80cm x 30cm x 45cm (31" x 12" x 18"), by packing everything I could into it. Françoise took charge and carefully arranged everything I thought I might need. This included my bike stand, tent, mattress, sleeping bag and some spare parts. In the lid, I fabricated an elastic net to store all my paperwork. Françoise drew up a list of medicines and creams she thought I might need, itemizing on a sheet of paper what each item was for. We taped that onto the lid as well. When the trunk was full, it felt kind of heavy. I didn't have a scale so I guesstimated the weight. I was almost certain it exceeded the 50-kilo limit. Rather than take some items out, I left everything in figuring I'd find out sooner or later if indeed it was too heavy to be accepted for transportation by the TSO people.

On December 30, I returned to Chateau de Vincennes to go through the process of becoming an official Paris-Dakar participant. Paperwork consumed the first couple of hours. The TSO staff was especially helpful in keeping the actual procedure of dealing with the many forms fairly simple. I had brought a few hundred small Canadian flag pins and handed them out liberally. From past experience I had learned that little gestures like this made cutting through red tape much easier. I was surprised to see that very few other participants subscribed to my way of thinking. One of the things on the TSO agenda was ensuring everyone had paid up all the various fees connected with the rally. There was the handing over of wads of cash for details such as the obligatory fuel package that covers the cost of most but not all of the fuel needed in Africa. Every competitor's picture was taken for the official Paris-Dakar website and rally ID badge. A cabin and bunk were also assigned on the two ferries that would take the competitors and their vehicles to North Africa. Stops at every one of the many booths meant more paperwork and rubber stamps. There was good-hearted banter and some chance meetings with competitors, old acquaintances and journalists. Everyone seemed to wear a jacket proclaiming allegiance to, or sponsorship from, one company or another. Team names and company logos from every corner of the world were in evidence. It was a regular zoo, but without the distinction between the viewers and the viewed.

When the administrative business was done, I checked into making arrangements for transporting the spare engine and parts. TSO recommended a Spanish-based company called Team Tibau Raids Assistance Services. Team Tibau offered an array of rally services that included among others, freight transportation for privateers. Late model Mercedes 4 x 4 and 6 x 6 trucks were used for this purpose. The company had an impressive six-year Dakar track record, moving goods from bivouac to bivouac without fail. The company's owner, Rafael Tibau, was directly involved in all the operations and even drove a race truck during the competition. That was good enough for me, so I rented space, charged by weight, in one of the trucks. Once that was taken care of I retrieved my bike from the van, which was parked in a secure area, and headed over to *Controle Technique* or technical control. This was the final requirement that would allow me to set off for Dakar on New Year's Day. During tech control, the competitors' bikes, cars and trucks are inspected to establish their readiness for the long journey to Dakar. The vehicles must not only meet stringent rally criteria, but also the minimum street-legal requirements for travelling in Europe. Safety items such as emergency flares, a signal mirror, lights, horn and a three-litre water container are obligatory. The XR650 passed the technical scrutiny easily, but more importantly to me, it met with nods of approval from many knowledgeable and experienced Dakar veterans. This alone gave me a significant boost in morale.

I had been a little apprehensive about technical control, wondering whether the bike, though meticulously prepared, was going to pass without some last-minute modifications. A mad scramble to solve a problem, or comply with a new rule or request I hadn't been aware of beforehand, was something I didn't want to have to contend with. While at the *Controle Technique* I crossed paths with Dominique Rochette, the

Frenchman who had prepared Paris-Dakar icon Stephane Peterhansel's bikes and race car many times. Dominique remembered me from my Yamaha days in Holland and greeted me with a warm handshake and friendly smile.

"Well, you said you were going to do this damn rally one day and I guess that day has come, eh Lawrence," he said. Not surprisingly, he was drawn to my Honda like a moth to a flame. Dominique knew what it took to ensure the mechanical aspects of a motorcycle and car were going to endure a rally like Paris-Dakar. The way he lingered over certain parts of the bike, smiling and nodding his head, sent a very positive message.

"Nice job Lawrence. You really seem to have covered all the bases. I don't think I could have done a much better job myself," he said. Receiving this master mechanic's blessing gave me additional confidence. I could hardly wait to hit the road. The first of three major hurdles that represent Paris-Dakar had been crossed: getting into the event without any kind of hassle. As soon as the bike had been tagged to prove it had passed tech control, I drove over to the Champs de Mars, the striking park that is home to the Eiffel Tower. From here, the exodus to Dakar would commence a few days later. I headed straight to the expansive *Parc Ferme*, the enclosed compound where all the vehicles taking part in the rally are sequestered. I dropped off my bike and that would be the last time I would see it until I fired it up to commence my journey to Dakar.

On December 31, the day before the start of the rally, I took Françoise along on a reconnaissance mission to the Champs de Mars. I wanted to familiarize myself with the layout of the place and know what to expect. New Year's Eve we spent hanging around the breathtaking Eiffel Tower, all lit up to celebrate the holiday season. We walked hand-in-hand, saying little, feeling close, lost in our own thoughts. Although I would be starting the long-anticipated adventure to Dakar the following day, and should have called it an early night, I was much too excited to sleep. Paris was bristling with its usual frenetic energy — even more so as the first year of the new millennium was about to be ushered in. Despite the dire predictions of the prophets of doom, the world had not come to an end in 2000. It had been life, business and pleasure as usual. Humanity was ready to ring in another New Year. We watched throngs of people make their way to the Champs de Mars. The *Parc Ferme* proved to be a major attraction for locals and tourists alike. After we had had enough of the excitement, I took Françoise to a chocolate shop and bought us some mouth-watering desserts. At midnight, fireworks lit up the sky around the Eiffel Tower. It was a magical evening — a perfect prelude to Stage 1 of the rally.

ChapTer 5

"Gentlemen and Ladies, start your engines"

Stage 1 — New Year's Day 2001
Paris, France to Narbonne, France
Liaison: 305 km — **Special:** 6 km — **Liaison:** 594 km
Total distance: 905 km

I slept very lightly the night of New Year's Eve, my mind totally preoccupied with the Dakar. I was too anxious — and not only that, fireworks went off until the wee hours of the morning. Before I knew it, it was time to get up. I had set the alarm clock for 4:00 a.m. but I was already awake. Even though I hadn't slept much I hopped out of bed ready to take on the world. I peered outside the hotel window to check on the weather. The morning darkness hid the fact that it was raining. Françoise and I had an early breakfast, which she whipped up in the flat hotel's kitchenette. After breakfast, we loaded the trunk, spare wheels, and all the gear bags and material into the Iveco van, which was being driven by a chauffeur to follow the rally as far as the south of Spain. Before setting out for my date with destiny I slipped into my racing gear and strapped on my Acerbis tool bag.

A pelting rain, falling in a steady pattern, confronted us as we left the hotel for the short ride to the *Champs de Mars* and the *Parc Ferme*. Despite the rain, I arrived in good spirits. It was shortly before 5:00 a.m. and the place was buzzing with activity. I had never seen this many people in one place at such an early hour. There was a distinct energy surrounding the place; you just knew it was a precursor to a major happening. The assistance vehicles, which were scheduled to lead the way, were just getting ready to set off. The bikes were slated to start the rally between 6:00 and 8:00 a.m., then the cars would get the go-ahead, followed by the trucks at 11:30 a.m. Françoise, a talkative high-energy person by nature, grew more subdued as the minutes until departure ticked away. Although she was 100% behind the undertaking, it wasn't easy for her to see me off. But this is par for the course for all couples. You don't want to think about the worst possible outcome, but you know there's always the chance you won't live to see the conclusion. We both knew we had to remain upbeat and in a positive frame of mind. Still, it was a heart-wrenching goodbye. We held each other for what seemed like a long time.

"See you in Dakar, okay?" was all Françoise managed to say as I finally pulled away from her.

"You bet," I replied strapping on my helmet.

Getting everyone sent on his or her way for the premiere stage of Paris-Dakar 2001 was tedious. Each competitor was required to depart for the long journey to Narbonne individually, via a presentation podium on Avenue De La Motte Picouet, which bordered the *Parc Ferme*. This was done according to plate numbers: the riders with the lowest numbers, being the fastest, started towards the back. In the scheme of things, the rider with plate No.1, Richard Sainct, started last. With my plate designation being No.84, I was ranked roughly in the middle of the motorcycle competitors, so I wasn't really affected too much by this procedure.

Facing 916 kilometres of open road on a motorcycle is daunting at the best of times. Pouring rain at about 3° Celsius made it even more so. The pleasant weather of a few days earlier had disappeared. But I was prepared for just about anything Mother Nature could throw at me. I had a waterproof Sinisalo jacket with electric jacket liner, pants, gloves and a full coverage Arai helmet equipped with a breath deflector. Handgrip heaters completed the package. I would be comfortable and warm. Michelin Sirac dual sport tires had been mounted to a third set of wheels so the ride would be smooth and safer. It also meant I wouldn't wear out a set of precious desert tires. I had fitted the Honda with a smaller forty-five-tooth rear sprocket to let the engine work less during the long highway stretches.

After my introduction on the podium was over, I was finally on my way. The moment I had dreamed about for so long had arrived. I followed the predetermined route out of town: east for a short jaunt down Avenue De La Motte Picoue, then north onto Avenue Bosquet. When I got to Quai Branly I turned left, rode past the Eiffel Tower, and continued west onto the magnificent Boulevard De Grenelle. From there the boulevard segued south onto Route 20 past the suburbs of Paris and into the countryside. By the time daybreak started to erase the darkness, the rain let up; but the skies remained cloudy. Some 300 uneventful kilometres later, which I did at a modest clip so as not to tax the motor, I pulled into La Chatre for the first special stage of the Dakar.

Special stages are the backbone of rallies and enduros alike. They are serious business and eventually determine the overall winner of the event. In essence, a special stage is a race against the clock on a course the competitor hasn't ridden before. In enduros like the ISDE, where specials are relatively short, a rider is allowed to walk the course to get a feel for the layout. In the Dakar, however, you don't have that luxury because the specials are over long distances. To commence a special stage, each rider or driver starts individually, separated from one another by 30 seconds. As soon as the start line beam is broken, the clock starts ticking. It stops when the beam at the finish of the stage is activated. Whoever covers the distance in the shortest period of time wins the stage. The following day's starting order is based on the outcome of each rider's individual time.

To ride a special stage may sound relatively straightforward but it actually requires a total change of mindset. The special stage is about unbridled speed, whereas the liaison stages have time limits attached to them. After coming off a liaison stage, which is designed to get you from one point to the other, you are suddenly faced with pulling out all the stops. Speed becomes the name of the game. Conversely, when you finish the special, you need to stay within the imposed speed limits. Ideally, during the liaison stages, you conserve physical energy, try to relax a bit and spare the bike. If you encounter problems getting to a special, however, you need to push the envelope to get there on time.

Well before getting to the special stage the sun had burned away the gloomy skies and the surrounding landscape was relatively dry. The quaint town of La Chatre, like others throughout France, had once been a Roman encampment. Some vestiges from that era, like the Roman-built bridge across the Indre River, still linger. The medieval buildings of the place make you feel like you're in some kind of time warp as you travel through the town's centre. As soon as the Iveco van arrived at the site of the special, I switched the Honda's road-tire shod wheels with the off-road wheels. At a mere 6 kilometres, the first special stage would be the shortest of the rally. It was laid out on what the local organizers called a "weatherproof" course. I guess this meant that even if it poured rain the show would go on.

Despite the moody weather thousands of spectators were on hand to watch the action. The first section of the stage was run on a narrow piece of pavement that eventually turned into a gravel farm road. The rest of the course was composed of heavy gravel straights, some low manmade jumps, and some really tight corners. Finally, the course returned to pavement as it made its way into a motorsports facility, where the stage ended.

By the time I got to ride the course, tall berms had been built up by the bikes that had preceded me. This was the first time I rode the XR in the dirt; the suspension felt good and the engine pulled strongly. The bike launched itself out of the corners like a dragster. I tried to go as quickly as I dared, always leaving myself a margin for error. The last thing I wanted was to see my Dakar end before even getting out of France! The test was fun and I felt good afterwards. I always feel at home riding off-road, and consider pavement, although a welcome sight sometimes, a necessary evil. After finishing the special stage, I rode back towards the autoroute to look for the Iveco van. There were so many support trucks and vehicles belonging to media companies and sponsors in the mix, I had reservations about being able to depend on the van. To my amazement it had actually shown up where it was supposed to. Now that the off-road segment was behind us, I changed the wheels again and roared off down a long stretch of toll road towards the next control passage. Ahead were 600 kilometres from La Chatre to the first overnight stop of the rally at Narbonne. It was a long distance by any standard — on a modified single-cylinder off-road bike the distance was daunting.

The idea behind the European special and liaison stages is to expose the French and Spanish public to the rally as much as possible. It more than achieves that objective. I was completely taken aback. Thousands upon thousands of people crowded along the highway to wave and cheer the passing cars, trucks and bikes. Every service area along the autoroute was packed with onlookers. The teams that were sponsored by Total and Elf pulled into their respective gas stations with the kind of fanfare and hoopla an advertising agency's dreams are made of. Motorsport aficionados had gathered in droves to get close to the professional drivers and riders, and their state-of-the-art racing machines. These are vehicles whose technology and design have been especially conceived for competition in the world's most demanding rally.

My Honda hummed along nicely between 130 and 140 clicks an hour. At that speed, with the taller gearing, the 649cc engine worked easily and sounded deep and throaty. The grip heaters kept my hands warm as toast and the long highway ride was actually quite enjoyable. Once off the autoroute, the towns and main intersections were so clogged with cars and spectators I was often forced to ride on the wrong side of the road to get past the clutter. But being part of this vehicular circus was a ball. I was having the time of my life and thinking, somewhat naively, that if this was a taste of what lay ahead, Paris-Dakar was going to be a blast.

At one point in the journey south, Team BMW's Joan "Nani" Roma, Andrea Mayer and Cyril Despres seemed to deliberately stay behind me. I wasn't sure what their game plan was, but when we sailed through some long, sweeping corners, I waved them by. I preferred to follow them. I still didn't want to push the Honda too much this early on. Roma took my cue and led Mayer and Despres past me like a high-speed freight train. Riding fast and aggressively, they piloted their large, booming BMWs past cars at every opportunity and soon dissolved into the distance. Despite my conservative speed I was making really good time. The kilometres disappeared behind me until finally I pulled into Montauban for the second control passage. In keeping with the huge party the rally represented, town officials had set up a ramp-like podium so each vehicle rolled to a stop to applause, cheers and whistles. All the drivers and riders enjoyed good-natured Montauban hospitality and were presented with a small gift of the local delicacy, *pâté fois gras*.

After receiving my pâté, I pulled into a parking lot to rest for a few minutes and grab a bite to eat. While looking for a spot to park the Honda, I noticed, to my horror, a cloud of steam starting to rise from underneath the fuel tank. The crossover hose between the radiators had ruptured and was spilling coolant all over the parking lot. While this was not a good thing, I considered it a stroke of luck that it had happened here. There was ample light — darkness had only started to settle in on a long day — and there was the possibility of some assistance. Although I was hungry, my stomach would have to wait. After frantically searching around for a hose and coming up empty-handed, the BMW team was kind enough to supply me with a piece of rubber hose to replace the Tygon hose I had installed to replace the stock hose, which needed to be re-routed to accommodate the larger gas tank. The Tygon is the most expensive fuel line available, but it obviously wasn't designed to handle the heat and pressure of a coolant hose. It was my fault for assuming something I shouldn't have. At least the rupture hadn't happened in the desert. That would have been a real disaster.

I replaced the hose and resumed the rest of the journey to Narbonne. My day, and my butt, had been saved thanks to the kind folks at BMW. Finally, between nine and ten that evening, road signs for Narbonne came into view. They were a welcome sight. Like most towns and villages in France, Narbonne has a long history, dating back to 118 BC, when it was established as a Roman colony. Its core boasts many and varied historical buildings in styles ranging from Gothic to Art Nouveau. And like any fair-sized city in France, it has a splendid cathedral. Narbonne's, called Saint-Just, dates from 1272. Most of these cultural treasures were lost on me, however, as I cruised into town. It had been a long day and I just wanted to see it end. The way things were shaping up, I'd be lucky to be in bed before it officially became tomorrow.

I rode into the centre of town towards a large covered stage that served as a podium and waited in line. Hundreds of people had gathered in front of the brightly lit platform. They cheered as each competitor rode or drove up onto the structure. After handing our time cards to a TSO official, a master of ceremonies asked each competitor some questions about their first day in the rally. Everything seemed to happen in slow motion. Lack of a good night's sleep and the long journey from Paris, had caught up with me and hit me like a sledgehammer. Suddenly I felt zoned out and sluggish. The only thing I wanted to do was get to the hotel, eat some dinner, and crawl into bed. Finally, I got the signal to ride up onto the podium. I handed in my time card, which almost dropped from my numb fingers, then approached the master of ceremonies for the brief interview. Despite my best effort and a relatively good command of the language, I responded to his questions like some tourist who had dropped out of French 101. The crowd, however, overlooked this and gave me a round of applause. At least I'd made more sense to them than a lot of the other competitors, who spoke no French at all. I mustered up a curt wave to show my appreciation and slowly rode off the podium.

I headed to the *Parc Ferme* to have my Honda sequestered for the night. It was a bit of a walk back to the hotel, so I approached two local people who were getting into their car and asked for a lift. My French seemed to have returned. They readily obliged, happy to be able to help out a Paris-Dakar Rally rider. When we got to the hotel, I thanked them for the ride and gave them both a Canadian flag pin. The gratitude with which they accepted the pins was as if I'd handed them a couple of gold coins. It reminded me of the high esteem in which Canada is held abroad, and how lucky I was to call it home.

I had hoped the Iveco van, which contained all my belongings, would have arrived by now but it was nowhere to be seen. I checked into the hotel and thought of one thing only: sitting down to a decent meal and then hitting the sack. To my chagrin the clerk informed me their restaurant was already closed. I was so hungry I could have eaten the flowers that were in a vase on the lobby desk. "The hotel just west of here has a café that serves cooked meals till eleven o'clock," the clerk assured me. I headed down the street and found the hotel at the end of the block. The café was crowded and noisy; the menu was limited to some finger foods and the national favourite, *biftek et frites* — steak and French fries. I opted for that and it went down like manna from heaven, washed down with two bottles of Perrier.

While I was having dinner, the Iveco arrived and it was parked in front of my hotel. I was finally able to retire, satisfied that, except for the glitch with the hose, the first day of my twenty-one-day adventure had gone rather well. The only thing left to do was to call Françoise and tell her about my day. It was good to hear her voice. She was back at her parents' place in Thionville, where she and Mia were going to stay for a few days before heading home to Canada.

"Congratulations, I'm really proud of you," she said excitedly.

"Oh. What did I do?" I replied without much enthusiasm.

"You mean you don't know? You recorded the thirty-fifth fastest time in the special stage."

Françoise had logged onto the Dakar website and checked

to see how I had fared. I hadn't expected to find out my results until the next morning. I was encouraged by this news. Considering the large number of riders I was up against, thirty-fifth wasn't at all bad. It meant a good starting position the following day at Chateau Lastours, just outside of Narbonne. The Italian Giovani Sala had won the stage riding a KTM, posting a time of 3:37:00. Because the special was so short, the times recorded were all very tight. Most of the pros finished within seconds of each other. Tenth place Cyril Despres put his BMW across the finish line just eight seconds behind Sala. The car division was won by the French driver Jose Maria Servia in a Schlesser/Renault/Megane buggy. He and his navigator Jean-Marie Lurquin logged a time of 3:43:00. As in the motorcycle class, the top drivers finished within seconds of each other. After chatting for a few more minutes we said goodnight. I could hardly keep my eyes open.

"Give Mia a big hug and kiss for me when she gets up tomorrow. Tell her daddy loves her a whole bunch," I said before hanging up. It was nearly midnight when I flopped down onto a nice comfortable bed. I knew that pretty soon I'd be sleeping in a tent in the desert. I instantly slipped into a deep, sound sleep. The following morning would see my fellow rallyists and I leave France for sunny Spain. From there, we'd be boarding the ferry for Africa and getting down to the nitty-gritty.

* * *

Stage 2 — Tuesday, January 2, 2001
Narbonne, France to Castellon, Spain
Liaison: 20 km — **Special:** 35 km — **Liaison:** 514 km
Total distance: 569 km

Departure time for Stage 2 was a reasonable eight o'clock, on the morning of Tuesday, January 2nd. The short, 20-kilometre liaison to Chateau Lastours would take us through Narbonne and into the hills surrounding the town. Chateau Lastours, a renowned wine-growing region in southwestern France, looks like it has been painted onto hills that stretch lazily for many kilometres from east to west. The area's south-facing slopes, rich red soil and temperate climate produce some of France's best red wines. The starting order was reversed again this day so I had a bit of a wait before my departure. As in Paris, reversing the starting order was done so that the fastest riders started last. But whereas the starting line in Paris was determined by the rider's plate number, here it was based on the times recorded in the special stage from the day before. The spectators had quite a climb and distance to walk to reach a good vantage point from which to witness the rallyists attack the special stage. While waiting for my go-ahead, I broke the monotony by chatting with the well-known Swedish enduro/rally rider, P.G. Lundmark. He had entered his first Dakar in 2000, finishing a remarkable eleventh overall. Like me, P.G. was a privateer. He mentioned that he funded much of his current Dakar effort by giving presentations and slide shows in his native Sweden. What surprised me was that the KTM-mounted rider had arrived a few minutes behind me the night before. "My support crew failed to meet me at the special test segment, and I had to do it on my street tires," he told me, explaining why he'd been a bit off the pace.

By the time I finally got the go-ahead to hit the road to commence Stage 2, it was close to 11:00 a.m. It was near perfect riding weather: there was a slight breeze, the sun was strong, the sky dark blue, not one cloud dotted the horizon. Just before starting out I spotted Franco Acerbis at the staging area. For a moment I wasn't sure if my eyes were playing tricks on me. But there was no mistaking the amicable Italian's cheerful, animated demeanour. To see a familiar face in this mass of strangers was a nice surprise. I'd known Franco, founder/president of Acerbis Plastics, a world leader in the manufacturing of aftermarket and OEM motorcycle parts, for many years. I called out and waved to draw his attention. Franco seemed as surprised to see me as I had been to see him. He jostled through the people milling about the starting area and joined me for the few minutes that remained before I had to take off.

We exchanged some small talk, and when I got the signal to leave he gave me a hearty pat on the back. "Give 'em hell Lawrence. I'll see you in Dakar on the twenty-first." I hoped Franco had some kind of psychic abilities.

The start of the special stage was an uphill, two-track road with shale-like rock embedded into the ground. There was a thin layer of moist clay spread over the surface and it was very slick. I rode cautiously over the 35-kilometre distance, not wanting to dump the bike. The course climbed higher onto the plateau, where eventually the landscape became shrouded in a heavy mist. Visibility was very poor and the going was dangerous. I pulled off my goggles and rode with a large margin for error, braking easily and using the inside lines. Finding the turns in the fog was nearly impossible. I caught and passed one rider and, until another came into view, remained on guard for any and all hazards. Once the next rider was close enough to reel in, I stayed behind him and used him as another set of eyes for what lay ahead. I followed his lead, ready to apply the brakes if he showed any signs of hesitation or if he went down. That way I could maintain a comfortable pace without taking undue risks. The tactic worked and I felt I was riding at a good steady pace. That is, until Lundmark and Alain Duclos flew past me like a pair of supersonic jets. It was as if these guys possessed bat-like radar and knew exactly what lay ahead. Finally, after what seemed like an eternity, the fog lifted and I whipped past the rider I had been following.

The special stage was longer and hotter than I was prepared for. I should have known what to expect. I was aware that this part of France didn't get really cold in winter, but at 15°C it seemed unusually warm. When I thought of Paris-Dakar I thought in terms of deserts. It was another lesson learned — you can never gather too much information. Towards the area near the end of the special stage the wet clay surface of the road was like riding on greased ball bearings. Advancing at a snail's pace was the only way to stay upright. I knew that one crash could throw it all away. Once past the finish line and into the control area, every competitor handed over his or her time card. I coasted to a stop and a TSO timekeeper held out his hand to accept my card. Team KTM's Richard Sainct won the stage with a time of 31:25:00. Sainct, winner of the motorcycle class in 1999/2000, riding for Team BMW, had been hired away from the German manufacturer by KTM. With Sainct, the Austrians were hoping to snare their first ever Dakar victory. Joan Roma kept BMW in the mix by taking second place for the day, less than a minute behind Sainct. Jean-Louis Schlesser, who had won the car division for the past two years, took the stage in his Schlesser/Renault/Megane buggy with a time of 30:33:00. He displaced his teammate Jose-Maria Servia, who finished fourth, 54 seconds down, as the provisional overall leader. At this point being at the head of the pack didn't mean very much. With eighteen special stages to go, holding any lead position was tenuous at best. Not till the halfway point do the prospective class winners usually start to present themselves. Still, nothing is certain until the finish line is crossed. Even if you're more than an hour ahead of second place, your Dakar can end at any time after a crash or mechanical failure.

By the time I got to the end of the special, the lead group of bikes were already on the liaison to Castellon. Not that I was overly concerned. It wasn't my intention to ride over my head in an attempt to be among the front-runners — winning the Dakar wasn't the carrot I was going for. I just wanted to finish. After finishing the special stage, just doing that seemed like it was going to be a tall order. I was already in a state of fatigue, sweating profusely and overheating. And this was just the beginning. The bike also concerned me — perhaps unnecessarily. I was projecting my own discomfort, convinced the motor needed air moving through the radiator, and took off without a second thought. Unfortunately, in my haste and tired condition, I left without collecting my time card. I rode along narrow farm roads towards the main highway and the service area where most of the privateer teams were making preparations for the ride farther south, or loading up their bikes in their respective support vehicles. In Europe, the rally rules allow the bikes to be transported in vans or on trailers during some liaison stages. Like most of the other motorcycle-mounted competitors, I choose to take advantage of this rule and decided I would load the xr into the Iveco for the 500-kilometre drive to Castellon, situated 80 kilometres north of Valencia, on Spain's east coast. As I pulled into the service area, it suddenly dawned on me that I had forgotten my time card. I felt my stomach knot up. This was not good. What should I do? Turn back or keep going? I was nearing Spain and had put quite some distance between the last checkpoint and myself. The thought of going back was not an attractive one.

I parked the bike, found my rule book in the Iveco van and quickly thumbed through it to see what this infraction would cost me. To my dismay I discovered that a 15-minute penalty was assessed for losing one's time card. When considering the alternative, retracing my steps to fetch the card, it was clear that it would cost me even more time. There was nothing left to do but take the penalty and make the best of the situation. I knew that the time card incident would ultimately prove to be a minor glitch in the overall scheme of things. I was certain to face more serious setbacks in the sands of North Africa. I often remind myself that there really is no good or bad when you get right down to it: things just are the way they are. As conscious beings we're moved to attach meanings to what happens to us and around us, effectively creating our own reality. With that in mind, I like to think negatives can be turned into positives. When I spotted the Iveco support van I quickly forgot about the time card. New ones are issued at the beginning of each stage, anyway. It wasn't the end of the world, just a 15-minute time penalty. On the provisional scoreboard, however, I dropped from a thirty-fifth overall standing to 125th. I would likely never reach that lofty ranking obtained in Stage 1 again, but I would definitely move through the pack and regain some lost ground.

I loaded up the xr into the van and we set off for Castellon. Being a passenger in a comfortable seat was a welcome break. It gave me the opportunity to catch up on some sleep and conserve precious physical energy for Stage 3. The Iveco was loaded to the brink and lumbered along at barely 110 kilometres per hour. It was already past noon and we were in for a long monotonous drive south. It never seemed to end. All I could think of doing was some basic maintenance to the XR. It needed to be thoroughly cleaned and given a general once-over. The oil had to be changed and the spokes tightened. There was another concern. When I'd loaded the bike into the van I had noticed a crack in the exhaust pipe near the joint where it met the muffler. It would need to be welded. Fortunately, I had the business card of a Honda dealer in Castellon who had a young rider entered in the rally. I was sure I could get the pipe repaired there.

I was glad to pull into Castellon and that Paris was a long way behind me. Located on the Mediterranean Sea's Costa-Azahar, Castellon de la Playa is the capital city of Castellon Province. The city sports modern avenues, narrow streets and old plazas. Modernist buildings, modern shops, shady parks and Gothic and Renaissance monuments contribute to the charm of the city, which was bathed in a glorious sunset as I opened my eyes. Dusk fell as we pulled into Boluda Honda. The shop owner welcomed me like I was an old friend. It was becoming more obvious each day that taking part in the Paris-Dakar Rally afforded one a kind of special status.

I explained to the owner what my problem was only to be told he wouldn't be able to weld the pipe. "Don't worry," he said, sensing my disappointment, "there's a shop not far from here that can do it. You can remove the pipe here and one of my men will take you." I set to work quickly. Time was of the essence and there would be some additional things to do when I got back. When the pipe was removed, I hopped onto the back of a scooter, piloted by one of the mechanics, and was rushed over to the welding shop. It was a hair-raising ride there and back, and one I wouldn't want to repeat. Fortunately, the mechanic was an accomplished scooter pilot. After we returned, I drilled out the pipe mounts and installed rubber mounts to curb the vibration and expansion of the long stainless steel exhaust that had caused the cracking. While at Boluda, I had the road tires removed and off-road tires installed on the spare wheels.

By the time the bike was finished and thanks were extended all around, it was close to 11:00 p.m. We followed a shop employee through downtown Castellon to the *Parc Ferme*. After the bike was sequestered, I had to transfer my trunk to the official TSO truck which would carry it directly to Africa with the other competitors' luggage. As feared, I had exceeded the maximum weight allowed.

"Hey, *mon ami*, do we look like Arnold Schwarzenegger or something? What have you got in there? A body you're planning on burying in the desert?" one of the TSO volunteers quipped. Point taken — I removed some of the heavier spare bike parts and set out to locate the Team Tibau support truck. I would have to store the parts with the rest of my stuff already aboard the vehicle.

When all the post–Stage 2 chores were completed we made our way to the hotel, which took some time to find. Once again, it was around midnight by the time I dragged my gear into my room. I threw everything onto the floor, took a shower, and crawled exhausted into bed. I tossed and turned until I fell into a restless sleep. Another day had gone by without a proper dinner.

* * *

Stage 3 — Wednesday, January 3, 2001
Castellon, Spain to Almeria, Spain
Liaison: 5 km — **Special:** 6 km — **Liaison:** 520 km
Total distance: 531 km

The day began in darkness. The entire contents of my gear bags were spread around the hotel room in an effort to ensure nothing had disappeared from the Iveco van, which had been parked overnight on the street in front of the hotel. When I was satisfied everything was there, I made my way down to the hotel bar to grab something to eat. To my dismay it didn't offer much in the way of breakfast. The lack of solid food was becoming a concern. I ordered some juice and fruit. I also asked for some hot water and made myself a bowl of Quaker instant oatmeal. As soon as I had finished my meagre breakfast I prepared myself for the final day of the European leg of the rally.

The Iveco's driver was waiting for me outside the hotel and we set off for the *Parc Ferme*. The streets of Castellon were a maze of narrow one-way roads that didn't make much sense in North American terms. Rather than try to figure out how to get to the *Parc Ferme* and risk getting lost, I hailed a taxi. After telling the driver where to go, I had the Iveco driver get into the cab. I wanted to drive the van myself and followed the taxi to the *Parc Ferme*. Once we made it there, I discovered that the special stage, which was to be held on the beach, had been cancelled after a disagreement between the organizers and the Spanish Motorcycle Federation. It seemed that plain, simple greed had spurred the federation to demand more money to allow the event to be run in their jurisdiction. The car and truck competitors didn't face the same scenario, and for them, Stage 3 was business as usual. On the comparatively warm, balmy beach at Castellon — a stark contrast to the cold, miserable start in Paris — the French duo Jean-Pierre Fontenay and Gilles Picard won the stage by 6 seconds in their Mitsubishi Pajero/Montero, just ahead of teammates Hiroshi Masuoka and Pascal Maimon. The third and final European Dakar stage was only 6 kilometres long, but the soft beach sand was enough to reshuffle the names at the top of the scoreboard. Masuoka and Maimon inherited the lead from Renault's Jean-Louis Schlesser and Henri Magne, who finished thirteenth after getting bogged down in the sand. Thanks to their victory Fontenay and Picard powered their way from eighth to third, a scant 14 seconds behind Schlesser/Magne.

While the car competitors were slugging it out on the beach, I used the unexpected time off to look after a few more mechanical details on the XR. When reinstalling the pipe the night before, I noticed the muffler also had a small crack in the welds near the front. And I still had to mount the small electronic compass that would be critical in the barren expanses of North Africa. I rode the bike over to the auto body repair shop where the owner and his staff had been so helpful the night before in welding my pipe. Everyone was very friendly and accommodating once again. The rally was a big deal in this town and it was obvious they wanted to help in any way they could, to the point of refusing payment for the second welding job. One of the shop's artisans also carefully ground away a small part of the front number plate to provide a nice spot to mount the compass. I stuck a Velcro strip down onto the aluminum ICO mount and pushed the compass into place. Now the bike was ready for Africa. We parted company with handshakes all around. A couple of photographs were snapped for posterity. I left these wonderful Spaniards with a collection of — what else? — Canadian flag pins. I also gave them a Euromaster map of the rally, which they immediately pinned to the shop's bulletin board.

Once the bike was reloaded into the van, we set off down the wide four-lane highway to the southern tip of Spain, a distance of 445 kilometres. Like many of the motorcycle competitors, I opted to have my bike transported the rest of the way rather than riding it. It took all day to rumble down the "del Mediterraneo Autoroute" but the weather was picture perfect. The sky was a pale blue and crystal clear. Not a whiff of cloud could be seen anywhere. I could see why this was a favourite holiday destination for many Europeans who live north of the Spanish border. The January weather was balmy to the point where a T-shirt was suitable attire. The Iveco's large windshield acted like a greenhouse. Soon I was overheating and drinking water almost non-stop.

The parched countryside crawled by as we kept a steady but sluggish pace in the overloaded van. By the end of the afternoon, we drove into the bustling southern port city of Almeria, located between the Sierra Nevada Mountains and the Mediterranean Sea. The ancient town, rich in history, serves as the capital of Almeria Province as well as being an important seaport. Overlooking the town from its hilltop perch is the famous Alcazaba, a sprawling Moorish citadel built in the tenth century. Almeria has a distinct salty air about it; the downtown area has the look and feel of an exotic port. The townspeople were obviously stirred by the excitement generated by the arrival of the rallyists, support vehicles and entourage of TSO people and journalists. The dock area of the city was jam-packed with cars, kids on mopeds and motorcycles, and hundreds of Dakar-crazed onlookers milling about.

We pulled the Iveco off to the side of the road in the harbour district and I got ready for the next day's ride. TSO had warned everybody to be ready to jump into action as soon as our ferry docked in Nador, Morocco. Getting suited up as the sun went down was a strange feeling. But I wanted to be sure I was ready for the start the following morning, even if I had to sleep with my gear on. I got my XR off the support van and rode over to a nearby gas station to fill its fuel tank to the brim. There was an incredible number of colourful race cars, bikes and support vehicles jockeying for access to the fuel pumps. Contributing to the chaos was the crush of spectators who seemed intent to remain where they were. Getting a first-hand look at the men, women and machines taking part in the famous Paris-Dakar seemed to be the only consideration. Everybody taking part in the rally had to squeeze in and around the crowd riveted to the spots they had staked out. Surprisingly, there were no incidents of pushing, crushed toes or flaring tempers. But, after all, this was as much show business as it was motorsport; without the fans there is no rally.

An eerie sense of anticipation gripped me as a bloody red sun dropped behind the sharp cliffs surrounding Almeria. The temperature was still balmy, yet I felt an unwelcome sensation that sent shivers through me. Ancient places seem to be imprinted with the many intrigues and twists of fortune and destiny that have taken place there. My imagination was getting the better of me. I suddenly longed for the solitude of the desert. I needed to shut out the din and frenetic pace of my surroundings. I took a deep breath in an attempt to exorcize the negative feeling that had come over me and retreated to the staging area inside the loading compound. It was a good place to wait until we were given the signal that the first of the two immense ferries that would take the rally caravan to Africa was ready to be boarded.

Searching for a more positive frame of mind, I struck up a conversation with a fellow rallyist named Guido Maletti, a friendly Italian motorcyclist who had also sought respite from the turmoil. Maletti, I discovered, was a fifteen-time Dakar veteran with many impressive finishes to his credit — often in the top ten. In this edition, he was riding a very meticulously prepared Kawasaki KLX650. His attention to detail was obvious. The bike was clearly well thought-out and designed to go the distance with comfort and ease of maintenance. I asked Guido for advice on how to set up my roadbook, which had to be inserted into an electric holder mounted on the XR's handlebars. In the Dakar, the electric roadbook holder is one of the most essential pieces of navigational equipment. It automatically scrolls the roadbook, which is printed on a roll of paper, onto a take-up bar. The roll itself is usually 6 inches wide and, depending on the length of the stage, its diameter can be more than the size of a fist to hold all the directions. I wasn't quite sure how to install the book and saw this as a good opportunity to find out.

"Ah, it is easy as one-two-three. Let me show you. The end of each stage is at the beginning of each roll and needs to be rewound. You start from the end, you see. Like this," Guido said as he taped the end of the roll to the feed-bar. He then proceeded to re-roll the entire book. "Once it's been rolled onto the feed-bar, the beginning of the stage is ready to be taped to the take-up bar, and you're in business."

While re-rolling the book, Guido carefully tightened up the windings occasionally. "There you go. Simple, eh?" he said as he snapped the holder's clear plastic cover into place. The procedure of loading a roadbook was complete. It was easy, but everything seems simple when you know how to do it.

I was glad to finally know how to use the roadbook properly. Without the roadbook, which is the rally's bible, you don't get very far. Each evening, competitors are supplied with the following day's book, which shows the route to be taken to the next destination and explains how to get there. There are three main indications on each panel: distances shown can be as little as 50 metres or as large as 50 kilometres. In the left-hand column, the distance is shown from the start of the stage. Below that is the distance from the last marker. To the right is a pictograph of what you should see around you. This could be just about anything that can be considered a landmark. Further to the right are comments, available in a variety of languages including Arabic, French and English. I primarily used the English version.

Once the word spread that we could board, I bid farewell to the Iveco's chauffeur and sent him on his way to return the van to Darry. I slowly proceeded to ride the XR across the large expanse of pavement to where competitors were being directed up the wide ramp and into the hold of the Swedish-registered ferry we had been assigned to for our passage to Nador. I felt a wave of excitement rush through me. With gusto I rode up the ramp into the ship's gaping interior. The European preliminaries and the liaison stages were behind us. The "real" Dakar was about to begin.

After the bike was parked in a safe spot, I found my cabin and promptly took off my gear. The cabin was a Lilliputian-sized cubicle with four tiny bunks stacked two to a side, flanked by a small sink and mirror. Before my cabin mates bunked in, I decided to hit the shower and refresh myself from a long, sweaty day on the road. To my delight, I found the shower had plenty of hot water. Life was good again. The trials and tribulations of the past few days seemed trivial now. Two and a half weeks later, I'd know just how trivial those first few days really had been.

When I emerged from the shower, some of my cabin mates had shown up and they were anxious to get washed up, too. We exchanged greetings as I stowed my gear, then I made my way to the cafeteria to have something to eat. Finally, I could sit down to a full-course dinner, which included curried chicken. I had the pleasure of dining with some top-level riders, including World Enduro Champion Kari Tianen, South

African Alfie Cox, Japanese rider Jun Mitsuhashi and P.G. Lundmark. I kept my ears cocked for any useful tidbits of information. P.G. ate like there was no tomorrow, guzzling Cokes and wolfing down his plate of food. When I asked him why he ate no chicken, he told me his system didn't contain the right bacteria to digest food like curry. He restricted himself to boiled potatoes, peas, and other staples. I followed P.G.'s lead and chose what I ate carefully.

During dinner the ship had left Spain and we were on our way to Morocco. The lights of Almeria grew more and more distant, replaced once we were on the open sea by an all-encompassing darkness. After dinner, I got my passport stamped and went to the ferry's exchange station to convert some of my money into Moroccan drachmas. Before turning in, I went outside to one the ship's decks to catch a moment of peace and quiet. I enjoyed some deep breaths of sea air and then went looking for my cabin. One of the other guys was already sleeping when I entered. I crawled into my bunk — it was time for some much-needed rest. I stuffed some earplugs into my ears, just in case one of my cabin mates snored. As I drifted off to sleep my last thoughts were of Françoise and Mia. I knew I was a fortunate man.

Chapter 6

The real Dakar

------ ------ ------ ------ ------ ------ ------ ------ ------ ------

Stage 4 — Thursday, January 4, 2001
Nador, Morocco to Er-Rachidia, Morocco
Liaison: 184 km — **Special:** 139 km — **Liaison:** 279 km
Total distance: 602 km

I didn't wake up until early the next morning as the ferry was approaching North Africa. I endured another restless sleep and woke up to thoughts of friends and family in Canada. I wasn't really feeling homesick — I'm used to being away from home — they just seemed to be on my mind. The day of the week, and what was going on back home, was irrelevant to me at this moment. I had much bigger fish to fry. I rolled out of my bunk, splashed water on my face, pulled on my riding gear and went for a quick breakfast. The body language of the people on board suggested the arrival of something big. Nobody could mistake this for anything but the important event it was.

After breakfast, I went outside where I was greeted by vast, inky skies, dotted with countless stars. I lounged about on the starboard deck; with forced patience I watched the distant shimmering lights of Morocco inch closer. I was like a kid waiting to be turned loose in an amusement park. I fought hard to contain my excitement, anxious to get the rally under-way. I needed to do something familiar in these unfamiliar surroundings. Riding a motorcycle was about the only thing that would qualify. Finally, not knowing what to do with myself, I decided to go down below. I wanted to check my bike well ahead of our arrival time in Nador so I would be ready when the ferry's massive door opened to disgorge its cargo onto the shores of Africa.

I followed the small overhead signs that led to the parking garage levels in search of my rally-prepped XR650. The hold of the ship was stifling and clogged with vehicles of every description. Motorcycles were jammed along the bulkheads; thick ropes were tied across the seats of each bike to hold them in place. Row upon row, wedged nose to tail, were the race cars and trucks that would compete with the motorcycles for the honour of being the first to reach Dakar. I clawed my way through the tangle of rubber, plastic and steel and finally spotted my Honda. It was trussed up against a far bulkhead next to dozens of other bikes. All over the hold overanxious car drivers were starting their vehicles. I shared their anticipation but not their haste. Their high-performance engines were blowing half-burnt fuel and toxic smoke into the interior of the ship. By the time I made it over to the XR650, the choking fumes from the idling vehicles nearly knocked me out. Within minutes, I was sweating bullets and gasping for air. I thought of Dante's inferno and decided it couldn't have been much worse than this. Suddenly, I longed for the bone-chilling temperatures and crisp outdoor air I was more accustomed to at this time of year in Canada, now a world away. My bike would have to wait. I didn't want to hang around in the noxious fumes any longer than necessary. I would return after we docked and deal with it then.

Nearly overtaken by nausea, I threaded my way back to the nearest exit that would give me relief, following a maze of tiny gangways to an upper deck. Much to my chagrin, I was greeted by acrid cigarette smoke in the steep and narrow stairwells. It was not as bad as the deadly fumes below, but far from a return to easier breathing. On my way up I met all kinds of people shuffling around in the stairwells. They seemed to be going in no particular direction: some up, some down. Everybody seemed driven by adrenalin or anxiety. Most were fellow rally-ists, readily identified by their colourful apparel. Many were dressed in driving suits or motorcycle riding gear; most carried helmets and gloves. Everyone, including myself, was gripped by Dakar fever. The closer we got to Nador, the more anxious we were to get on the road.

It was still pitch black outside when I reached an upper deck. It seemed that whoever wasn't down below was on deck watching the lights from shore draw nearer and nearer. I stood against the railing and greedily sucked fresh air into my oxygen-starved lungs. I was glad to see the docks of Nador almost within spitting distance now. The ship slowed notice-ably. Soon we were manoeuvring into port. The massive vessel came to rest against the dock with a resounding thud. This was it: Africa. No turning back! For the next eighteen days the Paris-Dakar Rally would unfold for me, hundreds of other competitors and the TSO staff and volunteers who were the backbone of this huge event. The character and cadence of the Dakar was about to change. The carnival atmosphere that defined the rally in France and Spain would give way to some-thing much more intense and serious. The war of attrition was about to begin.

As soon as we docked I wanted to rush below deck again, jump on my bike and get off the ship as quickly as possible. I decided to curb my enthusiasm, however, and wait. When everyone else headed below, I followed suit. Back in the foul atmosphere of the ship's hold, lack of sleep and high emotions had me quickly craving fresh air once more. My eyes stung from the fumes, even worse now as drivers and riders started their vehicles left, right, front and back. The sound of so many high-performance engines exploding to life was deafening. As I made my way to my Honda I took shallow gulps of air, ignoring to the best of my ability the chaos around me. Once I had the XR in hand, I purposefully wriggled it between the bikes and cars of owners who hadn't made it down yet. I manoeuvred the Honda as close as I could to the front ramp of the ship. The sooner I got ashore, the better I would feel.

Finally, when it was my turn to disembark, I mounted the bike and rode down the wide ramp onto terra firma. A rush of relief and exhilaration swept over me. I was in Africa. Soon I would be on my way to Dakar. But first there was the formality of clearing customs in Nador, home to some 180,000 Tarifit-Berber-speaking inhabitants.

The port city of Nador is located on the Bou Areg Lagoon in northeastern Morocco. Nador was designed as an industrial port, and that was the dominant feel of the place. In addition to loading and unloading ships from far and near, Nador is a trading centre for fish, fruits and livestock. There are no quaint beachside restaurants, no picturesque views of fishermen returning home at sunset. The city's most distinctive landmarks are the broadcasting towers of Radio Medi, easily visible from out at sea. At a dazzling 380 metres high, the towers are the tallest manmade structures in Africa. As a tourist, Nador was the last place you'd want to be; as a rallyist, it was a welcome site.

I got into line with the rest of the throng to clear customs. I expected a time-consuming delay while laid-back officials checked our documents. To my pleasant surprise, the Moroccan border police took only a cursory glance at everyone's passport. Once we were processed, we were funnelled a short distance into a large gravel parking lot. It took some time to gather every rally vehicle. Now the wait was long and drawn out. Once everybody had been accounted for, a gala breakfast was next on the agenda. I joined a crowded table with a group of other motorcycle riders that included Alain Duclos, an affable, talkative guy who hails from Bamako, Mali. Alain had been one of the riders who'd overtaken me during the special stage on the way from Narbonne to Castellon. Although considered one of the top riders in the rally, this was my fellow Honda-mounted rider's first Paris-Dakar. We sat, all of us wearing our riding gear, on small high-backed chairs under colourful tents. Every table came with the trappings one would expect in a fancy restaurant: bright white tablecloths, cloth napkins, sparkling silverware, crystal glasses and ornate plates, teacups and saucers. Breakfast consisted of some strange pancakes and sweet pastries that were tasty and abundant. The chilled fresh orange juice and hot tea went down like nectar. After the poor man's breakfasts I had eaten over the past few mornings, this was a pleasant change.

While we were enjoying the Moroccan goodies, local musicians dressed in native garb wandered about blowing horns and banging drums, gongs and little cymbals. Perhaps it was designed to set a festive tone; maybe they were a welcoming committee, as per Moroccan custom. It was a gesture that didn't really appeal to me at that time of day. A little peace and quiet would have suited me just fine. Maybe I wasn't quite as cultured as I'd like to think. Trying to glean whatever I could, I picked the brains of my breakfast companions. When do you line up? What about the time cards? Where do you get fuel? What . . . who . . . where . . . when? The veterans, perhaps amused by my babe-in-the-woods style, seemed willing enough to share their knowledge. There was so much to absorb. It wasn't easy deciphering the procedures ahead. As I would soon learn, it was always a challenge to maintain some sort of equilibrium during the rally. There were so many variables poised to upset the applecart. It would be essential to attend to even the smallest details, each of which contributed in a small way to being more comfortable, healthy and strong; or to being able to solve the problems that were about to confront us.

An hour or so after breakfast it was finally time for me to set out for my first Dakar bivouac. Getting everyone unloaded from the ferry and through customs, then fed and lined up in the proper starting order for Er-Rachidia was an involved procedure. We had only travelled a few hundred metres from the ship, but already fatigue was setting in. I hoped the actual physical act of riding would be less tiring. The 15-minute penalty I had been assessed for forgetting my time card at the end of the special stage on Day 2 would now be applied. Although I had recorded a reasonable time in the 35-kilometre special, which had seen me finish in fiftieth place, the penalty put me at the back of the pack in 125th spot. Not an ideal position to start my first day in Africa. Still, it was of little consequence in the long run.

Team BMW's John Deacon was one of those whom I found at the end of the starting order. This surprised me considering the Brit was a factory rider. Factory riders are the hired guns of the motorsport world. Although it's an enviable position to be in, the job comes with the added pressure of having to perform. Factory riders are expected to be in the front-running mix or to ride shotgun for higher profile teammates. There are a lot of wannabes in the wings ready to replace anyone who lost his edge. Deacon was not thrilled with the prospect of having to pass dozens of riders in the special stage, but if he was going to keep his edge, he had no choice. John was already under pressure, and this was only the fourth day of the rally. I, on the other hand, didn't have to worry about much of anything, except getting through the day.

I learned from Deacon that his bike had quit on him at the start of the special stage in Chateau Lastours, a reminder that even factory-prepared machines were not exempt from mechanical problems. Apparently, some wires had broken underneath the fuel tank of Deacon's BMW and the engine had simply stopped. It took half an hour to fix the problem, effectively eliminating Deacon's chance to win the rally. We talked briefly about the race and his BMW, a massive twin-cylinder race bike that was the culmination of a year's worth of work by an entire department of technicians. "I even spent a week at the German factory, wind-tunnel testing the aerodynamics of the body work," Deacon said. "Nothing was left to chance for this race and then a simple electrical problem went and threw a wrench into the works. Now, that's frustrating!" He went on to explain that for the 2001 Paris-Dakar, BMW had enlisted strong riders from each of their most important markets: England, the USA, France, Spain and Germany. The campaign was part of a marketing strategy to shift focus towards adventurous BMW models like the Boxer-engined GS, a bike that was very popular among long-distance motorcycle riders. As to be expected from a major factory like BMW — motorcycle-class winners of the 1999 and 2000 editions of the rally — their effort was polished and professional. The team consisted of no fewer than five riders, including four men on twins and one woman, German Andrea Mayer, on a single-cylinder 650. The backup infrastructure was impressive, with race support trucks and mechanics for each rider's bike. With such support, failure to complete the rally was unlikely but even the best of the best are not immune to Murphy's Law.

Once it was my turn to hit the road, I took off at a quick pace through early-morning Nador rush-hour traffic. I was finally on my way. Life was good and I forgot about being tired. Navigation was easy enough for this stage, which was basically designed as a warm-up to acclimatize everyone to their new environment. A police officer stood at every major intersection in town, waving us through in the proper direction. There were no lane dividing lines painted on the roads and passing rattle-trap cars and trucks became a free-for-all. Adding to the traffic mayhem were donkey carts that listlessly plodded along, and bicycle riders who weaved in and around parked cars. No one seemed to care about the speed I was doing. All kinds of people stood along the road and waved. Groups of carefree school-children carrying book bags lingered on the sidewalks to enjoy the Dakar circus. I'm sure many of them were going to be late for class. It felt like an auspicious day to be setting out for the long African segment of the Dakar: a wave of emotional well-being swept over me. When I'm riding a motorcycle, nothing else seems to matter. It's like being in an altered state of consciousness. I thought for a moment that even if I didn't get any farther than the outskirts of Nador, it would have been worth all the work and energy I'd put in thus far. I decided I would take things as they came, one hour at a time. Each stage completed would be bonus, regardless of how far I had come. Nonetheless, I still had every intention of reaching my destination and finishing the rally, even if it seemed against the odds.

The road out of Nador took the rally due south for 184 kilometres to the first special stage. The air, which was rather polluted, cleared up once the city limits were left behind. The pavement I found myself on was narrow and broken up along the edges. The bitumen tar covering was thin and fragile; potholes exposed the base of the road. It was clear that the budget in Morocco for road work was minimal. The rainy season must have played havoc with the road that stretched from Nador to just south of Taourirt, close to where the special stage was to begin. When I got to Taourirt, a small town not far from the vast reserve lake created by the El-Mansour Eddahbi Dam, I stopped to refuel. Some twenty minutes later, I arrived at the departure point of the special stage, which was basically in the middle of nowhere. Nearly all of the bikes were already parked waiting for their start time. Police with long bamboo staffs chased away the locals, who seemed to materialize out of thin air. It struck me as rather strange, but then this was Morocco, a country I knew very little about. The wait to get the go-ahead was once again long and uncomfortable. There were only flat stones to sit on and rest. Nearly every rider had to walk a short distance away from the parking area to relieve him- or herself. To urinate in public was second nature to everyone here, except maybe the odd uptight North American.

The first African special stage — still relatively short for a Dakar at 139 kilometres — started on a hard-packed dirt and rock road scarred with washouts. The track wound through a cork forest and eventually rose out of a valley onto a rocky edge, carved out of the hillside. It was there I noticed the "Maindru Photo" sign just before the point where a photographer snaps pictures of every rally vehicle that passes. The company specializes in events like Paris-Dakar. Once the rallyists are back home, they receive a contact sheet of photos from Maindru from which orders can be placed in various sizes. Of course, nearly everyone wanted a photo from this spot, because most made it at least this far.

The course led us up onto the rock-covered Biguil Plateau in the Moyen or Middle Atlas. Few cars had been through the track and it was narrow. I tried to follow single-track animal paths because the cows, or whatever made the paths, had kicked off the larger stones. Once the plain opened up, choosing lines was easy. My frame of mind was completely contrary to what I was accustomed to. There was complete freedom to choose where to place my wheels. There were no trees to restrict manoeuvrability or worn-in paths to follow as was usually the case in enduro racing. This mindset took some getting used to. Looking as far as possible ahead and deciding, at speed, which line to choose is an acquired art. I thought I was zipping along at a reasonably good pace but that illusion was shattered some 17 kilometres into the special. John Deacon, who had started behind me, wailed past at a high speed and in short order, disappeared into the horizon. I could only marvel at how fast riders like him go on those big flat BMW twins. Very impressive, I thought. John was definitely not going to lose his edge.

Staying focused was definitely a challenge. Looking around and taking in the vast breathtaking countryside was tempting. The landscape was so foreign to me, it was almost a shame to blast through it. But this was no tourist outing. Sightseeing and slacking off were luxuries I couldn't afford if I didn't want to end up as another statistic. Despite doing my utmost to concentrate on what was ahead of me, to my horror, I clipped a large rock. I felt the front wheel shake violently and feared the worst. I stopped in front of some spectators sitting on four-wheel-drive trucks watching the bikes race by. They gave me curious glances. Some shook their heads at my misfortune, or maybe they were thinking what a bozo I was. I couldn't see any broken spokes but the rim now had a significant wow to it. I had little choice but to continue with the damaged wheel. Trying not to make things worse, and to keep the bike from shaking, I stuck to a much slower speed. This resulted in a handful of riders passing me, but it ensured I made it to the end of the stage at Outat-Oulad-El-Hai. Not that my troubles were over — I had another 270 clicks to go on the liaison to Er-Rachidia.

Once through the arrival area of the special stage, I pulled off to the side to see if I could tighten my spokes a bit. The wow in the front wheel had become noticeably worse. The affected spokes had indeed loosened even more. While I was tightening them the disconcerting wail of a high-performance racing engine at full chat came within earshot. It was one of the Mitsubishi Pajero cars, approaching at a dizzying speed. I now realized I would be dealing with the dust and danger of being passed by aggressive drivers every day for the next two weeks. My plan to regain an early start time during this special stage, and to maintain it for the duration of the rally, was now out the window. One reason I had pushed myself during the first two timed specials in Europe was to grab an earlier start time the following days. The earlier you start, the less traffic you have to deal with and the fewer cars pass you during the day. This translates into a lot less dust to be swallowed and choked on. Because of the lost time card penalty my strategy to secure and maintain a start position in the top thirty-five was lost. To pick up positions I would have to work my way through the dust left behind by other motorcyclists and car drivers. In retrospect, it worked out for the better. I quickly came to realize that the rally days are so long and drawn out, a few minutes here and there really don't factor into finishing the Dakar. My goal was to finish. What position I would finish in was not important. Then again, I didn't want to be last, either. Finishing the Dakar was an accomplishment, but saying you were the last one across the finish line takes some of the lustre off it.

When I was satisfied the spokes were snug, I set out for Missour, a small town known for its deposits of a rare natural healing clay. A second fuel depot had been set up at the town and I stopped briefly to fill up the xr's tank. From Missour, it was a comfortable ride on a paved road that follows the Moulouya, northeastern Morocco's main river. The bike felt good and I rode at a steady pace. Other than seeing a few inhabitants — and Moroccan military in crisp green uniforms standing every five kilometres or so and at every bridge or vantage point where terrorists could potentially ambush rally competitors — the majestic Moyen Atlas Mountains were all I had for company. The high alpine air was invigorating and had a crisp clean bite to it. It was hard to believe that in a few days I'd be broiling in the Sahara Desert. A hard left up into a mountain pass, some 1,900 metres above sea level at the highest point, took me past places where there was still snow in the ditches. The road switched back on itself as it climbed up to the summit. Down the opposite side, into the town of Rich, it took a path through another pass that allowed just enough space for a narrow two-lane roadway. A short distance outside of Rich, I encountered the rust-coloured Gorges du Ziz. Etched out of sheer rock by the Ziz River over millions of years, the gorge features striking cliffs thousands of feet high, rising skyward so steeply, I was unable to see the top from the road.

The ride to Er-Rachidia was just about as I had imagined it. I had traversed similar landscapes in Egypt and the Baja Peninsula of Mexico. The distances are long and the terrain rugged and unforgiving. Dead-straight stretches of pavement link varied geographies. Villages are built around features that provide sustenance, such as water or fertile land suitable for agriculture. I finally arrived in Er-Rachidia, in the Ziz Valley on the northern edge of the Sahara, about nine hours after I had left Nador. I pulled into a gas station that by almost anyone's standards was hard to recognize. The place looked like a derelict shack in an out-of-the-way ghost town. There were no glass panes in the window frames. The ecological damage from leaking oil and diesel fuel, both on and around the property, was appalling. I figured it would take years to correct, if ever. But environmental issues are not a high priority in places like this. Garbage and junk of all kinds littered the streets and vacant lots of Er-Rachidia. Like many other towns in Morocco, Er-Rachidia served as a garrison during the French colonial period.

Despite the dreariness of Er-Rachidia, it was a welcome sight. I had made it to my first Paris-Dakar layover. As was the case with all of the bivouacs, the stop at Er-Rachidia was set up at an airport just outside of town. The Dakar bivouacs, or encampments, leapfrog ahead of the rally by air transport. Planes need a place to land safely, and airport towns along the designated route to Dakar are of vital importance. Without air support there would be no Paris-Dakar. Aircraft of various sizes move the equivalent of a small town across some of the world's most hostile terrain during the rally. For the 2001 event, seventeen aircraft and ten helicopters — two of which were air ambulances — were in use. As the rally progressed I found that "airport" was a relative term. "Airfield" or "airstrip" would have been more applicable. If a place had a tarmac and landing/take-off strip with maybe a ramshackle building or two, it qualified. This was the case in Er-Rachidia.

As I pulled up to the bivouac I noticed well-armed soldiers surrounding the entire compound, seemingly ready for action at the first sign of trouble. The place was already bustling with activity. The top factory riders had started arriving around four in the afternoon, followed by cars, trucks and more motorcycle riders. The procession wore on well into the night. Richard Sainct continued his winning ways. He completed the 139 km competitive section in a time of 1:16:01:00. For my part, it had taken me 1:45:14:00 to traverse the same distance, putting me across the finish line in sixty-seventh place. My time was good enough to improve my overall standing from 125th to ninety-fifth.

Special stage 4 had been a KTM bonanza. The Austrian manufacturer snared the top five finishing positions with Sainct, Carlo De Gavardo, Fabrizio Meoni, Alfie Cox and Kari Tiainen, in that order. The first BMW rider to finish (with a time of 1:18:34:00) was Joan Roma, close to two and a half minutes down from Sainct. At the top of the overall standings, Meoni jumped from seventh to second. Roma occupied third, followed by a string of KTM riders up to ninth place. In tenth was the next BMW, which belonged to the American Jimmy Lewis. With a win in the car class, Renault's Jean-Louis Schlesser regained the overall lead. He finished the special in a time of 1:12:12, nearly four minutes ahead of Mitsu's Jean-Pierre Fontenay.

Once inside the bivouac, I zeroed in on the cargo plane with the Yacco logo. It carried the privateers' personal trunks and spare wheels and was sponsored by Yacco, a French oil company that provided lubricants and assistance to the motorcyclists. I staked out a spot underneath one of the plane's wings, which would be my home for the night. This was in the heart of the privateer encampment and a favoured place by the riders to put up their tents. The first thing I did was retrieve my trunk and then pitch the Khyam tent Thierry Millet had recommended because of its simplicity to erect. The three-person tent, large enough to offer plenty of sleeping room and space to lay out my gear, went up in a matter of minutes. No pegs are required for the tent, making it ideal in areas with hard surfaces, like tarmac. After my tent was in order, I wandered around the vast bivouac to stretch my legs a bit and find the catering tent. As I made my way through the bustling little portable city, I tried to pick up as much as I could from what the more experienced competitors and old Paris-Dakar hands were doing. I quickly realized one of the keys to my survival would be to develop a basic routine: learn about start times, when breakfast and dinner were served, and where fuel was available and at what distance. Knowing the next day's code for the GPS was also critical. Acquiring and setting up the roadbook for each individual stage was equally important. There were so many variables to deal with, the actual riding seemed almost secondary. Many of the riders were working feverishly on their machines. They looked tired and ragged from the long day on the road. I wondered if I looked the same to them. When I finally spotted the large catering tent it was a welcome sight. Other than some energy bars, I hadn't eaten much since breakfast. There were no chairs set up in the tent and everybody ate desert style, sprawled across colourful carpets. I was so hungry I didn't even pay attention to what the meal was. It tasted surprisingly good.

When I got back to the Yacco plane all I wanted to do was sleep, but I knew I had to check the bike. Within an hour of sunset the temperature started to plunge. The night air was cool and fresh so I pulled on my jacket. The airport sat over 1,000 metres above sea level, and at night this time of the year the thermometer dips to just below freezing. I paid little attention to my bike that evening, other than giving the spokes of the front wheel a close inspection and tightening or loosening some of the spokes to make sure the wheel was true. I also checked the air filter. I knew it would be maxed-out handling all the sand and dust it had been subjected to. Not surprisingly, the fine talcum-like dust I had encountered on my way to Er-Rachidia had been getting past this vital engine-saving component. It was not a good sign. The motor would wear down extremely fast breathing in this stuff. The abrasive properties of the dirt would wreak havoc on the internal engine parts. The piston rings and cylinder bore would be the first to go; then compression would drop and the engine would lose power and burn oil. Ultimately it would just fail to start. I knew I would have to replace the filter every night if the engine was going to last. Satisfied the xr was ready to go in the morning, I crawled into my tent and hunkered down in my sleeping bag — wearing fleece from head to toe, including my toque — and fell into a sound sleep.

Chapter 7

Reality check

▬ ▬ ▬ ▬ ▬ ▬ ▬ ▬ ▬ ▬

Stage 5 — Friday, January 5, 2001
Er-Rachidia, Morocco to Ouarzazate, Morocco
Liaison: 57 km — **Special:** 333 km — **Liaison:** 182 km
Total distance: 572 km   83

My second day in Africa. I awoke around five and focused on
the immediate task at hand: to get dressed, repack my trunk,
eat breakfast, then settle into the saddle. After breakfast, I rode
to the start area at the gate of the airport and waited for my
number to come up. Soon I was on my way south to Erfoud.
The ride out of Er-Rachidia was rather frosty and I was dressed
to the max. I also had the electrically heated grips on to keep
my hands warm. It was a nice feature.

Although I was tired, I really felt like I was getting into the
rhythm of the race. I was no longer overwhelmed by the
thought of being in Africa, taking part in the world's premier
rally. Everything that had seemed surreal on my arrival in
Nador now took on a mantle of reality. The 57 kilometres to
Erfoud were on a paved road and passed quickly. Erfoud was
yet another small town that had been established as a military
post during the French colonial period. With its dusty red
buildings, the place has a ghost town atmosphere about it, yet
it is surrounded by some of the most spectacular scenery in all

of Morocco. On this day, Erfoud was where the special stage was slated to start. At 333 kilometres, it was the rally's first serious time challenge. The highlight of this leg of the Dakar would be the crossing of the Erg Chebbi dunes. I had heard quite a bit about these fabled dunes and, although a challenge to ride in, I was looking forward to them.

I arrived at Erfoud feeling somewhat invigorated by the cool riding conditions. There I found the legendary Hubert Auriol, dealing with one of the many problems that arose on a daily basis. This time, the main concern was over a fuel truck that hadn't shown up. Everyone was anxious to get the special underway. It was a long wait, but finally some barrels of fuel appeared in the back of an old truck. Somehow, Auriol always managed to keep the show on the road. I waited in line with the other motorcyclists for my turn to take on fuel. While queuing I struck up a conversation with Elisabete Jacinto, a feisty Portuguese woman who was doing the rally on a KTM. There were some features about the GPS that hadn't quite sunk in at the briefing during the *Control Technique* in Paris. I needed someone to help fill in the blanks. Elisabete was kind enough to explain what I needed to know. She told me the GPS automatically changes to the next waypoint once you pass within 200 metres of the previous waypoint.

"You can skip a waypoint by entering a series of inputs; that's really important," she said. "You'll find it will factor into the scheme of things as the rally plays out."

Having confidence in your navigation is an essential element for success in the rally. Actually knowing what you are doing is something entirely different. After Elisabete showed me the finer points of using the GPS, I felt a bit more secure, but I still had some misgivings about this wonder of modern navigation. We chatted for a while about our families until finally it was our turn to take on fuel. A while later I got the go-ahead to start the special stage. I set off along a rocky gravel road, no more than two cart tracks wide, with the larger rocks having been tossed off to the side. The track followed a shallow valley whose hillsides were covered in shale-like, square-edged rock.

Heavy dust, tossed into the air by the vehicles that preceded me, was once again a major issue. There was very little wind and the dust hung in the air like a thick haze. It gave the sun the eerie appearance of a muted ball of faded orange.

Despite the dust, I rode quickly. I caught up to a couple of other riders within the first 16 kilometres. Although risky, I decided to overtake them. The dust obscured so much of the road I reckoned it was much safer to lead than to follow. As the road rose out of the valley onto a plain, I quickly came up behind an ATV, one of only three in the rally. Not one of these one-person, four-wheeled all-terrain vehicles had ever finished previous editions of the Dakar. Because they are prone to mechanical failure and tire punctures, and are extremely tiring to handle, ATVs require a certain mentality to ride. The low number, or complete lack, of entries each year suggested that few people possessed the mentality to take up the Dakar challenge on one of these vehicles. As I came up behind the ATV, I found myself enveloped by thick dust. It was nearly impossible to see anything and I didn't want to risk a passing manoeuvre. I dropped back a bit but the dust persisted. I grew impatient, cranked the throttle and zipped off the track. I decided I would pass the ATV by riding through an obstacle course of various-sized rocks, dodging and darting in between them. It proved to be a poor decision. Full of fuel, the bike was extremely heavy and did not lend itself well to pinpoint manoeuvring. With the special tank full, the weight of the bike is close to 203 kilograms (450 lbs), a huge difference from the weight of a stock XR650 tank. Factor in the treacherous riding conditions, and you have a recipe for disaster. I was riding far too aggressively, and in no time at all I struck a large rock with the bike's front wheel. The impact resonated up through the forks and handlebars. *Clank . . . whack, whack, whack* — the handlebars shook like a jackhammer and wouldn't stop vibrating. Somehow I managed to avoid a get-off, but I knew I was in big trouble. I cursed myself for my stupidity. What a dumb thing to do, especially after hitting a rock just the day before. I was afraid that this time, my rally would really be over. Just 73 kilometres into the second day of the "real" Dakar and I was looking at a worst-case scenario. Despite the vibration, I was able to keep going. I knew I should stop and take stock of the situation but I was afraid to face the truth. It was like a flesh wound you don't want to look at for fear of finding out how bad it really is. I was in a state of total disbelief and denial. I slowed down, but kept riding. The wheel wobbled menacingly and I fought to hang onto my bike. Every rider I had passed, and many who had started behind me, soon overtook me.

The attrition rate in Paris-Dakar is very high. When it comes to first-timers, only one in three make it to the end. At this point, it looked like I was going to be one of those who took the *camion ballet*, or sweep truck, back to the bivouac. From there, the only thing left to do would be to make the sad trip home. It was an extremely distressing moment and I felt sick to the pit of my stomach. All the time, energy and work I had invested in the rally would go to waste. I would not become the first Canadian to reach Dakar. I felt the hopes of my countrymen riding on my shoulders. Nearly everyone I had met or come in contact with during the previous thirty years in the motorcycle industry knew where I was and what I was attempting. There was no escaping the scrutiny, no hiding. Media coverage of the event was being monitored by my family, friends, acquaintances and colleagues back home. Would they empathize or criticize? Panic gripped me. I was trying to convince myself that this had to be some kind of nightmare, one I would wake up from in a cold sweat inside my tent. I would get up and start my day all over again, remembering what happened in my dreams, and stay behind the ATV until it was safe to pass. But the reality of the situation gradually became clear. Here I was, somewhere in the heart of Morocco, my front wheel smashed and the world watching. All there was to do was to keep riding, hoping against hope I could finish the stage. To make matters worse, at the 18-kilometre mark, the ICO odometers quit. This was not good because now I wouldn't be able to determine the distance I had travelled in relation to the roadbook. I slowed down to a crawl and helplessly watched other riders stream steadily by me. This was hard to take because I knew I was a better rider than they were — at least when not making stupid errors. Maybe they were better riders after all; they seemed to be having no problems whatsoever. I finally pulled to a stop and got off the bike. I knew I had to gauge the extent of the damage to the wheel. It was bent all right, and broken spokes were proving to be a menace. One of them had been flailing around and had sliced the ICO odometer's wires. I grabbed a pair of pliers out of my Leatherman and removed the broken spokes. All I could do after that was hope the wheel would keep turning, and as long as it did I would keep riding. I started the bike and continued on my way.

I adapted my riding style to suit how my wounded bike behaved. This wasn't pretty, but I figured I would just go for broke. There was nothing else to do — other than give up. And that wasn't an option. The bad news was that I still had an inconceivable 520 kilometres ahead of me and I had no idea what to expect. The good news was that the wheel was somehow hanging in. The terrain became sandy. The course followed an *oued*, or dry riverbed. Generally, *oueds* are an indication that you're near more arable land, meaning there are small settlements or villages. In the desert, water always draws inhabitants. Remarkably, I was able to keep up with some of the other riders on this terrain. Encouraged, I pressed on. I had no idea of the distance I had travelled. The roadbook was now useless; I'd have to rely on following tracks and the other riders. I still wasn't up to speed with the GPS and hung onto the rear fender of French policeman Didier Py, riding a yellow BMW F650. He and another rallyist ventured out of the *oued* and struck out in another direction. The tracks and bearing didn't make sense, so I stopped and had a quick look around. Ahead of me lay some of the flattest and most desolate land imaginable; in the far distance there appeared to be a long ridge of sand dunes. At first I wondered if what I saw was real. But there was no mistaking the first "genuine" dunes of the rally. These were the Merzouga and Erg de Chebbi, the largest sand dunes in Morocco. Bathed in the golden glow of the afternoon sunlight, they were an awe-inspiring sight. The experienced competitors know the area well. The rippling dunes of Erg de Chebbi tower some 150 metres above the desert floor. They run in a line, almost perfectly in a north-south direction to the village of Merzouga and beyond. The dunes mark the western fringe of the Sahara Desert, dividing Morocco from Algeria. According to local legend, the dunes of Erg Chebbi were created by God to punish the inhabitants of Merzouga. Their transgression was the refusal to give shelter to a woman and her child during a festival. A sandstorm was unleashed and the village of Merzouga, as it was then known, was completely buried.

I headed towards the dunes praying I was going in the right direction. When, after a while, I saw the colourful flags indicating a rally checkpoint (CP), I was assured I was heading the right way. It was now around midday and the temperature was becoming increasingly hot. The bright sun was beating down mercilessly from a clear blue sky, its rays bouncing off the desert sand as if it were a gigantic solar reflecting panel. I rode around a number of small dunes towards the checkpoint. It meant riding more or less against the flow of traffic and several barbed wire fences. Quite a few people had gathered around the checkpoint. In addition to TSO officials were some spectators and the ever-present curious locals. As I rode by I noticed people, here and there, pointing at the Honda's twisted front wheel. I nonchalantly pulled up to the CP as if everything was going just fine. This, of course, was anything but the case. In addition to the problem with the wheel, the bike was starting to overheat and I was starting to feel slightly nauseous. I gave the TSO official my time card and he stamped it. He noticed the damaged wheel but didn't say anything. No doubt he was used to seeing damaged-but-still-functioning vehicles pull into his checkpoint. I had a quick look at the wheel myself and spotted yet another broken spoke. It was sticking out of the tire and bent over in a hook, polished to a high shine by the desert sand. I got off the bike and used my pliers to yank it out. I wondered if I should try to tighten the other spokes but decided to leave well enough alone.

"Some bad luck, eh?" the CP attendant said, stating the obvious.

"Just a bit," I said as if not overly concerned and handed him the spoke. "Here's a souvenir for you. Which way do I go from here?" I asked him in French, knowing many of the volunteers speak little or ño English. Even if they do, they appreciate it if you can communicate with them in their own language, or at least attempt to.

"Just follow the tracks," he said, motioning with the spoke to the numerous tracks in the sand. "Good luck," he said as I took off for the dunes. I guess he knew I needed it.

Sand is usually fun to ride in, but the dunes here were soft and treacherous. I rode with extreme caution, staying high on the ridges so as to not sink into a hole. Wasting time and precious energy digging myself out was not an appealing prospect. I noticed some photographers up ahead and knew I'd really have to watch where I was going. It is common knowledge among the rallyists that photographers always station themselves at the most interesting and challenging places along the rally route. These are the kinds of places where they know they can capture the most dramatic photos. If they were hoping I'd give them a dramatic photo op, I disappointed them; I stayed my course without any incidents. The dunes took some time to negotiate. The sand ruts were deep and nasty. I used the torque of the powerful 650cc Honda engine to pull me through, keeping the speed up and going as easy on the front wheel as possible. Just before the end of the sand dunes I pulled into another CP to have my card stamped once more. I was making slow time, but at least I was making time. My rally wasn't over yet. Once out of the sand dunes the course followed the Vallee du Draa, a very beautiful region of Morocco and a popular tourist destination. Along the valley a well-worn dusty road links small, remote villages tucked in amongst prickly, small-leafed trees. Low stone walls protect small plots of arable land, but few crops were being grown at this time of the year.

My cautious and sluggish progress saw me drop back even more, and I now had to deal with swift cars frequently coming up from behind. They rocketed past me as if I was standing still, making me feel more like a spectator than a participant in the rally. I also had to contend with a new menace scattered along the track: fine-powdered dust sinkholes called *fesh-fesh*. These pits are imperceptible to the inexperienced eye and hell to anyone unfortunate enough to wander into one. They are usually found where a trail narrows and the wheels of numerous vehicles have chewed up the earth in the same spot. A deep hole develops over time, then fills in with powdered dust. Riding a bike into *fesh-fesh* is a very trying, if not disastrous, experience. The motor's air filter can get plugged almost immediately and, worse, a bike can get stuck in it. If the hole is deep enough, you come to an abrupt stop without knowing what hit you. If you're riding fast enough, a somersault over the handlebars is often the result. It can also mean the difference between being able or not being able to ride another day. Fortunately, I didn't meet my doom in one of the feared *fesh-feshes* and I plodded my way to a village called Remelia, where the third CP of the day was located.

After getting my card stamped by the attendant, who also ignored my wheel, I rode over to the welcome shade of a nearby schoolhouse. An old acquaintance of mine, Peter Mayer, a journalist for the prestigious German motorcycling magazine *Motorrad*, was there taking pictures. He came over to greet me and at once noticed the ailing front wheel. The expression on his face signalled in no uncertain terms that the wheel didn't look good. But then, I already knew that. I explained what happened and Peter suggested I could improve my chances to reach Ouarzazate by doing some repair work. I knew there wasn't a whole lot I could do, other than replace the wheel.

"You won't know until you try," Peter suggested.

I propped the bike onto a chair and its side stand. I stripped off my jacket and toolbag and set out to try and straighten the wheel by tightening the spokes. It had worked the day before, but this time it turned out to be a bad move. The wheel was so tweaked, each twist of a spoke nipple pulled the wheel further away from true. It got worse! Now the tire was rubbing against the fork protector and coming close to rubbing on the fork tube. The only answer to that problem was to slice off some of the knobs on the side of the tire to gain extra clearance. After mulling over my situation, trying to remain in a positive frame of mind, I suited back up, said goodbye to Peter, and continued on my way. I had no sooner left the schoolhouse when, to my horror, the cars and trucks started overtaking me at a very fast rate of speed. Because the swirling dust reduced visibility to near zero, getting creamed by flying projectiles was a distinct possibility. The thought made me more than a bit apprehensive. Not having much choice in the matter, I stayed on course and ploughed onwards. I noticed some of the cars' navigators look at my damaged wheel and wriggle their hands when they saw how warped it was. Perhaps they thought they needed to draw my attention to the wheel, or maybe figured I was a fool for pushing on with it. Then again, maybe they considered me a die-hard competitor who would make it to Dakar. Well, at least to the bivouac in Ouarzazate. Much to my relief there were no close calls, and I coped with the raging dust like a regular desert rat. As the day wore on, I finally reached the finish of the special stage at Tazzarine. It had taken me nearly six hours to cover the 333 km: 5 hours and 57 minutes to be exact. This dropped my two-digit overall standing back to three digits. I was now in 107th place.

It had been another banner day for KTM: three of their riders claimed the top finishes. The Chilean, Carlo De Gavardo, led the sweep with a time of 3:14:17:00. Only twenty-one seconds separated him from the ever-present Sainct. Kari Tianen, in third, reached the end of the special 2:18:00 minutes later. BMW's Roma logged fourth based on a time of 3:17:10:00. The overall leaderboard continued to have Sainct at the top of the pile, now followed by Gavardo, Tianen and Roma. Fabrizio Meoni rounded out the top five. The Schlesser/Renault/Megane buggies ruled the day in the car division, with Jose Maria Servia and his navigator Jean Marie Lurquin snaring first place. Jean-Louis Schlesser and navigator Henri Magne followed in their tracks to take second. Jean-Pierre Fontenay and navigator Gilles

Picard kept Mitsubishi in the mix by rounding off the top three. They were 2:19:00 minutes behind Servia and Lurquin, who completed the stage in 3:25:55:00.

As in most villages in North Africa, the dust and filth in Tazzarine was inescapable. The village was comprised of ramshackle mud brick buildings called *kasbahs*, which were surrounded by primitive furniture, palm trees, mounds of garbage and rubble. Cows, goats, kids, dogs and dilapidated cars were scattered pell-mell throughout the village. I checked in with the TSO officials and got my card stamped. I dreaded to think of the time I had made on the special. The good news was that at least I had finished. I was still in the game. All I had to do now was get to Ouarzazate, a scant 182 kilometres away. After getting my card stamped I pulled up to a hole-in-the-wall store, hoping to buy a bottle of water and something to eat. Other than the water I craved, I found nothing but a large jar containing something pickled. I was afraid to ask the store clerk what it was. Flies buzzed everywhere and odd smells permeated from every nook and cranny of the dingy building. I pointed to one of several bottles of water lining a shelf. Not knowing how much the water cost, I counted out some coins and placed them in front of him. He scooped these up, nodded and flashed me a crooked smile. If I had any change coming I didn't get it. I couldn't wait to get out of this dismal place and hurried outside, afraid I might throw up if I lingered. I dropped into a chair at a rickety table underneath a palm tree and took a long drink of warm water. Trying to find a cold drink in a place like Tazzarine is like trying to find a cube of ice in the desert. But at least the water soothed my parched throat. At the next table, a group of young Germans chatted away as if this was just another day in paradise. I hadn't expected to come across tourists in this place, but then, in this day and age you can expect to find tourists just about anywhere on the planet. They told me Tazzarine was renowned for its orthoceras fossils, as if this would mean something to me. Still, I found myself asking what the heck orthoceras were.

"Orthoceras are a kind of mollusc; they're related to squids.

Millions of years ago, an ocean covered this area and the orthoceras swam in this ocean," one of the tourists explained. "They've been extinct for a long time, but they left some interesting shells embedded in the local limestone. Just east of here there are plenty of them." Well, I thought, you never know when you're going to get a lesson in palaeontology.

I was suddenly consumed by an overwhelming fatigue. I considered what lay ahead. This was only the second day in Africa and things were looking grim. I began to think that maybe I was way out of my league. I didn't feel this tired after three days of doing an ISDE. I came to the conclusion that the stress of the day's events was playing a large part in how tired I was feeling. It was starting to dawn on me that Paris-Dakar was every bit as difficult as its reputation made it out to be. Perhaps I'd underestimated the challenge. Maybe I was too old to tackle a 10,000-kilometre rally, much of it traversing an inhospitable desert. I wasn't sure how many more days like this one I could handle. The more these thoughts circulated through my head, the more I realized I was slipping out of character. I wasn't a quitter. I knew I had to reroute those negative thoughts into something positive. Paris-Dakar, if anything, is as much a mental challenge as it is a physical one — perhaps even more so.

After giving myself a mental pep talk I rode to the nearest gas station to fill up. Then it was off to complete the last 182 kilometres to Ouarzazate. I was glad to see the liaison section to Ouarzazate was on a paved road. After my ordeal in the desert sands, pavement was a welcome sight. At least the road should be easy on the wheel, I thought, but it continued to wallow intensely. I bit the bullet and kept going, hoping against hope I would reach my destination. Many occupants of the cars and bikes that slipped by me shook their heads or made gestures to the front wheel. Maybe this was part of a psychological strategy to undermine my resolve to keep going. The experienced guys can recognize rookies like me a mile away. They knew my chances of riding down the beach at Dakar were slim to none. It shouldn't have come as a surprise to me that I was drawing attention to myself. The wheel sent such violent oscillations into the front end I could barely keep both hands on the bars. My shoulders shook my head back and forth and I couldn't focus my eyes. Fatigue was an even worse enemy and I alternated holding down the throttle with my left and right hands.

After what seemed like an eternity, Ouarzazate, situated on a vast desert plateau on the threshold of the "Grand Sud," finally came into view. I was at once struck by how different it was from the other towns I'd been through in Morocco thus far. Not only is Ouarzazate the centre of Sahara tourism, it is known as the Hollywood of Morocco. International production companies have come here for years to shoot popular movies like *Lawrence of Arabia, Star Wars, Gladiator* and *The Sheltering Sky*. The studio outside town is a most impressive sight. The city's focal point is the long and wide Avenue Muhammed V, flanked by many modern buildings, including luxury hotels. Burning sands, snowy peaks, verdant oases, palm groves, lofty *ksours*, walled villages and magnificent kasbahs such as Taourirt and Ait Ben Haddou are among the wonders of Ouarzazate. When I pulled into the airport, I felt flushed with the sense that I had just executed a narrow escape from seeing my Dakar end in the sands of Morocco. I had literally laboured through this day by sheer power of will — or maybe it had been desperation. There is no question about it, I'd made it to the bivouac by the skin of my teeth. Some of the guys who had passed me en route — no doubt thinking I'd be coming into camp on the back of the sweep truck — gave me a thumbs-up when I coasted to a stop in the privateers' area by the Yacco plane. It felt good to be acknowledged for having made it to Ouarzazate. I got off my bike and felt a little weak-kneed and stiff. I did some stretches, took some long slow breaths, and walked over to the Yacco plane to retrieve my trunk. There were some camping spots left underneath one of the plane's wings and I pitched my tent. Then I started regrouping. Job number one was to remove the damaged front wheel and replace it with the stock Honda wheel. I used the custom axle Lou Costello had machined to adapt the wheel to the exotic Ohlins forks that had been installed on the bike. The axle and wheel fit like a charm, testimony to Lou's craftsmanship. While I was tending to the bike, one of the car drivers approached me and asked if I had a spark plug socket he could use. I was happy to lend it to him because I'm a firm believer in cooperative competitiveness and camaraderie. The driver promised to return the socket when he was finished with it and left to take care of the repairs he was doing to his car. Once the task of replacing the wheel was taken care of, I focused my attention on the broken wires leading from the sensor to the ico odometers. To do a proper job I needed a soldering iron, which I didn't have, so it was now my turn to do the borrowing. I asked around and soon found what I was looking for. Steph, a bearded Frenchman from Bretagne who worked for ERTF Navigation, lent me a small propane soldering iron from his array of tools. After reconnecting the wires, I returned the soldering iron to Steph, then performed one more critical chore on the bike: another air filter change. When I finished looking after the xr's needs, I wiped my hands and headed for the large tent where dinner was being served. Except for a few power bars, I hadn't eaten anything since breakfast. I was starving. Inside the half-full tent I kept mostly to myself, wanting to eat my meal quietly. I didn't have much energy left and I didn't want to spend it talking; I was still recovering from a trying day out in the desert.

Soon after I finished dinner I headed for the makeshift shower trailer and took a quick cold rinse. Feeling refreshed and almost like a new man, I hopped onto the xr and rode to the Total gas station outside the airport gates. After the wobbling and shaking of this day's ride, it felt kind of weird to be riding the bike with the new straight and true wheel. I still felt like I should be babying the machine, but soon enough I adjusted to riding it the way it was intended. I was already looking forward to another day in the saddle. My enthusiasm began to resurface. I knew that someday the trials and tribulations of Day 5 of the rally would seem humorous to me. I would be able to laugh because I had survived to race another day. I had dodged a bullet, but I'd never panicked or lost my cool. It was something I was pleased about. I was now even more confident that I would meet the Paris-Dakar challenge.

When I got back to my tent, one of my neighbours mentioned that the driver who had borrowed the spark plug socket had returned it while I was having dinner. I had thought that maybe I would have to chase the guy down to retrieve it, but he had left it in one of my boots. Most motorsport people treat you the way they like to be treated. The honour system prevails, and that's why it is rare to be turned down when asking for help. As I bedded down for the night, I wondered if it had just been dumb luck that I'd made it to Ouarzazate. But if luck had factored into the equation, then I shouldn't have hit the rock that damaged my wheel in the first place. Luck, or lack of it, is an interesting concept and we seem to use it to explain away a lot of what happens to us. Someone once told me that luck is for losers. If you depend on luck in life, you're spitting into the wind. Thomas Jefferson has been quoted as saying, "I'm a great believer in luck. I find the harder I work the more I have of it." Perhaps that is the way it is. You make your own luck. Whatever the case, the broken front wheel was another valuable lesson learned. I had fooled myself into believing that the special wheel I had installed was indestructible. Still, it had been good foresight to invest in the higher grade wheel. If nothing else, it set me up for some much-needed good luck after the bad luck of hitting the rock. A lesser quality wheel might have come completely apart upon impact. I would have been cooked right then and there. And I shuddered to think of the consequences if I had been pitched from the bike after a wheel collapsed. I wouldn't have been in any shape to race another day. I regretted not being able to rely on the Excel wheel anymore, but it had saved my bacon. The stock front wheel was top quality, but I knew I would have to proceed much more cautiously.

* * *

Stage 6 — Saturday, January 6, 2001
Ouarzazate, Morocco to Goulimine, Morocco
Liaison: 155 km — **Special:** 305 km — **Liaison:** 148 km
Total distance: 608 km

I woke up in early-morning darkness. It didn't seem quite as cold as it had been in Er-Rachidia, but the temperature couldn't have been much above freezing. I crawled out of my sleeping bag, got dressed and stuck my head outside the tent. Many of the other privateers camped underneath the wings of the Yacco cargo plane were also getting up. It seemed like everyone was emerging from their tents around the same time, as if on cue. Competitors from twenty-three countries were taking part in the rally — many divided along racial lines, ideology and creed. Still, as is usually the case when sports people get together for major events, differences are put aside and there's a general feeling of camaraderie. I had noticed the night before that even the drivers and riders from rival teams socialized. This is something you would never see at Grand Prix races. When it comes to a rally like Paris-Dakar, everybody knows they're in it together. Only when there's racing going on does individualism surface. I wasn't slated to start till some time after 7:00 a.m., so I took the opportunity to circulate a bit and introduce myself to other riders. Early on, the general atmosphere had been a little tepid. People had been courteous, but not much more than that. Now, almost a full week into the Dakar, everyone started loosening up and becoming more talkative. One common topic of discussion that came up was the ever-present Moroccan military. Like at the bivouac at Er-Rachidia, the boys in green uniforms surrounded the compound at Ouarzazate. Some of the riders half-jokingly said they felt like they were in a prison camp. I'd heard stories about previous editions of the rally, where somewhere along the line personal possessions and bikes or cars had been stolen at gunpoint. Some of the guys seemed concerned about this but it didn't carry much weight with me. You can get held up at gunpoint just about anywhere these days. The only difference is that if it happens in your own town you might make the local news; if it happens to you during the Paris-Dakar you're likely to make headlines worldwide.

It was still dark when it was my turn to start Stage 6. The large Baja Designs HID headlight cast a strong beam of white light into the black void. I was happy to be underway again, especially considering how close I had come to seeing it all end the day before. The stage from Ouarzazate to Goulimine consisted of long tracks across very dry terrain, the dust was once again severe. I faced incredible stoney plains that stretched for kilometres on end. On this day, I rode like I should have been riding all along: with utmost caution and extreme respect for the elements. I paid close attention to the roadbook, making sure my odometer matched the distance indicated between waypoints. Everything seemed to jive. In front on me, the tail lights of bikes ahead disappeared around corners and over hills, then reappeared when I turned the same corners and crested the same hills. The road climbed high into the Atlas Mountains. Crisp mountain air stung my face like needles as the temperature dropped. The slopes of the rock faces closed in on me as the elevation increased. The Honda's open-exhaust note rattled against the rock faces as I rolled the throttle back and forth. Its rich throaty sound was music to my ears: a mechanical symphony that told me the XR's 649cc motor was running problem-free. The narrow paved road snaked along the cliffs. The pass through the ridge was very steep and treacherous. A low rock wall lined the outside of the turns and the tight switchback corners clung precariously to the side of the cliffs. If I make a mistake here and crashed over the edge, they'd never find me. It would literally be into the abyss — over and out. Gradually, a breathtaking globe of fiery crimson began to peek out from behind a distant mountain range, then quickly rose into the sky. It was one of those special moments that overwhelm the senses. I felt euphoric. Moments like this made it all worthwhile: all the dreaming, planning and preparation that had gone into the rally were being parlayed into the adventure of a lifetime. The Dakar was taking me places — both in reality and in my mind — that couldn't be reached in any other way. I was beginning to understand why many veteran competitors kept coming back year after year.

As the sun's rays began to illuminate this desolate corner of southern Morocco, they revealed a straight stretch of road that dropped down out of the mountains onto a low plain. It was a welcome sight. I was looking forward to getting out of the dangerous mountain pass. No sooner had I entertained that thought that I actually found myself somewhere on the plain, cruising along at a nice clip. Although I had been totally focused on my riding, I seemed to have covered quite a distance on the plain without really being cognizant of it. It was like time had ceased to exist. It was the sound of another motorcycle that snapped me back into the moment. I had caught up to Mike Hughes, an English privateer, also Honda-mounted, but on the smaller xr400. I wanted to overtake Hughes, who seemed intent on staying ahead of me. It looked like we were going to play cat and mouse for a while but then I noticed another rider, further ahead, parked at the side of the road. I decided to let Hughes go for the time being and check on the stranded rider. Hughes also slowed down. He no doubt was as willing as I to assist our fellow competitor. He glanced over his shoulder but kept going when he saw I was turning around. I rode back to the parked bike, which sported the No. 81 plate. I soon learned it belonged to Philippe Peillon, a rallyist from Gabon. Peillon was also riding a Honda xr650 so I at once felt some kinship with him.

"I'm out of gas," he said in French, expressing his frustration with a hopeless gesture. I could understand his exasperation; there was a planned fuel stop a short distance away at a gas station in Tazenakht. I told him to push the bike into the centre of the road and get on. He looked at me questioningly, not sure what I had in mind.

"Don't worry, I'll get you to Tazenakht," I said as I put my left foot against the exhaust pipe of his xr.

"You're kidding me, right? You're not going to push me there," he said.

"That's exactly what I'm going to do," I replied, pretty confident my plan would work. I slipped my bike into gear and proceeded to push him to the gas station, which fortunately was only about a kilometre down the road. I got up to second gear and it only took a few minutes to get to Tazenakht, famous for its traditional wool and goat's hair Atlas rugs. I was relieved, as no doubt Philippe was, to see the gas station, on the edge of town.

While refuelling I learned from a grateful Peillon that we had a mutual acquaintance back in France, none other than Thierry Millet, owner of Accelere Motos in Metz. Thierry had prepared Peillon's bike for the Dakar. Ironically enough, I had noticed the XR in Thierry's shop when I went there to have my Michelin mousse inner tubes and desert tires installed. Peillon's bike wasn't the only rally machine in Thierry's shop at the time. I was stunned by how much work the bikes he was preparing needed. He was waiting on rally kits and components for the fuel tank set-up, which were coming from Formule Top in Paris. Vincent Bourgoise, the owner of Formule Top, had two Polish riders in the rally as well. Vincent and his riders were based out of the same Team Tibau support truck I was. During the rally, I spoke often with Vincent. We even exchanged spares and helped each other on occasion. At one point later on in the rally, I noticed Vincent and his mechanic closely examining my XR. They had made what I considered a major error in the design of the fuel delivery system, and their kit was virtually untested. It was evident that pumping fuel via a fuel pump directly into the carburetor was not the way to go. The carburetor was designed to accept gasoline by gravity flow. The needle valve in the float bowl was designed to work in this way and no other. The kit Formule Top produced was made of fibreglass-reinforced plastic. The tanks, fairing and seat were nicely designed with a well-thought-out air filter system. It drew fresh air through a filter mounted on top of the main fuel tanks. But because it was an untested design, it required extensive work every evening. I saw Vincent mixing up fibreglass resin daily to repair holes that were wearing through the brittle plastic tanks. The following year, they would have a similar kit with the fuel tanks made of aluminum. Another lesson learned in the Dakar.

I started out for the special stage. For a while, I traversed a veritable wasteland that seemed like the remnants of some long ago holocaust. It didn't take much imagination to believe I was on some other world, some desolate place that could sustain neither man nor beast. The xr took a merciless pounding but I rode as fast as I dared, without taking hard hits and risking any damage to the wheels or suspension. Standing on the footpegs for long stretches at a time and picking lines among the rocks was tiresome and frustrating. As soon as the track cleared and I thought I was finally free of the rocks, more would suddenly appear. With temperatures hovering around 20° Celsius, the weather was relatively cool for this time of year and made for comfortable riding. Like the previous day the special was again 300-plus kilometres; this time it was 305 clicks, twenty-eight less than Stage 5. While this is a negligible distance under normal circumstances in a rally, depending on the terrain, it can seem like an eternity. Starting in a majestic stretch of palm groves near a small anonymous town called Foum-Zguid, the first 100 kilometres of the special ran over tight, winding tracks at the foot of the Atlas Mountains. After that, the tracks segued into the spectacular Oued Draa across dry, stony riverbeds and rocky outcrops. Heavy cloud cover and light rain, however, cast a certain drabness over a region famed for its dramatic scenery. The high-speed nature of the tracks favoured the bikes on this day, so I was able to ride at top speed. I got processed at all three cps very quickly and reached the end of the stage at Fam El Hisn — yet another nondescript town — in good order. With a time of 5:04:36:00, I recorded a ninety-first place across the finish line, a nice improvement over the previous stage. I derived some satisfaction from knowing I had put in a good day's ride.

For the first time since the rally began, bmw finally got a stage win, thanks to Joan Roma. The Spanish enduro/rally master traversed the wicked terrain from Er-Rachidia to

Ouarzazate in 3:13:39:00. But that was the only good news for the German manufacturer. Their rival Austrian counterparts occupied the next eight positions, starting with Tiainen and Sainct, who capped the top three. In the final analysis Roma only moved up one notch, to third place in the overall standings. Sainct stayed at the top of the board and continued to reinforce his status as the odds-on favourite to win a third Dakar. The Schlesser/Renault/Megane buggies again dominated the car class, but with Schlesser and navigator Magne taking the win this time and teammates Servia and Lurquin grabbing a close runner-up just 42 seconds off the pace. Schlesser and Magne, who covered the 305 kilometres of the special stage in a time of 3:17:24:00, remained provisional overall leader while Servia and Lurquin skipped into second at the expense of Mitsubishi's Fontenay and Picard. The French duo finished third in the special, almost eight and a half minutes down from Schlesser. They were followed closely to the end of the stage by their Mitsubishi teammates Masuoka and Maimon.

Once the special stage was behind me, it was clear sailing the rest of the way. About 35 kilometres north of Goulimine, the final destination of Stage 6, I stopped at some hole-in-the-wall town called Tagant. I had spotted a service station with an adjoining carwash and decided to give the Honda a thorough washing. I was planning an oil change that evening and wanted the bike as clean as possible. The powdered dust came off quickly and the bike looked almost showroom-clean once more. While spraying the xr with water, I suddenly felt the urge to take a shower. I wasn't too optimistic that there would be one available but on the off chance there was, I thought I would ask the attendant anyway. He spoke reasonable French so communicating with him proved to be no problem. He animatedly nodded his head and told me there was a very nice shower at the back of the building. He led me to an adjacent door that opened on a completely tiled shower room. An on-demand hot water heater hung off the wall, but no matter how he tried, he couldn't get it to work.

"No problem, no problem, I will fix. I come right back," he

TO DAKAR AND BACK

said as he shuffled out of the room. Some five minutes later he returned, but his idea of fixing the water heater was to bring me a pot of hot murky water. With the hot water he supplied a half-used bar of soap and bottle of shampoo that was nearly empty. Despite the less-than-ideal amenities I was glad to be able to wash up. After dousing myself with the hot water, washing my hair and scrubbing myself, I let the cold water that dribbled from the showerhead flow over my body for a few minutes, then towelled myself dry. I felt mentally and physically refreshed but putting dusty riding gear back on seemed to defeat the purpose of showering. After both my bike and I were as clean as could be, I set out for the bivouac in Goulimine, a city of some 110,000 wedged between two mountain ranges in the sub-Sahara. Approaching Goulimine, some twenty minutes after leaving Tagant, I was struck by the surrounding landscape, which was stunningly bleak. The brown pastel buildings of the town blend into the parched brown hills, which stretch towards the mountains in the background. For many centuries, when camels had been the main mode of transportation in Northern Africa, Goulimine had been known as the "Gateway to the Sahara," a centre for camel caravans travelling into the Western Sahara Desert. To retain some measure of its once-important camel-trading heritage, Goulimine hosts a weekly camel fair and, each July, an annual camel festival.

As I rode towards the bivouac, again protected by Moroccan army personnel, it was with the satisfaction that I had just chalked up another successful day in the Dakar. Other than my transcendental experience in the mountains and pushing Philippe Peillon to the gas station, the day had been uneventful. I made my way to the small airport outside of town and cruised into the bivouac. A yellow banner was strung over the entrance proclaiming, "Welcome to Goulimine." I couldn't believe what confronted my weary eyes once inside the compound. Dozens of RV tourists had invaded a section of the bivouac, their rolling bungalows parked in a long line. Men and women sat on lawn chairs in groups, waving to the rallyists as they went by. Some of the tourists were drinking pastiche and playing *boules*. For a moment I thought I had been transported to some campground in the south of France. So much for being in the desert, I thought. I had expected a carnival atmosphere during the French and Spanish stages, even locals gathering to welcome the rallyists in the bivouac towns in Northern Africa, but definitely not a bunch of rally-obsessed Europeans in some out-of-the way place in Morocco. I dutifully waved back to the welcoming committee and rode on to join the rest of the riders who had already made it to the bivouac. I looked for a place to hunker down for the night and, once my tent was pitched, went about the business of changing the xr's oil, oil filter and air filters. Late that afternoon, a TV camera crew stopped by the area where the privateers were stationed, wedged in between a Russian-built turboprop aircraft and the Yacco plane. I was kind of surprised when the crew approached me, seeing there were plenty of other riders around. The director asked me if he could shoot some footage of me slaving over the bike after a hard day in the saddle. I had already finished doing the maintenance I had planned, but I happily complied with his request. I briefly became an actor, going through the motions of working on the Honda. Later, I heard my brother-in-law had seen me on French television that evening, "working" on the xr.

After the video shoot wrapped, I cleaned my hands and headed to the catering area for a much-needed meal. It was quite a long walk to the food tents, where a display of photos honouring Morocco's royal family had been posted. I hadn't even known there was such a thing as a Moroccan royal family, never mind that the present dynasty, the Alaouite, dated back to the seventeenth century. I learned that King Mohamed vi and his family are descended from the prophet Mohamed and, in addition to being king, he is *Amir al-Muminin* or Commander of the Faithful. Preparations were also underway for another cabaret-style show, which had been the highlight of the previous Moroccan bivouacs. The carnival atmosphere was somewhat overshadowed when tso director Auriol made an announcement at dinner that the Front Polisario had made threats to disturb the rally. The Polisario, I soon discovered, was the political wing of a group of approximately 200,000 Saharawis, indigenous people who'd lived in the Western Sahara until they were displaced by the Moroccan military and forced to live in refugee camps across the border in Algeria. The area of their ancestral home, between Morocco and Mauritania, has been disputed for many years. The Polisario is opposed to the Moroccan occupation of the West Sahara and now they were jumping on the Paris-Dakar media bandwagon to get some worldwide attention. The group's leader, Mohamed Abdelaziz, had issued a warning that his organization — labelled terrorists by the Moroccan government — was in conflict with the Moroccan military. He stressed that if rally competitors happened to get caught in the middle, the Front would take no responsibility. Abdelaziz's thinly disguised attempt at gaining media exposure worked: it drew the attention of the French Foreign Affairs Minister and rally organizers. Prior to 2001, the rally had been interrupted many times by anything from sand storms to floods to political unrest. Threats of terrorism were nothing new to Paris-Dakar. One year earlier, in 2000, the rally had ground to a halt in Niger when the Islamic Dissident Army vowed to attack competitors with full force. Not to be thwarted, TSO, at a cost of $5 million, airlifted the entire rally entourage to Sabbah, Lybia. After a delay of five days, the event resumed without incident. Fortunately, such dramatic measures were not required this time around. Roger Klamanovitz, the person in charge of foreign relations at TSO, managed to open the frontier so the rally could pass through to Mauritania undisturbed. We were told we would be safe as long as we didn't stray off the designated route. If one did, there was a distinct possibility of hitting one of the many landmines that were hidden near the border. Ever since we set foot in Morocco the military presence had been strong. I had felt like I was in a secure environment. Now I wasn't so sure.

* * *

Stage 7 — Sunday, January 7, 2001
Goulimine, Morocco to Smara, Morocco
Liaison: 53 km — **Special:** 420 km — **Liaison:** 16 km
Total distance: 489 km

At 100 metres above sea level, the night temperatures hadn't been as cold in Goulimine as at the previous bivouacs. I woke up toasty inside my sleeping bag and contemplated what lay ahead. It had been six days since Paris, and we were about to face the final Moroccan stage of the rally. Although we had been reassured, nobody could be 100% certain we were safe from an attack by the extremists. Other than that? It would be business as usual: traversing treacherous terrain and getting to the end of the stage in one piece. I got up, packed the trunk, and donned my gear. Breakfast was going to be served early. The first bikes were scheduled to leave at 7:00 a.m. for a short 53-kilometre jaunt to the start of the special. At 420 clicks, it was the longest of the rally so far. I decided not to walk the long distance to the catering tents again, opting to take my bike instead. While riding, I came across a lone figure walking in the darkness towards the tents. I had no idea who he was, but I pulled to a stop next to him and asked where he was going.

"Breakfast," he said. I invited him to hop on the bike, which he did without hesitation.

"Man, I can't believe how far you've got to walk to get a bite to eat around here," he said.

"Yeah, that's why I'm riding," I responded. A minute later we arrived at the large Berber tents where breakfast was being served. They reminded me of the tents I had seen in more than one desert epic as a kid. I tried to envision what it must have been like for the first Europeans who trekked across the Sahara. It must have been an adventure that made this modern-day rally seem tame by comparison.

I was about to part company with my passenger when he mentioned the Canadian flag sticker on the back of my Arai helmet.

"You're from the Great White North," he said. "You wouldn't

be or happen to know Lawrence Hacking, would you?"

I told him that indeed I was Lawrence Hacking, somewhat taken aback he had even heard of me.

"Well, isn't this a coincidence. You're just the man I've been looking for," he said enthusiastically, gripping my hand. "I'm Toby Moody, from Speedvision in the States. I'd like to do an interview with you. We've got a lot of Canadian viewers that would be interested in hearing from you, and how you're doing in the rally."

I was kind of flattered to be of interest to anybody, being a humble privateer whose main goal was just to finish the Dakar. Of course, a little positive media attention never hurt anybody. It comes in especially handy when you're looking for sponsorship support. And being seen in a potential 60 million households across the United States and Canada would be good exposure for the sponsors I already had. Speedvision is the premier motorsports cable channel in North America and was devoting some nine hours of coverage to the rally. I told Toby I'd be happy to do the interview and asked him if he wanted to join me for breakfast. Over a meal that offered a choice of cold meats, cheese, yogurt and cereals we agreed to meet up a few days later, when he'd have a Speedvision camera crew at his disposal to tape the interview. Although I enjoyed Toby's attention and looked forward to the interview, my mind was preoccupied. I knew it would be another long trying day of pushing the envelope.

The ride from the bivouac to the start of the special stage was on a paved road that was in relatively good condition by Moroccan standards — lumpy, narrow, and ill-defined at its edges. After that it was back to hell on two wheels. The track was fast, narrow, twisty and rocky once again. I never thought I would see so many rocks and boulders in the desert. When one thinks of a desert what comes to mind is sand. So far the wastelands of Morocco had been more about gravel and stony plains than pure unadulterated sand. Dakar veterans had assured me, however, I would get more sand than I could ever dream of soon enough. Still, the only way to race any kind of

terrain successfully is to forget the dislike you may have for certain elements and just go for it. I once asked five-time
motocross world champion Eric Geboers what his favourite
track was, and he told me they were all his favourite tracks. "If
I go to a track I don't like, I know I would already be at a disadvantage," he said. With that kind of attitude it's no wonder he
was the first motocross racer to win a world title in all three
displacement classes.

I was beetling along at a good pace about one-third of the
way into the special when I was passed by one of the Ford Pro
trucks. The trail of dust I was roosting must have obscured my
exact position on the track for the driver. He came so close it
startled the living daylights out of me. I instinctively veered off
the track and was immediately blinded by the wall of dust
stirred as the truck sped by me at breakneck speed. With rocks
strewn about like confetti on both sides of the track I was now
in very hazardous territory. The thought had barely surfaced
when I felt myself clipping the side of a hard object. It was a
dreaded rock, of course, and it washed out my front wheel,
causing me to crash into the rough terrain. Somewhere in the
distance I heard the aggressive sound of a high-performance
engine barrelling down on me. My biggest fear was being hit by
another speeding truck or an even faster-moving car. The dust
hung in the air like thick fog and I didn't know where I was. If
I had fallen back on the track after wiping out I would be a sitting duck. While the dust settled around me I quickly scram-
bled to my feet and wrestled the bike upright. Gasping for air,
I pushed the bike further to the right, away from the track.
Once I felt I was out of harm's way, I paused to gather my wits
and twist my body this way and that for signs of broken bones.
To my relief there was no telltale searing pain to indicate I had
indeed broken something. I knew I'd be sore and bruised later
on, but the main thing was I had survived the crash relatively
unscathed. I was more worried about damaging the bike, in
particular the fuel tanks and front wheel. Moments later
another truck flew by me some five metres away, leaving more
choking dust in its wake. As the truck's motor droned off into

the distance, it became eerily quiet. After the dust dissipated I inspected the xr for damage. My eyes automatically focused on the front wheel first, fearing a repeat of a few days earlier, but the wheel seemed okay. No broken or loose spokes, just a bit of a nick and scrape to the rim. Fortunately I hadn't hit the rock dead on. Everything else appeared intact and there were no fluid leaks of any kind. I was especially thankful the fuel tanks had been constructed of heavy gauge aluminium. The right-side tank was dented but it held tight. Once I had regrouped I worked up the nerve to try and start the Honda. Much to my relief, the trusty 649cc motor turned over with no problem. It was time to get back on my horse and resume the race. It had been a narrow escape and another Dakar reality check but I knew I couldn't dwell on it.

At the second control passage of the day, I passed through right behind Jean-Louis Schlesser, winner of the car division in 1999 and 2000. He'd stalled his Schlesser/Renault prototype buggy right in front of me as we exited the control zone. As I pulled up to the fuel dump I noticed his navigator Henri Magne and others pushing the car to get it running again. This outside assistance cost him an hour penalty, dropping the defending Paris-Dakar champ back to thirty-eighth position on the day and eighth overall. The stage from Goulimine to Smara was not kind to Schlesser: in addition to stalling his vehicle at the second CP he lost further time when his buggy suffered a punctured tire. Schlesser, who had enjoyed close to a six-minute lead at the end of Stage 6, now found himself 56 minutes behind the current leader, his Schlesser/Renault team-mate Jose Maria Servia. The likelihood that Schlesser would make up that much ground was slim. And from the way he was ranting he knew it, too. Attrition or serious problems for those ahead of him were his only hope to succeed at a three-peat.

* * *

Man cannot live by bread alone. There are rules as well, and nobody — even the marquee stars of the Dakar — is exempt from abiding by the rule book. Schlesser's penalty was based on rules 12 and 12.2 of the rule book. Rule 12.2 states that in off-road rallies, towing is authorized outside transit zones and the *Parc Ferme*. Rule 12 states towing, pushing, or any other form of moving a vehicle, other than by its motor, is not allowed. It's a matter of telling you what you can't do rather than what you can. Penalties for infractions apply to everyone, although how they are applied varies from case to case. Knowing the rules and deciphering the rule book is one of the more difficult aspects of the rally. The rules are written in a strange fashion and, of course, the French version is gospel. The rule book is open to interpretation and it helps to know what you can get away with.

The experience of a French rider named Gerard Barbezant provides a good example. Barbezant did the 2001 Dakar wearing a fancy custom-made leather riding suit. It had a clear plastic cover over his race number. It was evident he had some serious financial backing. He must have spent the whole year knocking on doors of the large companies looking for sponsorship money. His website tells the story: an impressive roster of high-tech industry businesses had attached their name to his. Barbezant was no stranger to the Dakar: he had made previous attempts to finish the rally on small-bore 125cc machines. My first contact with this quirky character had been at the finish of Stage 1 in Narbonne. I was patiently waiting my turn to ride up the finish podium's steep wooden ramp when Barbezant suddenly appeared out of nowhere. Hundreds of spectators crowded around the stage to hear what the Dakar competitors had to say. French rally hero Stephane Peterhansel, who was driving a Nissan in the production class, was being interviewed. Barbezant started edging his way towards the ramp and kept yelling Stephane's name in a bleating tone of voice. I let Barbezant go ahead of me, thinking maybe he was someone of importance. He didn't acknowledge me and rode up onto the podium as if he was some kind of VIP. Peterhansel and the announcer weren't sure what to make of the intrusion. Puzzled, they watched Barbezant as he removed his helmet and then simply pushed his way into the interview. I thought this was kind of rude, regardless of the guy's status. Later on, I learned that Barbezant was anything but a figure of importance. He was more of a Paris-Dakar pretender. Barbezant was manipulating the rule book and trying to finish the rally by taking the start of a stage, riding around to the road, and then getting to the finish on the same path used by the assistance vehicles. He would bypass the checkpoints en route and just take the imposed time penalties when he arrived at the finish line at the end of the day. His plan worked, until he was actually forced to ride the difficult off-road sections where no other options were available. The last time I saw him was the morning after the rest day in Atar. We were parked on the road leading out of the airport waiting to be given the start signal for the liaison stage. There were nearly fifty motorcycles in line. Off to one side, Barbezant was half squatting with his riding pants down in full view. He made no attempt to take care of nature's call behind a wall or building. There is no shame on the Dakar, so the saying goes. In the end, at Nouakchott, after missing eleven control passages and taking every piece of pavement possible, Barbezant disappeared without a trace, as most non-finishers do.

* * *

I arrived at the bivouac in Smara fairly early. According to the results it had been almost six hours of riding, with only 16 kilometres of liaison after the finish of the special stage. The long 420-km competitive section was one of the roughest and rockiest I had encountered thus far. And as the rally course headed south to the border with Mauritania, the temperature rose, too. At the start of the stage it had been a comfortable 15° Celsius; by the time I reached the finish it was over 25. The track had been very rocky, smoothing out a little after the halfway mark, but littered with jumps, bumps and dips the rest of the way. Still, taking everything into account, this had been a good stage for me time-wise. I completed the special in just over five hours to snare seventy-sixth spot. My time card recorded 5:04:36:00. This was only an hour and a few seconds more than it had taken the winner, Isidre Pujol Esteve, on the factory KTM, to complete the stage. At the end of the day, I had moved up in the overall standings to ninetieth on the provisional scoreboard.

Although I had managed to get to Smara without any real problem other than the crash, Stage 7 took a heavy toll in the motorcycle class. A number of front-runners, including Kari Tianen, Alfie Cox, Cyril Despres and Giovani Sala encountered mechanical problems that cost them dearly on their time cards. And the morning's *piste* opener, Joan Roma, had gotten lost, taking the lead group with him. After hearing about that I felt kind of good. Not because Roma and a bunch of others had gotten lost, but that it could even happen to the top guys. So far, I had managed to stay on course. Obviously, I was doing something right and it gave me some satisfaction. But I knew I shouldn't gloat; the rally wasn't even half over. Despite getting lost, Roma had still finished the special in sixth place. With a time of 4:09:11 he was only 6:42 off the pace set by Esteve. The Spaniard led a KTM sweep of the first five finishers, which included Fabrizio Meoni in second place, P.G. Lundmark in third, Jordi Arcarons in fourth, and Richard Sainct fifth. Defending Dakar champion Sainct remained in the overall lead, 5:08:00 ahead of Meoni and 7:31:00 ahead of Roma. In the car division Hiroshi Masuoka and his navigator Pascal Maimon won their second stage of the rally in their Mitsubishi Pajero/Montero. They moved up the board to third overall from fifth. Even though they'd had to contend with two tire punctures and a dead battery along the way, fellow Mitsubishi driver Jean-Pierre Fontenay and his navigator Gilles Picard moved back into second. Fontenay trailed Schlesser/Renault's Servia by just 8:37:00. It was looking like Renault was going to have a serious fight on their hands if they were going to win again.

It was around three o'clock when I pulled into the bivouac. My stomach was growling so I headed for the catering tents to look for something to eat. This had been the first time I had actually arrived early so I wasn't expecting much; the main meal is usually served between 7:30 and 9:30 p.m. All I managed to scrounge up was a piece of bread and some cream cheese.

Still, I couldn't help marvelling at the efficiency with which the catering company handled the huge undertaking of feeding the huge entourage of competitors, volunteers, staff, mechanics, journalists, doctors and hangers-on. Two Antonov 66 airplanes and a number of refrigerated trucks were used to move some 153 tons of food and a mobile kitchen with twelve ovens from bivouac to bivouac. Three teams of about twenty people each worked around the clock in shifts. An advance team, travelling in refrigerated trucks, worked a day ahead of the rally, setting up the next bivouac with local help. That way there was always some food and water available for anyone who got to the bivouac early in the day.

When I finished eating and drinking some water, I prepared the xr for the next stage. This included a change of tires and a close inspection of the entire bike. Fortunately it had survived the crash having suffered just some cosmetic damage and a dented fuel tank. Once the bike had been taken care of, I got cleaned up a bit and considered my next move. With some time on my hands, I decided to ride into town and look for a *telephone cabine*. I wanted to call Françoise and let her know I was still in the mix. I was aching now from my gravel-surfing crash, but I decided to leave that part out. Someone directed me to a storefront that housed a number of telephone booths. The place was tended by a burka-clad woman who poured out a handful of tokens in exchange for a small amount of money. To my surprise overseas calls from Morocco were easy and reliable. I entered a *cabine* and dropped my weary bones on a stool. Once the overseas number was dialled the reception was as clear as if I was calling an extension in my own neighbourhood. It was good to hear Françoise's voice. I realized how much I missed her and our daughter Mia. Françoise told me her brother had seen me on TV, and she was full of questions about how the rally was going. I assured her everything was going fine and told her I was looking forward to seeing her in Dakar. She didn't question the fact that I would make it and said, "Don't you worry, I will be there." I kept dropping tokens into the telephone's coin slot for as long as they lasted. As the units indicating the time left ticked away, I began to wind down the conversation. We had just said our goodbyes when the call was terminated.

I rode down the main street and was struck by how most of the buildings were small and predominantly painted red. I stopped in front of a walk-up hotel and went inside to inquire about the possibility of taking a shower on the premises. The clerk manning the front desk told me showers were indeed available for non-guests at a fee of fifteen French francs, which amounted to about three Canadian dollars.

"You'll have to supply your own towel, soap and shampoo," he added, when I told him I wanted to use the facility.

"Okay. I'll be back," I said and left to look for a towel, soap and shampoo. I was also thinking of perhaps picking up souvenir like a T-shirt, but the small stalls that served as stores had almost nothing of interest: very basic staples were all that was available. I spotted a barbershop and thought I would see if there was any shampoo or soap available there. And it was a good opportunity to grab a haircut and shave. I wandered into the shop and was welcomed by a well-dressed and well-groomed haircutter. I was a little nervous about having someone wield sharp instruments around my head, especially when he brought up the subject of religion almost immediately. I guess once a religious centre, always a religious centre. The barber told me everyone in Smara was Muslim; I guess this meant I was an infidel. I commented on how nice the town looked, trying to move the conversation away from anything confrontational. I know better than to talk religion or politics, especially on someone else's home turf. That led the barber to tell me about the town's mosque, its only place of worship, which had a different architecture from other mosques in Morocco. I told him I'd check it out. Then he mentioned the *zawiyya* of the Blue Sultan, which he explained was a shrine and the home of a holy figure. I told him I'd check that out, too.

"Oh no, you can't go into the *zawiyya* because it is off limits to non-Muslims. But it is still well worth seeing from the outside," he said. I told him I'd go and have a look at it, from the outside. I was beginning to get the feeling the barber was toying

with me and that he was an all-right guy — just having some
fun with an infidel. The people in the barbershop were friendly
and helpful, too. I started to relax, thinking maybe I was getting
paranoid. Perhaps the Front Polisario's struggle with the
Moroccan military still had me a little spooked.

"You wouldn't have any soap and shampoo for sale, would
you?" I asked the barber, remembering my mission to buy some
so I could have a decent shower at the hotel. He told me he
didn't but he was very obliging and sent a young assistant out
to get some. After my haircut, and armed with soap and
shampoo, I returned to the hotel and showered. This was a real
luxury and something unheard of when the first Dakar was run
more than two decades previously. According to legend,
nobody showered for more than two weeks in those first races.

When I got back to the bivouac it was time for dinner. I
didn't feel like staying in the tent so I wandered outside onto
the carpet with a plate of pasta and a bottle of water looking for
some company to eat with. I came upon a lone figure wearing
a Mitsubishi jacket, sitting all by himself. I thought he might
want to be left alone but when he glanced at me and kept eye
contact I strolled up and introduced myself.

"Mind if I join you," I asked.

"Not at all. Pull up a seat," he said cheerfully. He nodded to
the carpet because there weren't any chairs to sit on. "I'm Fred
Gallagher. Pleased to meet you."

I sat down and between mouthfuls of pasta we exchanged
some rally small talk. I soon learned from the Brit that he was
Team Mitsubishi front-runner Kenjiro Shinozuka's co-driver in
this edition of the rally. Shinozuka was a high-profile driver
who had won the Dakar in 1997 with navigator Henri Magne.
Gallagher and I exchanged abbreviated verbal resumes and I
was impressed to learn he had won a number of FIA world rally
championships, driving with such esteemed pilots as the
Finlander Ari Vatenen, another Dakar veteran and former
winner. When Gallagher found out I was a first-time Paris-
Dakar entrant, he explained that if you can get out of Morocco
in one piece you can finish the rally.

"It's not the desert, it's not the dunes, and it's not the dust that will do you in . . . it's the rocks! Rocks are the end of many a rider's and driver's valiant attempt at the Dakar," he said. "They can be your worst enemy. You simply must avoid them at all costs or be prepared for the worst."

I just kind of nodded my head to let him know I understood. I was wondering if he knew about my encounter with the rock during Stage 5. Gallagher also kindly mentioned, tongue-in-cheek, that if something happened you could still get to Dakar by road in a couple of days. "That way you can always say you rode across Africa," he said with a half smile. "You wouldn't be the first, I'm sure." After he mentioned that tidbit of information I was certain he knew of my encounter with a rock and that I was lucky to have survived this far. Maybe he saw my chances of getting to Dakar as next to zero . . . or worse.

That evening I again skipped the 9:30 p.m. briefing at the bivouac. I hadn't attended these briefings up until this point because I was either busy working on the bike or fast asleep. But most of the key information was posted on a bulletin board the next morning for everyone to read. This particular briefing dealt with the border crossing into Mauritania. I would have preferred to get the information first-hand but I was dead tired and needed sack time. One very important point was stressed: landmines were not to be taken lightly! It was critical to stick to the designated *piste*. Wandering off it could prove fatal, and getting lost was definitely not an option.

Chapter 8

Baptism by sand

—————————————————————

Stage 8 — Monday, January 8, 2001
Smara, Morocco to El Ghallaouiya, Mauritania
Liaison: 9 km — **Special:** 619 km
Total distance: 628 km

This was my fifth day in Africa, the fifth day of off-road riding as I had never experienced it before. A reassessment was in order. Life was good — it had to be, I was living my dream. I felt content, physically and mentally strong, and in total control of the situation. I had overcome two potential rally-ending mishaps. My gear was comfortable and working well. I felt neither too hot nor too cold. The xr sounded as finely tuned as the instant I had first started it up. It was easy to ride and holding up well. Yes, life was good, but I knew it was time to raise my guard another notch. Whenever I get too cocky and confident on a motorcycle, something not so good happens. In a split second life can go from being good to, well . . . It was just over a week into the rally, but there was already a noticeable decrease in the number of vehicles on the start line that morning: 118 motorcycles, 100 cars, and twenty-seven trucks set out from Smara, Morocco to El Ghallaouiya, Mauritania. This translated into twenty-four fewer bikes, eighteen fewer cars, and ten trucks dropped from the lineup. Day 8 of the rally had an even longer special stage than the one from Goulimine to Smara. In fact, it would be the longest of the 2001 Paris-Dakar and the first real desert special. An old Dakar hand warned me that once the rally crossed into Mauritania things got serious. And here I thought things had been pretty serious in Morocco. I couldn't imagine it getting more serious than that. I was about to get an education.

The liaison to the special stage ended just nine short kilometres outside of Smara. From there, the ride was against the clock all the way to the desolate valley where the ancient, abandoned fort at El Ghallaouiya was situated, 619 kilometres away. A highly visible military presence was once again in place. Toyota Land Cruiser pickup trucks and Land Rovers were parked along the way, often with a large machine guns mounted in the back. Each truck, many of which were placed strategically on hillsides, sported a towering radio antenna. Groups of soldiers, armed to the teeth, stood near the vehicles on full alert. The Moroccan army had promised strong retaliation if the Front Polisario interfered with the rally. It looked like they were ready for a showdown, but I truly hoped it wouldn't come to that. The morning passed quickly and peacefully, the border between Morocco and Mauritania closing in by the minute. Whenever I approach a border crossing, no matter where it is, I feel a sense of anticipation and excitement. The heat, which would become progressively more oppressive the farther we travelled south, was still tolerable and I rode with my jacket zipped up. Small dust cyclones swirled across the desert floor like whirling dervishes, then petered out in the distance.

The terrain became more diverse. The constant rocks I had encountered in Morocco had given way to a sandy consistency. A jutting range of mountains rose skyward off to my right as I rode across a smooth *chott* — a dried lakebed — on a compass heading that varied up to 10 degrees. A whitish, almost chalk-like dust invaded my clothing, nostrils and pores. My ICO speedometers indicated 139 kilometres per hour across this stretch of smooth dried mud, the fastest I travelled during the rally in off-road conditions. I couldn't see far enough to be sure there were no disastrous pitfalls ahead. Although it was a tremendous adrenaline rush to be barrelling along at this speed, and it would improve my finishing time for the stage, I slowed down to an average of 100 kilometres per hour. It probably wouldn't have made much of a difference if I had run into some crash-inducing obstruction, but I felt more comfortable at a reduced speed. I also had less difficulty seeing what was coming at me. The course was marked with cairns, essentially piles of stones. But even without these it would have been easy to follow the path, considering about eighty bikes had already been through ahead of me. Once across the lakebed, the course headed south. The smaller rocks had been moved off to the side of the track, undoubtedly by hand, and lined up on each side; this created a small curb-like border. It struck me as almost decorative. I could appreciate the painstaking work that had gone into its creation, and it was a pleasure not to have to ride on rock-studded gravel for a change. The route followed the hillside on a low angle until it rose onto a wide-open plain. To my dismay it was strewn with rocks, but according to my roadbook, this stretch would end at the Mauritanian border, where the first checkpoint was located, 90 kilometres into the special stage. The road turned left onto a die-straight rock path, exactly a bulldozer blade in width and headed due west as far as the eye could see. Some broken and gnarled tarmac, just two to three metres long, left a puzzling question as to why anyone had attempted to pave a road in such a haggard part of Morocco in the first place. It looked like someone had started the road and gave up after the first load of asphalt was delivered. Once the tarmac ended the road was composed of smaller rocks that had the bike's wheels dancing across the surface. The Honda purred along happily at a speed fast enough to keep the wheels in the air and smooth out most of the small hits.

I reached the first CP of the day without incident. It was set up precisely on the border. To cross the trenches, and the no man's land in the middle that marked the border, a road had been ploughed through the mounds of sand. Ahead of me lay Mauritania and nothing but sand, sand and more sand. This is what I had expected, but I never thought the Sahara would look so intimidating. About the same size as the United States, it is the world's largest hot desert. Immense sand sheets, complex sand seas and dunes cover more than one quarter of its surface. Other physical features typical of this humongous sandbox are shallow basins, large oasis depressions, gravel-covered plains, plateaus and mountains. The Sahara boasts several pyramidal dunes that reach over 152 metres (500 ft) in height while the *draa* — a mountainous sand ridge — towers over 300 metres (1,000 ft). Ninety percent of Mauritania is covered by the vastness of the Sahara, most of it flat and sandy. I quickly understood that without proper navigation aides like the roadbook and GPS, one could get lost out here in the blink of an eye. For centuries crossings had been limited to a handful of camel routes that link the Mediterranean with sub-Saharan Africa. In the past, these caravan routes followed a thread of reliable wells, skirting difficult terrain such as mountain ranges or the vast oceans of sand. Favoured routes also varied according to regional political allegiances and the activity of nomadic bandits. It wasn't much different in 2001, with the added restrictions of modern politics, threats of terrorism and landmines. For all intents and purposes the Sahara remains, by and large, a vast, lawless region where the risks to travellers are not to be underestimated.

* * *

The border between Morocco and Mauritania is actually a big ditch and a wall of sand that has been dug across a massive expanse of wasteland by the Moroccan army. Straying outside the cairns in this area is a form of Russian roulette. The terrain outside the marked track had not been swept for mines; they could be buried anywhere, as was discovered by a rally support vehicle.

That evening, the talk of the bivouac centred on an incident that involved Elisabete Jacinto's support truck crew. The truck had wandered a couple of hundred metres outside the cairns and hit a landmine. The front wheel of the truck was blown off and the Portuguese driver, Jose Eduardo Ribeiro, lost his foot in the explosion. It was a blatant reminder that the Dakar is deadly serious. It was also a reminder that I should start attending the nightly briefings just to make sure I got the information first-hand. I remembered Auriol mentioning a few nights earlier that mines could be a problem if the tracks were not strictly followed. It sometimes takes an actual incident to drive home the fact that they are indeed out there. I learned later that Africa holds the dubious distinction of having the most landmines on any continent. The number is estimated at around 40 million, spread mostly in the northern countries. They are a serious threat that kill or maim some 12,000 people annually. The Western Sahara alone is littered with close to 100,000 mines, remnants of the 1975–1991 war between Morocco and the Polisario Front. It's the old story: the more things change the more they remain the same.

* * *

After getting my card stamped at the CP, I set out to traverse some serious sand — 526 kilometres of it all the way to El Ghallaouiya. The day dragged on and the heat surged upward into the 40°C range. The course took us across the Tropic of Cancer and into the hottest and driest climate in the world. Eighty-seven clicks into the Sahara, the rally route took us through the remote military post town of Bir Mogrein, an area known for its landmines and the place where Jacinto's support truck met its Waterloo. The 148 kilometres from Bir Mogrein to the second CP of the stage was very fast. The distance involved and complex nature of the sand left no room for error. Once through the CP, I lined up at the fuel depot that had been set up there and had the bike's tank filled to the brim. Back on the road, I began to experience trouble steering. The track's ruts were worn into the sand's surface and the front wheel wandered wherever it wanted to go. Under full fuel load, the Honda is unwieldy, especially in the loose, sandy surface I was now encountering. As the sand became softer and went for longer stretches, the front end took more and more strength to control. I decided to stop and tighten the Scotts steering damper I had installed on the handlebars in anticipation of exactly this kind of scenario. It took a few more stops along the way to dial in more damping and get things under control. I ended up turning the damping to nearly its highest setting, to the point that it required great effort to twist the handlebars. I kept thinking about how much such a small thing like the steering damper now contributed to my ability to keep going. Without it, I'm almost sure I wouldn't have finished the day. My arms would have given out in the struggle to keep the bars straight. The time I'd spent researching and analyzing the Dakar, and diligently preparing for it, was starting to pay off. This was brought home to me when an Italian competitor, also riding a Honda XR650, pulled up to me while I was stopped to wind in more damping. To my surprise he had nothing in the form of a damper on his bike and he was paying the price by wrestling with his handlebars.

"Very smart to have the damper," he said. "I wish I would have thought of that." Yes, indeed, you can never give these things enough thought. All that preparation had left me more comfortable, less fatigued, and more concentrated on my riding, not the bike. You can't go to an event such as the Dakar and discover, in the middle of the desert, you should have arranged for a steering damper and mousse inner tubes, or brought seemingly insignificant things such as earplugs or riding shorts. One item in particular comes to mind. I had brought a pair of full-length bicycle tights with wind-stop material on the front. I wore these under my Sinisalo riding pants for the first half of the rally, until it got really hot. I also wore them to walk around the bivouac at night. They were warm and functional and did their part, however minor, in keeping me comfortable.

As we rode south further into Mauritania, the sand became deeper and the dunes got progressively larger and more difficult to traverse. I was finally getting my first real taste of the Sahara and the quirky nature of this immense desert. It was a real struggle through the dunes, so I played it safe, following the tracks of bikes and cars that had preceded me. Each dune was crossed at its lowest point. The sand moved underneath the tires of the Honda in granular waves; crossing them was more like surfing than riding a motorcycle. Guiding the XR demanded a loose grip on the bars and resisting the urge to wrestle the bike for control. The only way to make progress was to work with the bike, becoming one with it. This was truly a case of man and machine becoming a single unit. I poked the front wheel over the edges of dunes, had a quick look, then nosed down the faces. So-called "witches' holes" were especially disconcerting. These holes are formed when high winds, channelled by the shape of the surrounding dunes, whip the sand into a hole. Depending on the softness of the sand, it is nearly impossible to ride out of one of them. I nearly got trapped in one not far from the final dune crossing. I rode around the circumference of the shaft until I ended up at the top, which was much like a "Wall of Death" circus attraction. Fortunately, the sand had been firm enough to allow this manoeuvre.

Two kilometres from the end of the stage lurked the final sting in the tail: the immense Erg de Maqteir dunes. Although the bivouac was only a short distance away, it may as well have been on the other side of Africa. In some places the dunes are as high as a fifteen-storey building, and the going was slow and treacherous. At one point, the blind side of a dune I was crossing proved to be a steep harrowing drop over soft, loose white sand. Two resourceful photographers were stationed at the bottom, waiting for riders who would provide their camera lenses with a big "endo." One such hapless rider was the Brit Michael Hughes. He was standing next to his downed XR400 nursing a bleeding nose. He had obviously misjudged the grade and tumbled awkwardly down the slope. I wasn't about to repeat his error. I carefully rode the front of the bike up to the edge and spun the rear tire into the sand. But then the Honda refused to advance. I stepped off the XR, which was lodged into the sand on the flat aluminum skid plate mounted beneath the engine. Holding onto the bike with one hand, I scooped sand away from underneath the skid plate with the other until the front wheel gradually tipped down the incline. I carefully got back on the pegs and gingerly coasted to the bottom. Learning proper sand technique comes with time and experience. If you bury the rear wheel, you court disaster. Spinning a wheel deeper into the sand has ended many a Dakar effort. It's simple: the chain sucks up the sand, which in turn tightens up the linkages, until the transmission shaft gets pulled back with so much tension the engine cases crack. The smart and most efficient method to extricate a bike from such a predicament is to tip it over on its side, opposite to the chain, until the rear wheel is out. Sand will slide into the hole the tire made, and with a bit of technique and strength all should be well. Next, you stand the bike up, gently feed out the clutch while pushing on the bars, taking care not to spin the tire at all. Sand is an unusual substance to ride in. It requires patience and a cool head. In the heat of the desert, these things are not always easy to maintain. Another rider had waited above me to warn oncoming vehicles that someone was working his way down the blind side of the dune. I was grateful for this fellow rallyist's concern. When I reached the bottom, I gestured a thank-you. Getting run over by one off those monstrous six-wheeled race trucks in a situation like this was one of my biggest fears. I restarted the Honda and continued on. Finally, a stone-covered valley floor marked the end of the dunes. It was a relief to get out of them before dark. I never would have thought a massive expanse of flat rocks could be such a welcome sight. The valley was about two to three kilometres wide, and the tall flags marking the location of the end of the special stage were at the far edge. The bivouac was placed beyond that at the old fort of El Ghallaouiya. My GPS arrow pointed straight to the final CP of the day. I rode the short distance standing on the pegs, maintaining a slow pace to conserve the front wheel.

I'd spent 8 hours, 36 minutes and 58 seconds on my bike to get from the start of the competitive section, after the short 9-km liaison, to El Ghallaouiya, a God-forsaken place in the middle of nowhere. Joan Roma, who logged the fastest time of the day, did it in an unbelievable 5 hours, 16 minutes and 41 seconds. He might as well have been on a freeway back home. In the scheme of things, I didn't do that badly, finishing seventy-third for the day and taking over eightieth place on the provisional scoreboard. Only three days earlier I had been at 107. Meanwhile, only two minutes separated Roma from car division winner Jose Maria Servia, who could count on some advantages riding the dunes in his Schlesser/Renault buggy. KTM's Richard Sainct followed the BMW of Roma to take second place for the day, nearly two and a half minutes down. The Frenchman did stay ahead of Roma in the overall chase, however, by just over five minutes. In the car class, four Mitsubishis filled the top five overall places at the end of Day 8. It wasn't time yet to start laying bets that the manufacturer was going to win its sixth Paris-Dakar, but the pressure was certainly on. Servia, who won the special a scant two minutes ahead of Mitsubishi's Masuoka, was still in control of the race to Dakar by some eleven and a half minutes over Mitsu's Fontenay and Picard. On this day, the Spaniard and his navigator Jean-Marie Lurquin had actually increased their lead by close to three minutes.

When I arrived at the El Ghallaouiya bivouac it was immediately apparent that it wasn't a full-fledged version of the previous stopovers. We were without backup support, the trucks were almost a day behind us, and there was no airport to speak of, just a small landing strip on top of the escarpment — *dhar* — that cut across the desert. Only a few helicopters and some short take-off and landing planes (STOL) had been diverted to Ghallaouiya. There were no tourists, no press and just a skeleton crew of TSO personnel consisting of doctors, catering staff and timing crews. Being without the support trucks meant we were also without our trunks: no tents, sleeping bags, spare parts or change of clothes. All I had with me was my riding gear, boots, helmet, goggles and what I carried on my person: a tool bag and some energy bars.

The lively bivouac scene I had come to know took on a different tone, almost sombre in nature. Other than a temporary gathering place for the rallyists, with the minimum support for survival, there was absolutely nothing but rock and sand as far as the eye could see. A grey sky and eerie wind blew up as the sun dipped below the edge of the cliff an hour or so after I arrived. Immediately the temperature started dropping and it cooled off quickly. The main tent was an old and flapping grey cloth, soiled, stained and decrepit. Filthy carpets were laid down underneath. The wind blew sand in one end and out the other. This was how the locals lived every day. No water, no washrooms, no stores, no amenities of any kind. El Ghallaouiya was a place that shouldn't be inhabited, but it was — not by many, but by some. Why they didn't look for somewhere else to live seems like the obvious $65,000 question. Surely, I thought, there must be somewhere better to spend your time on Earth.

I was forced into contemplating my own life, and how the Dakar was changing it. I was a spoiled Westerner who relied on, and took for granted, all the amenities of home. Here, I felt abandoned. The depressing remoteness was working on my psyche. In Ghallaouiya, my courage was being put to the test like never before. The accomplishments of the past eight days, the mere fact that I had survived, now seemed trivial. Seven more competitors had dropped out of this day's stage. I could have been one of them, but so far so good. Still, distressing thoughts were haunting me. The positive energy I had been accumulating months in advance of the rally was suddenly starting to abandon me. I had been spending this energy hand-over-fist trying to stay optimistic and focused. I realized how much familiar faces and human interaction had played a positive role in my psychological makeup and strength. I had dealt with all sorts of naysayers and negative comments prior to leaving, but I had turned these into strength — they only hardened my resolve. I knew I was a tough nut to crack, or I wouldn't be in the rally in the first place. I also understood that I had to deal quickly with these negative feelings I was experiencing. It was time to start seeing the bottle as half full again. I reminded myself that this entire venture would boil down to something I was going to be judged on for years to come — perhaps for the rest of my days. It was time to pull up my socks — wimping out was not an option. I found a pail of fresh water and splashed the lukewarm liquid on my face and hair, washed my hands without soap, then wandered around the encampment, looking for something, anything, I didn't know quite what. It took some inner strength to regain an even keel. Ghallaouiya would turn out to be a defining moment, in the rally and in my life.

To further distract myself from the funk I was in, I looked for solace in working on my bike for a while. For as long as I can remember, tinkering with motorcycles has always been good therapy. Soon my thoughts were focused on my Honda XR650, a wonder of engineering I had come to consider a dear friend. I wiped the bike down and exchanged the air filter for the one I had carried with me for emergency purposes. There are many things a motorcycle engine can handle (and keep running) — sand isn't one of them. For that reason I always made sure I had a spare air filter with me during the rally. Next, I rode a short distance from the bivouac to the TSO fuel depot and quenched the XR's thirst for gas. Once this was out of the way, I installed the roadbook for the next day's stage. This only took a few minutes, as the book consisted of just two pages. They were meant to guide us through the canyon onto the upper level of the *dhar* that overlooked El Ghallaouiya. There were no liaison stages on the schedule for Day 9; the entire stage was a navigation stage, a yacht race of sorts for bikes and cars with passage controls substituting for buoys. Unprecedented in a Dakar, this 515-kilometre marathon loop would include numerous dune crossings. I was definitely going to get more sand than I ever dreamed of.

After I had taken care of the bike's needs, my thoughts turned to finding some kind of blanket or sleeping bag to help ward off the cold desert-night air. I knew that without a cover I would probably lie awake shivering until dawn. After circulating for a while, I found a young local who agreed to rent me his sleeping bag for 100 French francs. No doubt, having the Paris-Dakar Rally pass through his backyard was a heaven-sent opportunity to make more money in one day than he would in an entire month. What he called a sleeping bag, however, turned out to be a worthless discarded piece of cloth. I certainly was not in a position to be choosy or do much haggling: the filthy rag would offer some warmth, and was better than nothing. I accepted his sorry excuse for a sleeping bag and headed back to the equally dilapidated main tent that would serve as my refuge for the night. I quickly staked a claim to some sleeping space by placing my helmet on top of the rented bag near two American riders. They were top-flight competitors with solid sponsorship backing. One, Lewis, was riding for the prestigious BMW factory team, and currently held down seventh overall; the other, Campbell, hovered in thirteenth place. I found some solace in the fact that we were all in the same boat. Here, the top guys shared the same hardships as the privateers, except that they still had a support team to look after their machines. I had dinner with the amicable Americans and we chatted until there was nothing left to do but go to sleep. But before turning in, I stretched my legs and went for a stroll to the medical tent to inquire about an injured rider. While there, I asked for a couple of aspirins to deal with the headache I'd been nursing most of the day. At El Ghallaouiya, preparing for bed was as basic as it gets: you lie down in what you are wearing and close your eyes. As I drifted off to sleep I thought about home, family, and whether I would continue to be able to overcome the conditions that were wearing me down. No, wimping out wasn't an option. Grandfather Burla would never have approved.

* * *

Stage 9 — Tuesday, January 9, 2001
El Ghallaouiya, Mauritania to El Ghallaouiya, Mauritania
Special: 518 km
Total distance: 518 km

As usual, the day started early. Waking up in darkness underneath the flapping tent that was home for the night was like waking up to a living nightmare. But all things considered, I had slept fairly well. The rag that had substituted for my sleeping bag had kept me relatively warm. And I had regained my desire to get on with the business of racing, which on this day meant a long special test that began and ended in the same location. I donned my riding gear, filled up my drinking system and joined the others for something to eat. Breakfast, which thus far had been a nice spread, was far from sumptuous this time around. Here it consisted of a simple piece of bread with jam, orange juice and tea. I felt the situation, and the rallyists' position in the scheme of things, had become somewhat laughable. Whatever glamour the Dakar holds for the outside world was far from evident at El Ghallaouiya. If not for the bikes, cars, trucks, helicopters and plane, the bivouac could easily have been mistaken for a ragtag refugee camp in the shadows of an old ruined fort. The atmosphere was sullen, the stress and apprehension almost palpable. Everyone looked haggard, in need of a bath and a shave. Being here, voluntarily taking part in a potentially life-ending undertaking for no other reason than some ego-fulfilling urge, seemed like far-from-rational behaviour at that moment. I needed to take it all a little less seriously and see the humour and absurdity. I decided it was best to view my predicament as a comedy rather than tragedy. I noticed that those who adopted a cavalier attitude seemed to be dealing with life in the rally much more easily. After breakfast, I pictured myself doing the 518-kilometre loop from El Ghallaouiya and back, and got ready to again prove my mettle in the sands of the Sahara. At 7:30 a.m. the first bike, piloted by Stage 8 winner Joan Roma, set off. As per rally protocol, riders were sent on their way at thirty-second intervals. It was a matter of overtake or be overtaken.

With no landmarks other than the mountainous dunes and passes, navigation would play a major role in the special stage that was Day 9 of the Dakar. The first section was a short, but difficult, ride up a rocky gorge which led to a pass on a high plateau on the cliffs on one side of El Ghallaouiya. The gorge was the site of the ancient abandoned fort, originally placed there to control the movements of people travelling from both directions across the cliff that separated the lower valley from the higher plateau. Riding in the spectacular gorge was far from easy, especially with a full tank of gasoline. But this was the only feasible way to traverse the cliff, and the best passageway to the higher plateau from the lower valley. Sand was extremely soft, and rocks, both large and small, were strewn about helter-skelter. Having no direct line through meant riding into the lowest point and slowly manoeuvring the XR around the obstacles. I reasoned it was better to take my time and not drop the bike rather than struggle to pick it up again. Needlessly wasting energy was something I didn't want to do. After a while the canyon narrowed down in some areas to about 100 metres (300 ft) in width. Steep rock faces flanked it on either side. There was no clear path through the pass; the climb out of the gorge led to a gravel road and past the small landing strip where the STOL and helicopters had touched down the previous day.

There were three GPS waypoints and control passages to contend with once on top of the *dhar*. I picked lines across the tall dunes and followed the GPS arrow in an as-the-crow-flies direction. The sand was so soft, getting underway on level ground required a push to prevent the rear wheel from digging in. Skirting around some of the towering impassable dunes meant long detours to get back on course. I followed other riders' tracks up and over ridges, poking the front wheel over the tops and then slowly making my way down once I was sure the path was safe. This day was a long exercise in endurance and riding skill. At any moment one could make an error in judgment and throw it all away. One bad decision, one overly optimistic slice of enthusiasm, could have me buried in sand, overheated and expending energy I would need later for riding. It seemed like up until El Ghallaouiya and the majestic dunes of Erg de Maqteir, I had had only a cursory introduction to the Sahara. Now I was beginning to realize how dangerous and unforgiving this desert could be. I reached the first checkpoint, 61 kilometres into the stage, without any kind of trouble and at a relatively good clip. The next 120 kilometres or so, which took us in an easterly direction, were wide open and technical. This is where the key contenders pulled out all the stops to make up time; once in the

TO DAKAR AND BACK

The crated bike makes it through customs in Luxembourg.

Paris, Parc Florale, Vincennes outside Technical Control.

Denis Rozand and I in Dakar. I called him my "Ange Guardien" or Guardian Angel
— he summoned a truck to get me out of a potentially Dakar-ending situation.

My Honda XR 650 R became a well-traveled celebrity for years after
the Dakar. Here it is in the Canadian Motor Sports Hall of Fame beside
my old friend Ross Pederson's Suzuki motocross bike. Ross won many
Canadian Motocross championships. I am here at a special evening
at the Hall of Fame, with Dave Lloyd on the left, and Ralph Luciw.

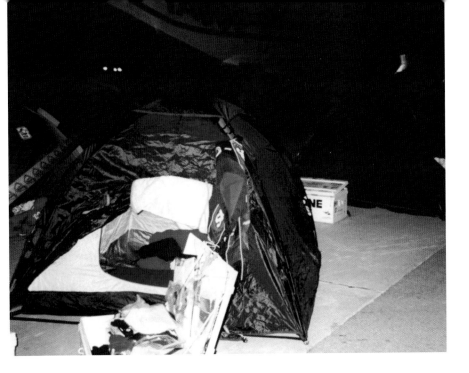

My tent and trunk set up in a bivouac beside the Yacco plane.

The bivouac at the airport in Smara, Mauritania. I had time to ride into the town centre and have a haircut and shower.

The TSO volunteer team later on in the rally.

A typical bivouac scene. Yacco is a French oil company that provided the airplane to transport all the privateers' trunks and supplies.

P.G. Lundmark's complete set up, bike, trunk, pair of boots and a covered sleeping bag. With the minimum he accomplished the maximum — winning Stage 11.

Here is the personal assistant I hired in Atar. He washed my air filters and seemed pleased with the energy bar I gave him.

Steph, from Bragne, worked for ERTF, the company that supplies the GPS units and support for the competitors.

Eric Aubijoux finished 16th overall and called me "Canadien." Here in Dakar he's all smiles. (He was killed in an accident in the 2007 Dakar rally.)

This is Masha, Jun Mitsuhashi's mechanic. Masha came to my rescue when I had problems in Bakel. It is quite possibly more exhausting to be a mechanic on the Dakar than a competitor.

Michael Hughes, number 97, finished the Dakar rally and went on to compete a few more times.

Here we are, the XR 650 and I, in action. I spent all day in this position.

You pass by locations and scenes that are not easy to reach by any other means when you enter the Dakar Rally.

This is the bible of the Dakar, the road book. It describes each day in detail and features time schedules, course conditions, refueling points and a general map of the route.

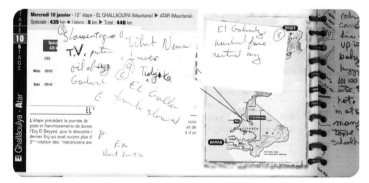

The pace of the rally is extremely fast. You have no time to dwell on the past. The basis for this book is written in the Post-It notes I stuck on each day's route description.

This particular day in the road book is from El Ghallaouiya to the rest day in Atar. I struggled in the deep sand and heat, but reaching Atar was one of my goals.

This is Phillipe Bermudes and Jun Mitsuhashi, both great guys. I rode with Phillipe four and a half days. Jun now competes successfully in rallies in four-wheeled vehicles.

In Dakar, at the celebration party, with two TSO volunteers and two other riders — M. Diallo from Senegal, on the far left, and Stephane Grignac on the far right.

This is Dominique Vian; he helped everyone he could. He won the "Lanterne Rouge" award for last place finisher. I loaned him my shoes in Atar so he could go into town.

With Alain Dulcos in Dakar. Obviously happy to get to the end, Alain went on to compete at the top level in the Dakar. He won stages and enjoyed factory-level support until he crashed and was seriously injured.

This is the bivouac in Atar, Mauritania, on the rest day. You can tell by the corporate planes in the background.

The Dakar rally medical assistance card. The organizers provide a very high level of medical care, emergency or otherwise, to all the competitors.

Guido Maletti, the Italian Dakar veteran, hit a cow a few days from the finish and broke his collarbone. He helped me install my road book correctly the first time.

On the finish podium with my old friend Jean Luc Sagnou — or "Darry" as he is called.

A joyous moment. Riding onto the podium with Françoise on the XR behind me, and TSO event director Hubert Auriol with the microphone.

Lac Rose or the Pink Lake in the background: the famous destination for all Dakar hopefuls.

A typical village scene in Africa.

A store in Dakar. I was more appreciative of what we have at home after visiting places like Mauritania, Mali and Senegal.

The rewards of months of hard work, time, energy and thousands of dollars invested . . . riding a well-prepared off-road bike across some of the most stunning terrain on the planet.

The last day of the rally, we are both tired and happy. Françoise supports what I do to no end.

massive dunes they were, like everybody else, obliged to proceed at a slower pace, although compared to rookies like me, they were still flying. Heading south, towering dunes were encountered from the second CP onwards for some fifty clicks. The dunes were replaced by sand and camel grass for another fifty clicks, then another unending stretch of dunes until the third CP. At 278 kilometres into the stage, CP3 marked the farthest point of travel south. It was also where the refuelling depot was located. From there, the marathon loop turned back in a northwesterly direction towards El Ghallaouiya.

Checkpoint No.3 was hidden behind some large dunes that held in the searing heat like a blast furnace. In addition to the large six-wheel-drive truck loaded with drums of fuel, a TSO Land Cruiser and the two helicopters were at the site. Shade was at a premium, cast only by the vehicles and the awning that covered the official who was stamping the time cards. When it was my turn to get gas, I was waved away and the fuel truck pulled away to service the helicopter. I screamed to the driver that I was on the clock and needed gas right away, but to no avail. He kept going as if he hadn't heard me or didn't care. He knew that the factory guys had already passed through — by this time the only riders looking for gas were the privateers.

"Just ride over and get fuel at the same time they're filling the helicopter," a neatly dressed pilot suggested. "I'm sure they won't mind."

I followed his advice and did my best to bite my tongue. Complaining to the fuel guys wouldn't do much good. They proved to be quite sympathetic to my dilemma and tried to calm me. I got the fuel I needed and was on my way.

On the ride back north towards the third GPS waypoint, I fell in line with KTM-mounted Philippe Bermudes, a likeable Frenchmen of Spanish descent. Neither of us seemed intent to outdo the other and this developed into the first in a series of days that we would ride together. As I got to know Philippe I learned that he owns and operates a thriving fruit-and-vegetable distribution business in Paris. "We sell a lot of produce every day; tons of it, actually," he told me, without sounding boastful, during one of our conversations. Pretty impressive I thought. So was his skill as a motorcyclist and rallyist. He struck me as a courageous person, one who pushes his own limits while remaining humble. Following the GPS arrow as close as we could to a waypoint that took us for quite a distance west, we were joined by the Japanese rider Takao Hosono. The same long rows of monolithic dunes encountered on the way south had to be crossed again going north, and they stretched off endlessly towards the horizon. Traversing them once had been tough enough, doing it twice was much harder, especially with the newly filled tanks of fuel. Manoeuvring through them now was even more tricky and hazardous. The dunes were farther west from where we first encountered them, and they came with new pitfalls. Philippe, Takao and I rode around the ends of these dunes or crossed over at the lower elevations, which at times were still as high as 50 and 75 feet. The sand hid steep drops on the windward sides, which held any number of traps that would cost precious time and energy to get out of. We proceeded cautiously along without incident and arrived at the next GPS waypoint.

To our surprise there were no other visible tracks. No one else had come this way. When we looked back we could see no one following.

"Now what?" queried Hosono, who spoke next to no English.

"Well, I think we just follow the GPS to the next point. That's where the last control passage should be," said Philippe.

The dunes were now lower and the sand firmer. We were able to ride much faster and make up precious time. Only the frequently encountered camel grass kept our speed in check. Camel grass is one of the more persistent hazards of desert rallying. The desert floor is often interspersed with clumps of dry grass. These sit on top of hard mounds of sand that resemble a camel's hump. I started to see more tracks and the odd four-wheeled vehicle off in the distance, travelling on converging vectors towards the same point we were heading for. Tiny specks sped across the vast horizon, indicating hundreds of people spread over thousands of acres of sand. It gave us a new appreciation for the logistics of the Dakar, and the immensity of the security measures needed to ensure competitors had some sort of backup in case of emergency. The final CP of the day was at the same location as the first. After getting our cards stamped we headed due west for the short ride back to the pass into the gorge to Ghallaouiya. On top of the cliffs that overlooked the Erg de Maqteir an immense rock garden spread across a great plain. Shards of flat black rocks appeared until they covered more of the desert surface than the sand did. Soon it was a matter of riding across the rocks, avoiding the larger ones that could damage the bike or send one flying over the handlebars. The GPS arrow pointed straight over an escarpment to the final waypoint, which was tucked beneath the cliff ledge and hidden in the shadows. Finding the right way down proved nearly impossible, as few tracks showed the way. It was a matter of riding across the rocks while standing on the pegs. Patience was the operative word here, but Philippe seemed to have run out. He seemed intent on getting to the finish line as quickly as possible. I chose to remain some distance behind him and take my time. I had already gone on two blind dates with hidden rocks and wasn't too keen on another one.

Takao wisely opted to stay behind me. Sure enough, the Frenchman's hastiness caught up with him just moments later when he struck a rock large enough to bring him down in a spectacular crash. He and his KTM slid across the rocks, both eventually coming to rest in a tangled heap. Philippe didn't get up right away; he just lied there prone against the bike. This could mean any number of things and I feared the worst as I rode over to him. I had seen far more innocent crashes with dire consequences for both rider and machine. But by the time Takao and I got to him, Philippe had managed to sit up. No doubt he was hurting some, but like any hardcore competitor he made light of the crash and laughed it off.

"It's still better to hit a rock than a landmine, eh?" he said with a crooked grin. "At least I'm still intact. I'm not so sure about my bike, however."

In no time he picked up his KTM and Philippe gave it a quick once-over. It had some dents and scratches but otherwise it seemed fine, too. He got the bike started without a problem and we took off. This time he stayed behind me and Takao followed our reserved pace to the opening of the pass, which took a bit of searching to find because it was hidden from view. As we dropped along the edge of the aircraft runway, my bike sputtered and stopped. It sounded like it had run out of gas. I knew this couldn't be the case, because I had enough fuel left to get back to the bivouac. After checking the internal reservoir, I fiddled with the fuel taps and determined that no gasoline was reaching the reservoir. In the true spirit of what the Dakar is all about, another rider stopped and asked if he could help. After I explained the problem, he offered me a length of fuel hose which I used to blow into the fuel caps, hoping I could push fuel up into the reservoir. To my relief, it worked — the motor started as if it had been completely overhauled. The old quick fix saved me this time, but it's not something you can always rely on. I kept my fingers crossed that I would be able to get to the bivouac, some sixty clicks away, without any further problems.

We eased down a rocky path that led past the ancient fort and into the sandy downhill pass. Descending into the narrow valley was no easier than it had been going in the opposite direction. To my amazement, I didn't recognize much of anything along the way, even though I had ridden through the same spot that morning. It seemed like someone had come behind us and changed the decor. I would have liked to have had a closer look at the abandoned fort, but I didn't want to stop and I couldn't afford to be distracted as I rode on. The sand was displaced and ruts were now a tangle of lines leading into abutments of rocks. I struggled with the sand and dumped the bike a few times when my strength gave out. It was extremely tough going and nearly impossible to hold a line and direct the bike between the massive rocks that were embedded in the sand. I'm sure I was not a pretty sight with my feet dangling, paddling through the sand and fighting to stay upright. Philippe and Takao were having equal difficulty, but managed to keep things on two wheels. I told them to keep going and not wait for me after my first fall. I finally reached the finish line, 9 hours and 41 minutes after setting out, and made my way to the bivouac. I had improved on my overall ranking once again, however, now taking up seventy-eighth spot.

The top riders were already at the bivouac when I arrived, relaxing while their crews worked on their bikes. The Spaniard Pujol had grabbed his second stage win, leading a KTM sweep of the first three places, with Giovani Sala and Carlo De Gavardo, in second and third respectively. Pujol brought home the bacon in a very respectable time of 5:22:33:00, preceding Sala by 1:20:00 minutes and De Gavardo by 2:53:00. It had again been a banner day for KTM. Eight of the Austrian machines finished in the top ten for the day, a tour de force showing at the expense of the defending BMW team. Lewis, finishing twelfth, was one of four BMW riders to end within ten minutes of Pujol. Included in the BMW group were John Deacon in fourth and Fabrizio Meoni in fifth. Richard Sainct, in ninth, was the last of the top KTM finishers. The Dakar 2000 winner kept his overall lead, however, nearly five minutes ahead of Meoni.

Meanwhile, in the car division, Jutta Kleinschmidt took her Mitsubishi Pajero/Montero to a seventh career Dakar stage win. Jean-Louis Schlesser and Henri Magne continued to make up for their Stage 7 fiasco by finishing second for the day. They followed Kleinschmidt and her navigator Andreas Schulz home with a time of 5:23:07:00, a mere 25 seconds behind the lead duo. Rounding off the top three were Kleinschmidt's Mitsubishi teammates Masuoka and Maimon. They moved into second overall at the expense of teammates Jean-Pierre Fontenay and Gilles Picard. The Frenchmen had struck a deceivingly high clump of camel grass at over 120 km per hour and had flipped their car onto its side. With the help of yet another Mitsu entry — Carlos Sousa and navigator J.M. Polato — they managed to get the car upright and continue the stage, but without the benefit of power steering and a clutch. They still finished a very impressive seventh place, 14 minutes behind Kleinschmidt. All hopes of Kenjiro Shinozuka repeating his previous Dakar victory went out the window. His Mitsubishi developed yet another electrical problem that forced him to return to the bivouac to get the car repaired, missing two critical passage controls in the process. As a consequence, Shinozuka and his navigator Fred Gallagher were hit with ten hours in penalties for each checkpoint missed, dropping them from twelfth overall to sixty-seventh, more than 28 hours behind the lead duo of Servia/Lurquin in the Renault/Megane buggy. A day earlier, the Mitsu duo lost one and a half hours due to an electrical problem, while holding down sixth overall on the provisional scoreboard.

By the time I got back the support trucks had arrived and the bivouac was almost fully populated again. Only most of the journalists and tourists were absent — they would be waiting at the next bivouac in Atar. Lights, generators and bustling team crews now animated an area that in the morning had been a barren wasteland. The Tibau team truck was there, too. But I still didn't have my spares trunk. The Yacco airplane, like most of the others, had been unable to land on the short strip outside the bivouac. I, and the other privateers, would not see our trunks again until we got to Atar late the following afternoon. After drinking some water and taking a breather, I checked out my bike. I had encountered no further problems with the reservoir and everything seemed fine. I had a spare element and proceeded to change the used one. Other than changing the air filter the xr didn't need work, so it was going to be a carefree evening. Before dinner I went to retrieve the standard tso-issue cloth duffel bag, which I had aboard the Tibau truck. Now that I had my sleeping bag and tent, I was able to enjoy at least some semblance of civilization for the night. And I had another spare air filter for the xr.

Chapter 9

Halfway there

▬ ▬ ▬ ▬ ▬ ▬ ▬ ▬ ▬ ▬

Stage 10 — Wednesday, January 10, 2001
El Ghallaouiya, Mauritania to Atar, Mauritania
Special: 435 km — **Liaison:** 5 km
Total distance: 440 km

137

After sleeping two nights in the hellhole of the El Ghallaouiya encampment, I began to feel resilient to the point of almost liking it (the operative word being "almost"). My appreciation for material things and the comforts of the Western world were deeper rooted than I had ever imagined. I thought of being at home in Canada, where all those wonderful machines do everything for you, where cold and hot running water, central heating, air conditioners, big-screen televisions and computers are regarded almost as necessities. I wanted to hug our dishwasher and say thank you for making life easier. I imagined myself having a shower with an unlimited stream of hot water, then sitting down to a juicy steak washed down with an ice-cold beer. Sure, back in the real world there are things to contend with like mortgages, road rage, car payments, credit card payments, taxes and telemarketers. But after a taste of Morocco and Mauritania, I was already looking forward to the stresses and tribulations of everyday life in what surely has to be considered the land of milk and honey. Patience, I told myself, patience will deliver. Just rewards were only a few weeks away. When immersed in an event like the Paris-Dakar Rally, twenty-one days seems like an eternity. Yet it's just a tiny slice of the time one spends over the course of a natural lifespan. Then again, the situation I found myself in wasn't exactly a prison sentence. It was something I had chosen to do; a challenge I had taken on as a human being hungry for new experiences and adventures. And new experiences and adventures were what I got — maybe more than I had bargained for. I knew I should embrace every moment, regardless. But I was looking forward to seeing this through to the end and getting back home. Then I could treasure the memories for the rest of my life, and I'd have one heck of a story to tell my grandchildren some day.

The first bikes were scheduled to leave El Ghallaouiya for Atar at 7:10 a.m. No longer was it cool in the morning. The climate had noticeably changed. In addition to the daily challenges presented by the rally, heat was really becoming a factor. Morning temperatures of 20°C became 38° by noon and hovered there until late afternoon. And the days were getting longer. The sun was rising at 7:24 a.m. and setting at 6:28 p.m. When I left Paris the sun rose at 7:46 a.m. (although you wouldn't have known it because of the dark cloud cover), and disappeared from the sky in Narbonne at 4:22 p.m. At this time of the year I was used to the sun rising at 7:40 a.m. and setting at 4:50 p.m. Temperatures could drop as low as -20°C, close to -30 with the wind chill factor, and there could be as much as a half metre of snow outside my door.

* * *

Stage 10 marked the halfway point of the rally. Traditionally it is one of the toughest on the schedule. Like the previous day, another long and demanding special, starting in El Ghallaouiya, was in store. At 435 kilometres it was only 73 clicks shorter than Stage 9's marathon loop. A short, five-kilometre liaison to the bivouac in Atar was tacked on the end. Although it had some stony tracks, camel grass and gravel stretches thrown in for good measure, the special was mostly sweeping sand with twisty sections. This meant high speeds most of the way. There was no shortage of dunes either. The highlight of the day was the crossing of the Erg El Beyyed, the descent of the Aghreijt Pass and at the finish line, the crossing of more dunes. After successfully handling everything that had been thrown at me so far, I had no doubt whatsoever that I would make it to Atar. As I set off across the stony valley floor leading out of El Ghallaouiya I hoped I would never have to look at these unmerciful rocks again. Fred Gallagher's warning about the rocks spelling the end of many a Dakar effort echoed through my head. But I had survived the rocks of Morocco, so according to his logic, I should make it to Dakar. The course out of El Ghallaouiya followed the now familiar valley for a short distance. I was happily buzzing along until, some 12 kilometres into the stage, I came across a grim sight. BMW's Joan Roma had crashed hard and was lying on his back beside his bike. A rider I recognized was kneeling over the young Spaniard holding his hand. Another was standing nearby with a worried look on his face. This was not good, and I felt my stomach knotting. Seeing a fellow rider involved in a bad accident is always disconcerting. It's a flagrant reminder of the dangers and possible consequences of racing motorcycles. Still, if you dwell on these things, you lose your edge. When that happens it's time to park your bike and hang up your boots. I circled around the scene once as the first helicopter landed thinking that maybe there was something I could do. This is a natural instinct. But other than get in the way I served no purpose, so I continued on. I rode at a reserved speed for a while until my main focus returned to the job at hand, not thinking of Roma's condition.

Picking the best or correct line offered many choices. The valley floor was covered in loose gravel and looked as if it had been subjected to serious flooding in recent months. But now there was no hint of water anywhere. The heat was so stifling, a glass of water would evaporate in a New York minute. I passed some clusters of dwellings that were little more than makeshift tents. Here and there curious children watched me ride by while they tended to a few scrawny camels or goats. I wondered what kind of future, if any, was in store for these children of the desert. I thanked my lucky stars to have been born in a country that offered a future to anyone willing to grasp one of the many opportunities available. Off to my right, a large line of gigantic white sand dunes rose abruptly towards the dark blue sky. The GPS arrow pointed directly up into the dunes towards one of the highest ridges. There was no mistake: the course was sending us into the majestic Erg de Maqteir once again. I noticed some journalists' vehicles parked on a step in the sand. I knew right then that this was going to be a difficult and trying passage. Photojournalists are the rally's vultures, circling around scenes of misery for their prey. I rode onto the crest of a small butte not far from a female photographer. She was holding a camera fitted with the appropriate telephoto lens so she could get intrusive close-ups of riders and drivers struggling in the dunes. I paused and took a look at what lay ahead. I wanted to be sure I was making a good line choice. Down the blind side of the dune, I could see two men labouring to dig their buggy out of a witch's hole big enough to hold a couple of trucks. It was current car division leader Jose Marie Servia and his navigator Jean-Marie Lurquin. The photographer, who no doubt had already taken pictures of them, walked over to me and pointed up to the steepest, most chewed-up line. It had all the makings of a trap if there ever was one.

"It's that way," she yelled. "Go that way . . . that way!" She kept motioning towards the same spot, really intent on me taking that line.

"Calm down, lady. If it's all the same to you I'll decide which way I'll go," I yelled back.

She shrugged her shoulders and focused her camera towards Servia and Lurquin, slaving away trying to free their buggy. The Schlesser/Renault/Megane duo, who had enjoyed the overall lead since Stage 7, spent a few hours freeing themselves from the hole. This proved one thing: in the Dakar, first place can be a very tenuous thing.

The dunes that had to be crossed now were the tallest I'd seen thus far. The sand was soft in some parts and solid in others. I chose to ignore the line the journalist suggested and rode up the dune face to the side where the sand was firm. I slowly ascended each step and stopped on a firm ledge to plot my next move. I wound around on the highest spots, carefully choosing the best line. It was time-consuming, but a much better alternative to having to dig myself out of a hole, or tumble head-over-heels down an incline. A number of other riders were in my company. All applied their own strategy in a bid to find the best way out of the dunes and into the flatter sands of the desert. At the crest of each dune crossing I slowed and poked the front wheel over. Sometimes the downhill side was incredibly steep and required meticulous manoeuvring to safely descend to the bottom. Some of the lower traverses were just as tricky. One in particular caught me out, much to my chagrin. I rode about one metre to the left of the existing tracks and, as the front wheel descended, it ploughed into a sinkhole and disappeared. Other riders passed a few feet away without a problem. I flopped over into the broiling sand and stared in disbelief at the half-buried XR. I dragged it inch by inch to solid sand before trying to stand it up. The sun's rays blazed down like a blowtorch, sucking the oxygen out of the air. I tried to imagine myself back home in frigid temperatures shovelling snow out of my driveway. Freeing the bike from the clutches of the sand under these conditions was one of the most exhausting things I had ever done. I was afraid that if I had to do this once more before getting out of the dunes, I wasn't going to finish.

The first two control passages came and went. The third, at 208 kilometres into the stage, had a fuel stop as well. Again there were numerous high dune crossings and some treacherous drop-offs. The course switched back and forth through mini dunes, low waves of sand interspersed over a harder gravel base. Finally, the GPS arrow and tracks headed straight for some medium-red sand dunes with tufts of camel grass. The tracks wound between the taller dunes with the sand well-chewed by the vehicles that had gone ahead of me. Elisabete Jacinto and her *porteur d'eau* — or follower — Pedro Machado rode into the heavy sand just ahead of me. I was impressed with her resolve. Elisabete suffered a great deal in this rally. She struggled in the sand, Pedro never straying more than a few metres off her stern. She did all her own navigating, and only when the bike was on its side or stuck did he come to her assistance. In severe sand dunes he led the way, reading the dunes and taking lines that may have been longer and slower, but ultimately safer. Pedro was a solid rider who had stepped up to the plate when their support truck and crew were taken out by a landmine on the Mauritanian/Moroccan border earlier on. I followed them for a good distance, trying to learn the firmest lines in the massive piles of windswept sand. Pedro had obviously done this before; he knew how to choose the easiest path through the monstrous sand dunes. Pedro struck off towards higher ground, looking for firmer sand to find a way across. This time I decided to stick to the beaten path, which also looked like the path of least resistance. After the time-consuming and energy-draining experience with the sand hole, I felt inclined to take no more chances. The scorching heat and slow going was starting to take its toll, not only on me, but on the xr. The motor was starting to overheat. I stopped, twisted off the hot radiator cap, and peeked inside. To my alarm the rad cores were showing. In a futile attempt to add fluid to the cooling system I whizzed what I had in my bladder into the radiator, but the amount wasn't enough to make a difference. A car was stuck not far away, so I walked over to the driver and co-driver, hoping they could help me out. It looked like they had been digging for a while and probably weren't in the best of moods. But they were my only chance for the time being. They glanced at me with questioning looks on their faces when I approached them.

"Would you happen to have any extra water you could spare?" I asked, getting some blank stares in return. "It's not for me. My bike's radiator is getting low and my engine is starting to overheat. Anything you can spare would really be appreciated," I added, thinking that might make a difference. Quite often under competitive circumstances a mechanical problem is easier to relate to than a personal problem.

"Okay, okay, just give us a minute here," said the driver. "I think we're ready to roll. Let me see if I can get the car out." He climbed behind the wheel and sure enough, the car was free of its trap. Both the driver and co-driver gave me a bottle of water each, although neither knew the other had done so.

"Maybe I can return the favour some time. Thanks a lot," I said and plodded back to the xr. I carefully poured the precious liquid into the rad, twisted the cap back on and started the bike. Everything was copacetic — I was on my way again. The deep sand was very rutted from the passage of numerous vehicles so I see-sawed back and forth on the bars, standing on the footpegs to maintain good balance. The gps indicated Checkpoint 4 was not far away; only about twenty kilometres or so. By now, however, twenty clicks might as well have been forty. I was thirsty, tired, and felt like a fish in a frying pan. Using the distance indicator on the gps to motivate myself, I kept going. At last I could see where the sand dunes flattened out and with a final thrust, navigated down the steep face towards the flags in front of the cp. It was a relief to see other people and have the end of the day within reach. I had travelled 393 kilometres; 42 remained on the special; then the five kilometres of liaison to the bivouac.

The tso crew offered up a large bottle of water. I poured it down my parched throat until I couldn't drink any more. After quenching my thirst I checked the bike's radiator again to verify the water level. It looked fine, so I was in good shape to continue. As I got ready to pull out of the checkpoint, Elisabete Jacinto and Pedro Machado were just coming in. She looked beat but showed no sign of giving in. I thought she was one tough lady. As I set off the sun slowly started dropping out towards the horizon. I took off down the laterite valley floor, following a two-track road that had few straight stretches. Suddenly the Honda's motor started gasping, as if thirsty for fuel, then finally gave up the ghost. I checked the internal reservoir. It was dry, yet plenty of gas sloshed around in the bottom of the tank. My fuel pump wasn't working. I opened the rear tank's fuel tap and blew into the overflow hose to pressurize the system. Fuel filled the reservoir and I managed to get the bike started again. It was a puzzling problem. I thought maybe I was dealing with a vapour lock, something many privateers had fallen victim to already. Fortunately, the following day was the mid-rally "rest day," and would give me the necessary time to investigate further. I waved down a TSO Toyota Land Cruiser and asked the driver if he had some duct tape — which he did. I wanted to try to insulate the fuel lines with pieces of shiny Mylar film I had cut off my emergency blanket. I couldn't make a good insulating cover over the fuel hose, so I rigged up a piece of hose to one of the breather hose spigots on a gas tank cap and zip-tied the hose to the handlebars. Now I could blow air into the tank and push gasoline into the reservoir so the motor would keep running. It ran rough, however, idled high, and overheated, but at least I was making progress. I caught up to the TSO Land Cruiser and without stopping handed the borrowed duct tape to one of the passengers while I rode alongside the vehicle. I gave them a "thank-you" wave and accelerated away down the winding track, heading in a westerly direction.

The sun was now flat on the horizon and shining directly into my eyes, making it hard to see where I was going. This was a bit disconcerting, as the final stretch to the end of the special stage was over stony ground. I slowed down and kept looking straight down ahead of me. At last I spotted the end of the stage. The vertical flags marking the finish point flapped vigorously in the breeze. I let my thoughts and concentration ease up and wander. It had been another nearly ten-hour day of riding — I clocked in at 9:42:56:00. Stage winner Alfie Cox brought his factory KTM home in a time of 5:02:04:00. Impressive, to say the least! It had been another good day in the rankings game: I had finished sixty-ninth in the stage and now found myself in seventieth place. Not only had I made the halfway mark of the rally, which had been one of my goals, I had kept a pace that saw me move up thirty-seven positions from the rather dismal 125th place I had dropped to after my Stage 2 penalty. Meanwhile, Hiroshi Masuoka led the car division with a time of 5:10:24:00. The Mitsubishi driver and his navigator Pascal Maimon were now at the head of the scoreboard. Servia and Lurquin, thanks to getting stuck in the witch's hole, had dropped to fifth. Their Renault teammates Schlesser and Magne had made up a lot of ground since being hit with the time penalties during Stage 7, finishing in second place. They were back in contention holding down second overall, trailing Masuoka and Maimon by just thirty-five minutes.

I was looking forward to getting to the bivouac and out of the saddle so I could kick back my heels. I rode at a leisurely pace towards Atar, which was silhouetted against the arc of the sun's rays. It was a glorious and uplifting sight, spoiled, however, by the tons of junk scattered along both sides of the paved roadway including large truck axles, dump boxes, and the skeletal remains of ancient cars and trucks. I continued this way through the streets of Atar, with its dark brown mud-brick buildings. Here and there a crude electrical pole rose above the boxy structures, drooping wires feeding power into the houses. There was no obvious city planning here: buildings were placed askew from one another. In the early 1990s, heavy rains and floods had destroyed large sections of the traditional architecture of Atar. Still, this oasis town remains one of the largest settlements in northern Mauritania and a key market centre for the vast outlying region. Steady streams of nomads pour into town to buy and sell goods, consisting mostly of foodstuffs and animals. People were going about their daily business and kids waved furiously as I passed. Many of these ragged-looking children ran into the street with outstretched hands yelling, "*Cadeaux-cadeaux*" — "Gifts-gifts". I had heard Mauritania was one of the poorest countries on earth, poor even by African standards. Seeing kids run fearlessly out into the street, begging, shouldn't have come as a shock, but it was unsettling nonetheless. Here I was riding a motorcycle through their town — for no practical purpose — spending more money than they would accumulate over their lifetimes. When I rode into the bivouac I was flushed with a sense of accomplishment. I had reached the second of three goals I had set for myself. The first was to clear technical control in Paris; the second was to arrive for the rest day in Atar; the third was to ride down the beach at Dakar. I reasoned that if I made this far I would be strong enough to finish. Even if the remainder of the way got more difficult I would be buoyed by the experience gained so far.

After the wretched conditions of El Ghallaouiya, it was good to be back in a full-blown bustling bivouac much like the earlier nightly stopovers. And we had some outside company. A planeload of VIPs and package-holiday tourists had been flown from Paris to Atar by TSO. I assumed the reason for this was to give these city slickers a chance to the experience life in a Dakar bivouac and to rub shoulders with the stars of the show. No doubt they'd be provided with many of the comforts of home, not roughing it like those they had come to observe. For the most part they looked out of place, strutting around neatly dressed and groomed, they stuck out like a sore thumb. Local taxi *brousse* cars were driving back and forth, taking the visitors into the city or sightseeing in the area. One of the attractions of Atar, I had been told, was a French fort that was built during World War II. I thought of the movie *Desert Fox*, with James Mason playing the German general Erwin Rommel. It's hard to believe that major battles which would affect the eventual outcome of the war had been fought in North Africa.

As soon as I stepped off the bike I was approached by a grungy local kid who looked about twelve years old, but I wouldn't have wanted to place a wager on it. Judging someone's age is a difficult thing to do in Africa. Generally the life expectancy of people here is much shorter than in the western world because of poor nutrition. The boy could have been much older than he looked.

"Would you like me to do some work for you? I do a good job and work cheap. Maybe I can wash your clothes," he said with a smile, in good French. I had expected him to ask for a handout and was quite moved by the fact that he thought more of himself than to just go and beg for money.

"Sure. Why not? But where do you plan on doing that? I didn't think there was much water around here to be washing clothes with," I replied.

"Oh, we have plenty of water to wash clothes," he said. "Come, I'll show you."

I followed him to what was the airport terminal building. I asked if he could arrange a place for me to clean up.

"No problem," he said, leading me into the square cement terminal building. Inside was a washroom of sorts. It was a disgusting place and stank to high heaven. I avoided all contact with any surface other than with the soles of my boots. I paid 20 francs for a pail of lukewarm water to be delivered to the washroom and, standing in my riding shorts, washed, shampooed my hair, and shaved in the reflection of a broken piece of mirror propped up on the sink. Despite the dismal surroundings I felt refreshed. When I left the washroom I noticed a group of women squatting over plastic pails of water in the stark waiting room of the terminal. One older woman scrubbed away at my jacket and pants with zeal. I guessed my laundry boy was a bit of an entrepreneur, going around looking for clients while the ladies did the actual washing. Or maybe they paid him a fee for finding work for them. I paid the boy twenty francs and collected my stuff. Clean pants and jacket would go a long way to rejuvenating me for the second part of this journey. Outside the terminal the warm evening air dried the water off my body and my hair very quickly. I felt great. I forgot how tired I was and that I was hungry enough to eat a horse. I had more than twenty-four hours off the bike ahead of me. Not since I had left Paris had I had enough breathing room to gather my composure and carefully look over the Honda. I strolled back to the Yacco plane where my motorcycle was parked and where I would set up camp for the next day and a half. I exchanged greetings and pleasantries along the way with some of the competitors I had gotten to know. When I got to the Yacco, I hung my laundry on the cables that lift and lower the rear-door ramp. As usual, I set up my tent underneath one of the wings of the plane. What had become a tightly knit band of privateer motorcyclists were doing the same. I looked around and couldn't help but smile. I was far from home but I knew it couldn't get any better than this.

The wind started picking up in intensity, whipping up dust clouds that swept across the area where the race teams were set up. Fortunately, we were upwind in the shadow of the planes and out of the worst of it. I tossed the rest of my riding gear into my tent and chatted with a few of my neighbours. I learned that Joan Roma wasn't the only motorcyclist struck down by the hand of fate that day. Less than a hundred kilometres into the special, Richard Sainct had crashed hard, ruining his navigation equipment. Although he had hurt his shoulder he resumed the race, only to have his KTM quit on him not long after that. It was an inglorious end for the 2000 Dakar winner who, as overall leader since Stage 2, seemed poised for a three-peat. With Sainct out of commission, fellow KTM rider Fabrizio Meoni replaced him at the head of the pack. The Italian had finished the stage in third place behind Cox, about two minutes down. Second place stage finisher, Jordi Arcarons, also KTM mounted, moved into second overall, trailing Meoni by twenty minutes. Meanwhile, Roma, third in the overall motorcycle rankings, had suffered a torn knee ligament when he went down in the valley outside of El Ghallaouiya. Once again his Dakar had ended in disappointment and grief. Roma had been stopped either by injuries or bike problems ever since his first Dakar in 1997. That he was a contender had never been in doubt. The twenty-nine-year-old Spaniard, whose impressive resumé included two gold and three bronze ISDE medals, had won nine Dakar stages, including three of them before his crash in the current edition.

By the time I headed for the catering tents an all-encompassing darkness had enveloped the area beyond the bivouac. The hum of numerous generators droned as dazzling lights illuminated the immediate compound. It was a fair hike across a dirt-covered open area to where dinner was being served. Outside of the lighted areas inky darkness cloaked the uneven ground. Walking about was a constant stumble and required a headlamp or a flashlight. On my way I encountered a young European tourist, riding a Suzuki DRZ, who was looking to report that he and a group of companions had come across a stranded competitor. I pointed him in the direction of the administration tents. The stranded rider had been cold and shivering when they came across him. They'd lent him some clothes and agreed to help him get to Atar. Although the likelihood of being left stranded in the desert is pretty slim in the Paris-Dakar Rally of the twenty-first century, it can happen. Had the tourists not spotted him, chances are good he would not have been missed until early morning. Finally I arrived at the food tent, which had a festive ambiance. Everyone who had made it this far had reason to celebrate. But the celebrants, despite their elation and freshly washed appearance, looked like they had just survived ten days in hell. I'm sure I didn't look much better.

* * *

Rest Day — Thursday, January 11, 2001
Atar, Mauritania
Rest Day
Total distance: 0 km

Dozens of fellow competitors had dropped out by the Atar rest day. All had seen their dreams dashed before the end of Stage 10. One rider, Thierry Vigneron, had exited as early as Stage 1. In many ways, the rest day was as much the psychological halfway point as it was a chance to rest. If you got this far, you felt much more confident in your chances of completing the remainder of the journey. Of course, one could get overconfident and be lulled into a false sense of security — it's never over until it's over. By now, I was becoming accustomed to the rally's routine. Although it had only been a week and a half, it felt like I had been doing this forever. I had become totally immersed in the Dakar. It had become my only reality.

The night before, I had gone back to my tent immediately

after dinner. I didn't wake for another ten hours. Still, I felt like I could have slept for another twenty-four. Had it not been for the incessant droning of the myriad generators inside my head, despite my earplugs, and the rest of the sounds permeating the bivouac, from hammers hitting metal to the starting up of engines, I probably would have slept through the entire rest day. I felt like a walking zombie; and no doubt this was how most of the rallyists felt. Their tired, haggard faces at dinner stick in my mind to this day. What I found most interesting was the changes that were sweeping over the competitors, from the privateers to professionals. The difference between the status of the car and truck drivers and motorcyclists narrowed as the drama played out. Time is the great equalizer in the Dakar, except that the factory drivers and riders had a lot more pressure on them to deliver the best possible results. I'm not sure how being a factory rider would have affected my general composure and performance. Other than coming out of fray with more money in my bank account, I believe it would only have left me even more frazzled.

Everyone had their own way of dealing with adversity. The ones who dealt with it best were the ones most likely to finish: at least if their vehicles held up. While some retained their sense of humour and kept things in perspective, others didn't. The changes in people are what make Paris-Dakar fascinating: like goldfish in a bowl or characters on television. Thanks to the extensive media coverage, competitors were under constant scrutiny by a worldwide audience of motorsport enthusiasts. Some 100 press, radio- and photojournalists, and another 140 television staff, accompanied us from bivouac to bivouac. Media helicopters were in the air from the time a stage started until it ended. Some 250 hours of television coverage was devoted to the 2001 race, and more than 175 countries broadcast Dakar footage. Not surprisingly, French TV led in the number of airtime hours with twenty-four; the cable station Eurosport was good for another twenty hours on top of that. Even people who have little or no interest in motorsport are drawn into the theatre that is Paris-Dakar. With so much in-your-face attention paid to the event, it's hard not to take notice. Total viewers reach into the tens of millions.

* * *

I had to chuckle at the thought of this being called a rest day. Only a few of the riders and drivers had the luxury of actually resting. These were the guys and gals who were on factory or heavily sponsored corporate teams, flanked by mechanics, service people, chiropractors, masseurs and the like. Then again, the pros are the hardest-working competitors in the Dakar. For the majority of privateers this was hardly a day of lazing about. Not having to ride meant a day spent working on bikes or cars. I was not spared, having quite a few mechanical issues to attend to as well. My first priority was to find out why the XR had been running strangely prior to arriving in Atar. It had acted like it was running out of fuel even though there was plenty in the tanks. I pulled the main fuel tank and the seat off the frame to investigate the source of the problem. I had intended to replace some of the fuel lines with more substantial tubing, so I was relieved to discover that the problem was simply that the vacuum line that led to the fuel pump had melted and was leaking. This was the reason I had experienced a lack of fuel delivery once the fuel level dropped to the point where the gasoline was no longer gravity fed. Initially I'd thought it was as a result of the fuel line vapour locking, something many of the other bikes were experiencing. This was not the case. The fuel system worked perfectly, other than the fact that the Tygon fuel line was not heat-resistant. Fellow privateer Alain Duclos gave me a piece of foil-wrapped aviation fuel-line insulation and I replaced the vacuum hose with a black rubber reinforced piece of line.

Once I had the fuel problem cleared up, I took the wheels off the bike. I delivered them to the Euromaster truck to have new tires and mousse tubes installed. I took the receipt and leisurely strolled back to the Yacco plane encampment and continued working on the bike. For once, I wasn't in a hurry. The stopover in Atar presented the first real opportunity for me to relax. The stress and pressure were off for twenty-four hours and it was a nice feeling. The Honda came apart easily. Everything seemed in good working order. There were no leaks, very little crash damage and no loose bolts or nuts. The highly touted XR650 was living up to its hype.

Not all privateers were busy working on their bikes, however. One of the Japanese riders, who was on a rented Challenge 75 Honda XR400, lay in his tent the whole day. Challenge 75 is an off-road bike shop in Paris which, for a fee, offered a rental and support service to contest the Dakar. The riders dropped off their bikes at the end of each stage with the support crew and the next morning they were serviced and ready to go again. Not a bad way to do things if you have the money (and no sponsors). Still, even if I'd had an abundance of cash I wouldn't go that route. I have always preferred to pack my own parachute, so to speak. If anything went wrong, at the very least I would know how to fix it — and no one else could be blamed for something being overlooked. It is part of my philosophy to take full responsibility for whatever it is I get myself involved in.

Rest day was also visitors' day, and a time for schmoozing. Many of the rally's feature sponsors, companies such as Euromaster, Columbia Sportswear and Total sent representatives to have a look at things first-hand. Most of them were with the group that TSO had flown in. BMW people arrived in an extremely large and expensive corporate plane that was said to be the fastest private jet available. A small BMW logo adorned the vertical stabilizer; plastic engine covers protected the openings to the turbines from blowing sand. The jet had a cluster of lavish tents set up underneath it — the homes away from home for execs used to being pampered. Unfortunately for BMW, their team was struggling at this point, so the atmosphere in their camp was subdued. Conversely, the KTM crew was totally upbeat. Though they had lost their star rider, Sainct, they were still armed and dangerous with the likes of Meoni, Arcarons, De Gavardo, Pujol, Cox and Deacon. Good old P.G. Lundmark, was in the mix, too.

I was wrenching on the Honda when Toby Moody from

Speedvision came by to ask me if I wanted to be part of an inter-view at 1:00 p.m. I had forgotten about the interview but, need-less to say, I was happy to oblige. Being seen on television screens across North America was a psychological boost and I knew Honda Canada and the rest of my sponsors would love it. After Toby left, I finished up with the bike and got cleaned up so I would be presentable for the interview. I met Toby at the humongous Hercules airplane that housed a complete television studio. We entered the massive plane — more commonly used for military and humanitarian operations — through a canvas dust chamber that featured an outer and inner door. Sand was not welcome inside the studio: it spelled disaster for the delicate equipment. Toby showed me around the cavernous interior like a tour guide. This was his world, the nuts and bolts that allowed him to bring his viewers into the experience of Dakar. The entire craft was air-conditioned and darkened. Control panels and monitors were about the only source of light. The cool air was a welcome relief from the desert heat, and I could see myself hanging around inside the plane/studio all day. A number of video technicians were hard at work piecing together bits and pieces on the Dakar for Speedvision's cable subscribers. It gave me a new appreciation for the work people like Toby and his crew do. The feeling inside the studio was entirely different from what was going on outside in the bivouac. I may as well have been back in the Western world. While I waited my turn to be interviewed I was offered lunch. Not surprisingly, the television crew's food was much better than what the rallyists were fed and was prepared by a different catering company. Among the goodies were fresh yogurt from France, puddings and other tasty desserts. It was a virtual feast and one I shamelessly indulged in. Eventually I sat down with Toby, the two American KIA drivers Darren Skilton and Curt Le Duc, and the American motorcycle riders Lewis and Campbell. Besides being the only Canadian — the other two had dropped out of the rally early on — I was the lone privateer present and looked a little out of place. But it made for good television: the Canuck privateer sur-rounded by the four American factory stars.

After the interview, I was thrust back into the real world of the rally and the drab surroundings of Atar. I headed back to the privateer motorcyclists' area. I lingered here and there chatting up some fellow competitors I had gotten to know, asking how things were going and exchanging a few words of encouragement. I also ran into the illustrious Stephane Peterhansel again, one of the most famous of Dakar icons. Since 1991, Stephane had won the Dakar a record six times, riding a factory Yamaha. Now he was competing in a car, looking to become the only competitor besides the equally famous Hubert Auriol to win the rally in both the motorcycle and car classes. I knew Stephane, a very unassuming and modest man, from my days at Yamaha in Europe. Motorcycling is a small world. The same people show up all over the planet, sometimes year after year, sometimes a decade later, but the camaraderie is always there. No matter what your status, celebrity or unknown, there is a certain bond between people who race motorcycles or cars. Stephane and I exchanged pleasantries for a while and when we parted company he said he'd see me in Dakar. So, in addition to Françoise and Franco Acerbis, I now had one more person to prove right.

The day felt as if it were endless. After ten days on the go, standing still seemed strange. It was like your body and mind had become programmed to deal with life in continuous motion. Time passed much more slowly than it did when riding. After the TV interview, and shooting the breeze with Stephane, I spent the rest of the afternoon working on the XR. I changed the oil and filter; replaced the friction plates in the clutch; installed new brake pads in both the front and rear; replaced the sprockets and chain and the chain guides, plus the rubber swing-arm protector. I commandeered the same local kid who had looked after the washing of my clothes and had him clean my supply of dirty air filters. I had him wash each one in a pan of gasoline to remove the oil and thick layer of dust that had accumulated; then, using a pail of water, I instructed him to wash the filters with soap, and finally rinse them with clean water. When he was done, I had nearly a dozen filters hanging out to dry.

Before the new tires were mounted and installed by the Euromaster guys I had enough time to eat dinner. I also wandered over to sit with some of the TSO volunteers at the temporary fly-in cargo depot. Most of the personnel that make Paris-Dakar so memorable are the volunteers. These are people who want to be involved in something larger than life, people who want to be part of the show. Not everybody makes the grade as a Dakar volunteer. They are carefully selected by TSO and assimilated into the overall organization of the event. It's not a job they're doing for money. It's about bragging rights and rubbing shoulders with ambitious dreamers and motorsport legends, or legends in the making. It's about taking part in a memorable adventure and experiencing the challenges of the actual competitors not just vicariously, but up close. The volunteers, like the competitors, "live the rally." They have a ringside seat at an unpredictable drama that unfolds daily, feeling and sharing the trials and tribulations of the competitors. This, no doubt, is what brings many of them back to the rally year after year.

"I always take my annual vacation to coincide with the Dakar. It's the most unique three-week adventure there is," one veteran volunteer told me. "Only the Dakar can offer something like that. I don't mind loading trunks in and out of airplanes to be part of it."

The four gentlemen who took care of the motorcyclists became good friends as the rally unfolded and they offered enormous moral support. Seeing their welcoming faces at the end of a tough day buoyed my spirits immensely. The positive energy given off by some of the volunteers was infectious. It's the kind of energy that can make the impossible happen, spurring you to dig deeper than ever before. I truly believe the presence of these individuals increases your odds of finishing the race. Sitting down with these guys at the end of a long day was priceless to me. While most other competitors stuck to their campsites, busy fixing things or sleeping, I spent time with the volunteers whenever possible and generally had a great time.

The spirit among the volunteer staff at the cargo depot was, as usual, elevated and jovial. They didn't have to endure the hardships of the drivers and riders but they worked hard and had earned a bit of rest, too. As the sun turned to a blaze of orange, reds, purples and yellows low in the sky west of Atar, I listened to their stories of past Dakars and some of its more memorable competitors. They even offered me some tasty snacks and a small glass of cognac. I normally don't drink liquor but on this occasion I had a nip. We made a toast to the Dakar, to friendship, to Thierry Sabine and to France. It didn't take much of the silky-smooth cognac to go to my head.

"Well, guys, it's been a pleasure, but I have to go and pick up my wheels and put them back on my bike. See you all tomorrow night," I said, and made my way to the Euromaster truck. By the time I had the wheels installed on the Honda nightfall had descended. In the distance, over the drone of the generators, I heard the sound of disco music. It was party time for the VIPs and tourists.

I crawled into my tent, put in my earplugs and went to sleep.

* * *

Stage 11 — Friday, January 12, 2001
Atar, Mauritania to Nouakchott, Mauritania
Liaison: 34 km — **Special:** 432 km — **Liaison:** 37 km
Total distance: 508 km

The special stage kicked off at a small decrepit village called Ain Attaya, thirty-four kilometres outside of Atar. The entire rally route ran in a southwesterly direction parallel to the main road that connects Atar with Nouakchott, near the Atlantic coast. Unlike the road, however, the course was anything but straight. There were a lot of twisty sections and dunes to be crossed, which also ran parallel to the main road. Here, the prevailing winds blow from the northwest and, with little elevation change to deflect the wind, the sea of sand has waves much like the ocean itself. The sand seems endless in this region of Mauritania. The land is parched and baked by the sun nearly year round. The wind is dry and strong; sweat evaporates instantaneously and dehydration takes only a matter of hours if one is stranded in the desert. The day's ride consisted of another long stretch — this time a total of 508 kilometres, 432 of them being special stage. At the previous night's briefing the stage was billed as "easy" — to facilitate re-entry into the rigours of the rally after a day of rest. The Atar-to-Nouakchott stage proved to be just that, except for one hiccup that saw me and a number of others, including Team Mitsubishi's Hiroshi Masuoka and Renault's Jean-Louis Schlesser, get lost. The special was a navigation stage; it started on a mountainous massif and then followed the bed of an *Oued* for a few kilometres to come out onto a desert zone that stretched some 300 kilometres into Nouakchott. The terrain varied from deep sand to hard grey powder, which turned to thick clouds of dust under the grinding motorcycles, cars and trucks. More than half the route was designed for top speed. Estimated total running time for the pros was pegged at around five hours. I wondered how close I could come to that, not that I was out to set any speed records and risk jeopardizing my race.

I rode in a reserved manner most of the day. My focus was on staying upright and maintaining a secure pace. After getting off the paved road that took the liaison stage from Atar to Ain Attaya, forty kilometres of soft sand and twenty-five kilometres of stony terrain had to be covered to the first checkpoint. From there it was a mixed bag of conditions including another thirty clicks of stone-covered sand, forty clicks of hard sand, and fifty clicks of gravel that led into a welcoming oasis. From there the remainder of the special — some 250 kilometres — consisted of long stretches of sand between rolling dunes. Twenty kilometres before the second control passage, which served as a refuelling depot, I learned another valuable lesson in navigation. The course ran along the edge of a range of hills towards some sand dunes. At one point the tracks veered off to the right and continued straight ahead. I slowed and looked down at my GPS. The arrow pointed straight at the CP. I followed it and soon I found myself riding into the checkpoint, where I lined up behind Alain Duclos to refuel. Later that day, I outsmarted myself by striking out off the beaten path to avoid some larger dunes. The GPS arrow indicated I should travel straight ahead over the towering dunes. I decided to choose one side of a line of dunes as opposed to the other. As I rode along, I was slowly being drawn away from the right direction by an abrupt ridge of dunes covered in low vegetation. At one point I passed right in front of a Tuareg tent. Here in the middle of nowhere, more than 300 kilometres from the nearest town, a tent stood alone. I couldn't believe my eyes. As I rode by, a man emerged from the shelter. He stood up tall and stretched his arms high into the air sending a distinct message that said, "What in the hell are you doing here?" It definitely wasn't a friendly, "Welcome to the neighbourhood" gesture and it compelled me to twist the XR's throttle in case he decided to bring out his rifle. Maybe I was being a bit paranoid but I didn't want to take any chances that this man considered me a threat to his existence. The Tuareg, like the Saharawis, are a displaced people and have, since the early sixties, launched a number of rebellions against their oppressors. They have a reputation for being fierce warriors and I didn't want to find out just how true the reputation was. I looked back and watched the Tuareg disappear back into the tent, satisfied that I was rapidly riding out of shooting range. The feeling of being alone in no-man's land struck fear into me and I made a vow to stick as close to the course as I could from then on. I turned around a safe distance from the tent, making sure I wouldn't come anywhere near it again, and backtracked to the point where I should have stayed on course to begin with. The track led onto a dusty mining road, suggesting that some form of civilization might be nearby. A few tin signs with painted messages on them were stuck in the gravel at the infrequent splits in the road. I thought back to the conversation with Duclos. He wasn't kidding when he said it was easy to get lost. Once I was back on the right route, I made sure I stuck to it, and to my relief I was getting close to the end of the special. I looked over my shoulder — something I do on a regular basis to see what's behind me — and saw a large race truck bearing down on me. I decided to get on the gas rather than deal with the ensuing dust he'd kick up if I let him pass. I managed to gain some distance on the truck and made it to the end of the special stage without a hitch. I got my card stamped, recording a time of 8:30:47, then took off on the paved road that led to Nouakchott. I finished in seventy-first on the day, which moved me into sixty-fifth. The Honda had performed flawlessly and the problem with the fuel delivery seemed to have been solved. The extra work I had managed to perform on the bike during the rest day no doubt contributed greatly to how well it ran. It had been a relatively smooth day, except for getting lost and crossing paths with the Tuareg.

P.G. Lundmark, contesting only his second Dakar, showed his mettle and the calibre of his riding skills by winning the special in a time of 4:23:46:00, an impressive 4:18:00 minutes faster than Carlo De Gavardo. Lundmark led a troupe of KTM riders to the finish that stretched all the way to eighth place. Fabrizio Meoni, who completed the stage in seventh, seven and a half minutes behind Lundmark, strengthened his hold on the overall lead by one minute over fellow KTM rider Jordi Arcarons. De Gavardo held down third, followed by Pujol Esteve and Alfie Cox in fourth and fifth, respectively. With these five riders, KTM had a stranglehold on the 2001 Dakar's motorcycle division. Jimmy Lewis, the top BMW rider on the provisional scoreboard, ranked sixth, just over two hours behind Meoni. It looked like it was going to be a slam dunk for the Austrian manufacturer. In the car division Jose Maria Servia and navigator Jean-Marie Lurquin scored their fourth stage win driving the Schlesser/Renault/Megane buggy. Mitsubishi's Hiroshi Masuoka saw his overall lead shrink substantially, from thirty-five minutes to twelve. Getting lost in the desert, puncturing a tire, and dealing with engine problems saw him finish eighth for the day, 52:35:00 behind Servia. Jutta Kleinschmidt jumped into second place on the overall scoreboard thanks to a second-place finish behind Servia. Team Mitsubishi Portugal's Carlos Sousa and his navigator Jean-Michel Polato drove their L200 Strakar to third place, strengthening their hold on third overall, 13:13:00 behind Masuoka, and just over a minute behind Team Mitsubishi Germany's Kleinschmidt. As in the motorcycle division, one car manufacturer was dominating the rally and it looked like Mitsubishi was rolling towards victory. Jean-Louis Schlesser, another driver who got lost on this stage, finished tenth for the day and dropped from second overall to fourth. He and his navigator Henri Magne would have to make up 39:20:00 minutes on Masuoka if they were going to recapture the lead for Renault.

It had been another successful day and one less between me and my goal. I knew I wasn't there, but with each stage completed I felt more confident. I was happy to find myself in Nouakchott, the capital of Mauritania and by far the largest city of the Sahara. Being near the Atlantic Ocean made me feel less isolated and closer to home. Nouakchott is a burgeoning sprawl of a city with strange-looking billboards that advertise everything from soft drinks to water pumps. It's a city located in one of the poorest countries on earth, but judging by all the Western-style advertising, you'd have to come to the conclusion that the people who live here have money to burn. In fact, most of the country's wealthy elite live here but an influx of poor people has created many slums. Riding through Nouakchott is a study in contrasts. The city was built in 1958 to serve as the nation's capital and was intended to support a population of 15,000. By the early years of the twenty-first century, it was a city of over half a million. This sudden sprawl, however, had nothing to do with economic growth, and much to do with the recurring droughts that have plagued the Sahara for the past twenty years, forcing young people, families and small communities to abandon their traditional way of life. The city has not only been under siege by a wave of newcomers, but by the encroaching Sahara as well.

The road into the suburban area near the airport was wide, with stone curbs and a centre divider. The airport compound was fenced in and secure. This was the most modern airport the rally had visited so far, not surprising considering the importance of Nouakchott in the region. You don't want to welcome important visitors and dignitaries to your country via a capital city that doesn't at least have a decent airport. Once at the bivouac it was the usual routine of getting my trunk from the Yacco plane, setting up my tent and checking over my bike. The airport terminal had a clean washroom, the first one I had seen thus far, and I washed up before heading to the catering tent to grab a bite to eat. Like many of the privateers, I used my bike to ride back and forth to where dinner was served. After a long day in the saddle, walking close to two kilometres each way was not an attractive proposition. After dinner I borrowed a satellite telephone to make a quick call home and assure Françoise that everything was okay, promising I'd call her again as soon as I could. After my call home I spent a few minutes catching up with some of the TSO volunteers at the temporary fly-in cargo depot. The depot sported a huge pile of tires, boxes of goods, and various items pro teams and some of the more seasoned privateers had flown in by the freight-forwarding company Lemoine. Collette Herlin was the friendly and helpful person in charge of this operation. In Paris, I had delivered spare tires and tubes to her station at the *controle technique*. She weighed them and charged by the kilo. It was a service that was integrated into the organization and, in addition to using Team Tibau, I had asked Lemoine to ship spare tires and mousse tubes to Atar. If I ever did Paris-Dakar again, I would have added a clean set of spare riding gear more appropriate for the weather conditions for the second half of the rally. I'd also ship clothes to change into after riding, plus some items for the bike, and a good supply of granola bars — things that are bulky and take up space in the already-crammed trunk. Sometimes you really have to walk the walk before you can talk the talk. Despite my intense preparations, these were things that hadn't occurred to me.

For some reason I didn't feel as tired after Stage 11 as I had after the previous stages. Perhaps I was so used to being tired that I didn't notice anymore. Maybe the rest day had revitalized me. Then again, it had been a relatively easy stage that didn't see me wrestle with the bike. Still, I turned in early. Stage 12, from Nouakchott to Tidjika, was certain to be a killer and included a demanding 580 km competitive section and an overall distance of 654 km. According to the roadbook, dune crossings and navigational challenges were going to be the order of the day. The first half, through sandy valleys that ran between high dunes, was going to be very fast. Because of recent rains, camel grass and clumps of vegetation promised to be the biggest hazards at high speed. The second half of the special offered similar technical challenges as Stage 10, navigating over massive dunes. But I wasn't too worried. I had done well under the same circumstances a few days earlier, and I felt like I could handle just about anything now.

Chapter 10

Drowning on dry land

▬ ▬ ▬ ▬ ▬ ▬ ▬ ▬ ▬ ▬ ▬ ▬ ▬ ▬ ▬

Stage 12 — Saturday, January 13, 2001
Nouakchott, Mauritania to Tidjika, Mauritania
Liaison: 71 km — **Special:** 580 km — **Liaison:** 3 km
Total distance: 654 km   163

Other than a group of bikes gathered around at the side of the
road, the start of Stage 12 wasn't much different than any other
day in the African hinterland. Some early-rising locals watched
the proceedings and talked amongst themselves, pointing at
the bikes and the riders. With our riding gear on we must have
looked like alien invaders. Actually, we *were* invading their
country, and no doubt this looked like an ostentatious display
of Western affluence and excess. But there is an upside to it all:
Paris-Dakar pumps a lot of money into the economies of the
countries the rally passes through. And TSO is involved with
additional projects that benefit these countries in many ways.

I left Nouakchott for Tidjika at 6:25 a.m. The first bikes had
started to leave the bivouac fifteen minutes earlier to ride the 71
kilometres of paved road to the start of the special stage. The
route took us into the heart of the desert again, due east away
from the coast. The special served up 580 kilometres of sand
and dunes with a few stony sections thrown in for good
measure. Could we expect anything less? The cars were slated

to begin leaving the bivouac at 7:40 a.m. I had a bit of a head start on them as usual, but that didn't mean I wouldn't have to contend with being passed by the front-runners, driving their cars as if their lives depended on it. It was a relatively smooth ride to the start of the special on the asphalt-covered road. The first checkpoint of the day, where a fuel stop awaited us, was 265 kilometres away. Once into the desert the track was twisted and the pace fast; I was able to generate some good speed. The track sliced past the odd thorny tree and rubbery, broad-leafed plants that grew throughout the low dunes. When I clipped the plants they spread a sticky white sap over the arms of my jacket. With the xr full of fuel and the sand inconsistent and rutted, I erred on the side of caution as had become my habit. Between the start of the stage and the first stop the dunes morphed from molehills to towering giants. For the most part I followed the tracks laid by the bikes before me, verifying the correct route with the GPS and the roadbook. The roadbook was accurate, but in many cases my odometer wasn't corresponding with the distances it noted. As a backup I referred to a compass, which I used mainly for navigating across open plains or *chotts* — dry lakebeds. The compass was small and hard to read, especially when the sun shone directly on its face — which was nearly all the time.

Much of the landscape between Nouakchott and Tidjika consists of parched, sandy earth. It was a scene that could have been taken from a Salvador Dali painting. Dead trees poked out of the ground. Rarely, some sort of vegetation could be seen. A fierce, hot wind blew directly at me as I rode across the seemingly endless *chott*. The wheels shook up and down across the uneven surface of the lakebed. The front wheel kicked up the powder and sent it directly into the air box, which is mounted low on the left side of the bike. In no time the foam air filter element was caked with fine red dust, which eventually would pass through and wreak havoc inside the engine. The pelting dust was unrelenting. It blasted with such force into my face it felt like my skin was being peeled off. Great chunks of curled, dried mud broke into powder as the xr's tires were flying over the lakebed. The clouds of dust were the thickest I had seen so far. I thought it couldn't possibly get worse, but "worse" is a relative term. I tucked into a low crouch behind the number plate and took shallow breaths so as not to suck in too much of the lung-clogging material. I finally understood what was meant by "drowning on dry land." I was unable to see any other vehicles ahead or behind me, or to my left or right. It was a dangerous situation. If anybody or anything stood directly in my path it could spell disaster. I could easily slam into a fellow competitor, camel, native or obstacle without any kind of warning. If I stopped or fell I would most likely do so in the path of another rallyist. While keeping a steady speed — not so fast as to risk a fall, and not so slow that I'd be caught by another rider or get bogged down — the XR sang its throaty exhaust note into the murky cloud. I was losing track of time and distance in an abstract hellhole hundreds of kilometres from civilization. The only way to be sure I was on the right track was to refer to the GPS screen mounted in the centre of the handlebars. The roadbook told me the large trucks in the race were to take a detour around this gigantic dustbin. At least they were one less thing to worry about.

When I was finally past the end of the lakebed, I noticed a camel with a lone rider perched upon it. He was wrapped from head to toe in pale blue cotton, with only his eyes, peering out from behind his Shemagh headdress, visible. What in the world was this fellow doing here, I wondered. He had to be days from the nearest water or fellow human beings. Unlike my run-in with the Tuareg the day before, I didn't feel threatened. The nomad and his camel projected a sense of serenity and oneness with the environment. I was struck by how the diversity of the world's people was caught by this moment: one the product of another era on a leisurely journey using a mode of transportation thousands of years old, the other a nylon-and-plastic-clad denizen of modern civilization on a high-tech motorcycle charging headlong on a strict time schedule. Something that could so profoundly lay bare the differences between two worlds would be difficult to imagine.

The man of the desert most likely had little knowledge of what it was to be someone living in the West. He was also likely a lot less harried by the daily vagaries of life. He wouldn't know about keeping up with the Joneses, constant change, conspicuous consumption, or the general dissatisfaction that plagues so many in a world where one's worth is measured by bank account balances. I wondered if he too pondered the circumstances that brought us together on this desolate piece of real estate, and what reason I might have to be there making all this noise and commotion, passing by him at such high speed. I wondered if he wondered what it would be like to be me. I certainly tried to envision myself as him.

It was becoming increasingly hot. Glaring sunlight poured down on the white sand, which acted like a gigantic mirror that reflected it back towards the sky. My black riding gear absorbed the heat and I welcomed the fast-moving air that funnelled past me as I sped along. In conjunction with the heat from the exhaust beneath me, the sun, which was to my left, was literally baking my left foot. All I could think of was dousing it in a pail of cold water. The day was getting difficult to the point where I really wanted it to be over as quickly as possible. But I had a long way to go and knew I had to persevere. I followed two distinct wheel ruts that led over the crest of a ridge. I pulled on the throttle hard and kept my momentum up to keep the bike going straight through the golden sand. From this vantage point I could see large rocks, sixty to seventy feet high, sticking out of the sand like jagged monoliths. The GPS indicated a waypoint close by. I followed the arrow down and around one of these rocks. The landscape was magical, a hollow of sorts. Judging by the shape of the sand formations, wind must have howled across the *chott* like a hurricane and swirled around the rocks, depositing tons of silica in the same shapes that snowdrifts settle around the corner of a barn on the prairies — only ten times the size.

After crossing the fourteen clicks of stony terrain about halfway into the special, I reached the first checkpoint and refuelled my bike. I didn't waste any time taking off again, hoping to get through the next two CPs in good time. Twisting tracks through sand and camel grass took me to Checkpoint 2, 379 kilometres into the special. After that, a second layer of sand dunes had to be traversed. Another stretch of level sand, spiked with camel grass, led to the final CP of the day. Not long after leaving the second CP, I'd come across the Polish rider Jacek Czachor on the No. 57 Honda. He had the clutch cover off his bike and was trying to remove the clutch basket. It appeared that his clutch had seized, and it was obvious he was dejected because he didn't have the right tools. Czachor didn't speak much English but we managed to communicate nonetheless. He explained to me he needed a big socket to take the clutch basket apart. Unfortunately I didn't have the socket he required and could do little else but wish him luck and continue on my way down the sandy two-track excuse of a road towards Tidjika. The going from the second checkpoint to the third was tight and rugged. Very loose sand ruts wound around large, ancient dark rocks and camel grass lined the road. Making things more difficult was a steadily increasing wind that had been building since earlier in the morning. Sand was blowing every which way, making it extremely difficult to see what lay ahead.

The third and final checkpoint was hidden from view behind an immense pile of round boulders. Suddenly the CP appeared in front of me, as if conjured up out of thin air. A group of children jumped around and shouted as I rode towards the tall flags. They were in front of a small corral made of oddly shaped wood. Their home appeared to be a ragged, makeshift lean-to, thrown together out of dead trees and torn bits of cloth and burlap that flapped in the wind. No adults could be seen — only a couple of scrawny goats kept the kids company. As was usually the case when I came across indigenous people, I wanted to stop and find out more about them. I wanted to understand what motivated them, what they felt, what their dreams were. My Western way of thinking made it hard to comprehend why they were here in this desolate place, one that seemed to offer no sustenance of any kind, and where no right-minded human would want to set up a home. But I had time for nothing but the task at hand. I found Alain Duclos — whom I kept bumping into en route — and his countryman Jean-Philippe Darnis at the CP. They had just finished doing some repairs to Jean-Phi's bike and were taking a rest in a shady spot by the TSO Land Cruiser. I gave the Frenchmen a curt wave and handed my time card to one of the volunteers on duty. As the rubber stamp he wielded inked a smudge on my card, he mentioned that I had come through from the right direction, something not everyone had done.

"I'm glad to hear that. I've been doing my best not to get lost today," I replied, then rode around behind the Land Cruiser and parked the bike next to the No.102 Honda of Duclos and the No.103 Honda of Darnis.

"Take a load off," Alain said, beckoning me to join him and Jean-Philippe in the shade.

"Don't mind if I do," I said and dropped down into the sand beside them. I pulled some energy bars out of my little knapsack and gave one to Alain and Jean-Phi. They tore into them like they hadn't seen food for a while. After munching my bar, I nursed a bottle of water, making it last as long as possible. Alain kept glancing at his watch, keeping an eye on the time.

"Well, we better get moving," he said to Jean-Phi. "We've only got forty minutes of daylight left and have 113 kilometres to ride to the end of the special." He turned to me and asked if I was coming.

"I'm ready when you guys are," I said, and dragged myself to my feet.

Just as we were ready to set out, Czachor rode into the CP. He had reattached the clutch cover and somehow managed to get underway. He pointed to his countershaft sprocket as he pulled to a stop in front of us. Oil was pouring out from behind the sprocket. There was no telling how long he had ridden it like that or how much oil was left in the system. This time I knew I would be able to help him. I had some spare seals with me and the circlip pliers needed to do the job. As there was no need for Alain and Jean-Phi to hang around, they bid us adieu and rode off.

"I'll catch up with you guys later," I said and proceeded to help Jacek. I didn't want to leave my circlip pliers with him in case I needed them myself later. We removed the rear axle nut so we could slide the rear wheel ahead to loosen the chain and remove the sprocket. It took a while to set things right but finally we set off along the twisty narrow track to the end of the special stage. Jacek nursed his bike so he had a better chance of making it to the bivouac; I decided to make up some time while it was still daylight and I quickly left him behind. My good deed would later be unexpectedly repaid. The team Czachor was with, Formula Top, would show their appreciation for helping their rider finish the stage by providing me with things I was short on.

Along the way to Tidjika, I came across an out-of-action Fabrice Monteaud. His big Yamaha 850 twin was lying on its side, the front wheel jammed into some large flat rocks. He had dumped the bike and gas was pouring out from a punctured fuel tank, or perhaps a broken fuel tap. I glanced down and offered a consoling look; there was nothing I could do but press on. The sun slipped slowly from the sky towards the now-visible horizon with the long shadows now camouflaging dangerous pitfalls. Fortunately, the terrain had become slightly easier, with a thin layer of loose surface covering a firmer base for the most part. The rocks were smaller and the trees taller; they spread out wide at the top like an umbrella. It looked like goats had eaten every leaf within their reach, and above that, the trees flourished. A while later I came across yet another Frenchman, Bernard Pascual. His Yamaha TT600 single was parked next to one of the TSO Toyota Land Cruisers. Seeing the Land Cruiser left me with a small sense of comfort, knowing that at least there was some company out here in the middle of nowhere. And it looked like Pascual was in need of aid: a woman wearing a TSO T-shirt was offering him a plastic bottle containing oil. In what seemed like only a few minutes, Pascual came scorching up from behind me, flying past like he was on fire. Not much farther along he had once again come to a stop. His bike was giving off a telltale smell of burnt oil and heat. I stopped briefly to see if there was anything I could do, but he just shook his head in resignation and motioned me on. His Dakar was over. Earlier in the rally, Pascual had told me No. 84 was a good number. He had finished three times with that particular designation but now he was sporting No. 34. I think there was a bit of resentment on his part that "his" number had been assigned to me. It seemed like he had made, perhaps for my benefit, one last attempt to show his prowess at desert riding before his Yamaha gave up the ghost. Though I'm not overly superstitious, I prefer an even number myself, and was glad to have 84. An even number is symmetrical. At the gym I always do an even number of repetitions of a given movement or exercise. The numbers flow — ending a set on an odd number seems unfinished. I was sure that when Pascual first laid eyes on me he never gave me a chance of finishing the rally. When I told him I came from a motocross background and that I had broken my front wheel the second day in Africa, he no doubt felt confident with prediction. Motocrossers have the unforgiving habit of turning the throttle on when something comes into doubt. Rally riders, on the other hand know when to turn the gas off and be safe. Few motocrossers, even those with world champion status, make good rally riders. To date, Gaston Rahier has been the only world motocross champion to make a successful crossover. The diminutive Belgian won the Dakar in 1983 and in 1985. The American Danny Laporte, 1982 250cc world motocross champion, and Austria's Heinz Kinigadner, 1985 250cc champion, are the only others who have come close. Laporte rode a Cagiva to second place behind Peterhansel in 1992. On a tragic note, three-time 500cc world motocross champion André Malherbe of Belgium crashed hard in the 1988 edition of Paris-Dakar. It was his first attempt at the rally and the accident rendered him a quadriplegic.

* * *

I left Pascual behind and gradually built up speed. I felt badly for him and thought it was odd that without his lucky No. 84 plate he wasn't going to finish the rally this time around. I wondered if that meant I was certain to finish, because I had the plate on my bike. Not long after I parted company with Pascual, the sun disappeared behind the hills directly over my shoulder. I stopped to change my goggle lenses from tinted to clear. Once darkness enveloped the desert I dropped my speed, keeping the motor down to first and second gear. Even though my big Baja Designs light cut a strong beam through the blackness, I could see only a short tunnel into the distance ahead. Fortunately the road improved slightly, but it was still rough going. For some distance, maybe twenty kilometres or so, deep sand ruts were all there was to follow. I rode with my feet out a lot. Balancing was difficult. At one point the bike plopped over onto the higher centre ridge that divided the two-wheel tracks. For a number of kilometres a maintenance crew had placed stones on both edges of the road. That proved to be of some help to me staying on course. The road rose up an incline by a series of switchbacks. I had no idea how high up I climbed or what lay past the edge of the road. I placed my face close to the edge of the Honda's windscreen as far forward as possible to gain an incremental amount of visibility. The navigation equipment sat in the dim glow of the single dash light, but reading the GPS screen was almost impossible. The occasional glimpse it afforded confirmed the distance that remained, but the device was useless as far as confirming the correct path — the road just wound back on itself too many times. The roadbook was also of no use at this point. The distance odometers couldn't be trusted, and I had no means of recognizing in the darkness of night any landmarks. I had little means of verifying that I was on the right track other than the occasional stranded competitor marking the way. It was like riding by Braille.

Riding at night without any points of reference gives you a strange feeling. It's like dog-paddling in the middle of the ocean: you know you're moving ahead, but you don't know the progress you're making. Without a horizon to fix on, my inner-ear equilibrium was all out of whack. It created one of those moments when you're left to think about who you are and what you're made of. I thought about Françoise and Mia. I thought about all my friends and what they would be doing at this time in the frigid January winter. It was about one o'clock in the afternoon back home. I knew most of the keen Dakar followers would have the website up on their computer and would be periodically checking the live updates as the competitors made their way through the checkpoints. I wanted to make sure that I was one of those still making progress.

Dizziness and fatigue were now my main enemies as I slowly plowed ahead into the pitch-black night. At one point I caught a glimpse of light from a settlement off in the distance. But that didn't mean much as far as assuring me I was heading in the right direction. I stopped whenever I came upon a stranded rider to see if he was okay. It seemed like this day was the end of the rally for quite a few. I asked each one how much distance was remaining. They all seemed to have a reasonable sense of how far we were from the end: twenty, nineteen, eighteen kilometres. At least the distance was growing shorter, and I was encouraged to press on. A few riders needed fuel but I wasn't keen on obliging them. What if I got lost? I might need every last drop of gas I had to make my way to the bivouac. On a few occasions I had made it to the end of a stage running on fumes. The last thing I wanted to do now was run out of gas because I had given it away to someone else. You want to help but reason tells you otherwise. I rode on for quite some distance, then came across yet another competitor who had run out of gas. It was Laurent Le Goff, riding a 400WR Yamaha. Like the others he asked if I could spare a drop or two. This time I thought I could take a chance on helping someone this close to the end of the line. I checked the XR's tank and it appeared to still be holding quite a bit of fuel. We siphoned a litre or so from my tank to his.

"That should get you to the bivouac if you ride conservatively," I told him. He inundated me with thank-yous and said he'd return the favour sometime if he could.

"Well, I hope that won't be necessary. I prefer not to run out of gas," I said with a laugh.

"Yeah, I know what you mean. If I do this again next year, I'll make sure I have a bigger tank," he said.

We started our bikes and got going just as a Mercedes race car blew past us. It's always a bit disconcerting when a four-wheeled vehicle comes upon you in the blink of an eye, even moreso in complete darkness. Le Goff took my advice and rode slow and I started putting a gap between us. The last few kilometres dragged on much longer than I expected. I fought to keep upright, paddling through the deep troughs that signified corners. To my dismay, I realized that in my exhausted state of mind I had forgotten to tighten the right fuel cap after helping Le Goff. The cap had disappeared somewhere into the darkness and gas was being sloshed all over me. The old adage, "No good deed deserves to go unpunished," came to mind. If it wasn't for the fact that blowing sand was sifting into the tank, it would have been funny. Fortunately I had good fuel filters that would keep the sand from getting into the motor. All kinds of questions shot through my mind: Can I really do this? Am I up to the test? What if this happens? And what if that happens? I was learning lessons only the Dakar teaches you — lessons about inner strength and the amount of resilience one has or doesn't have. I had used up just about everything I had in me but I knew I had to keep going. I wanted the chance to finish what I had started.

Finally, lights came into view far off in the darkness. They were tiny beacons of hope that gave me a much-needed boost in spirit. If ever there was a light at the end of a tunnel, this was it. I might finish the stage after all. The course took a winding route, and as far as I could tell there wasn't much change in elevation. Although I knew I was close to my destination it felt like an eternity before the dimly lit timing tent came into view. By that point I was wallowing in the sand ruts. I rode with my feet dragging, struggling for balance in the deep sand. I was paddling and pushing, doing anything to stay upright and keep moving forward. My brain seemed to be short-circuiting, barely able to send signals to my aching muscles to hang onto the bike and make it go where I wanted it to go. I was like a punch-drunk boxer against the ropes, wobbly and wavering.

Finally I went down like a ton of bricks. For all intents and purposes I was dead to the world. I had dumped the XR650 as if it was a bag of manure. I felt like I had betrayed this wonderful machine, the bike I had spent painstaking hours lovingly preparing — checking and rechecking each bolt, nut and washer — a machine that had become like a loyal friend to me. Somehow I crawled back onto my feet, and with the last ounce of my rapidly failing strength pulled the bike upright. It started right away and got me to the CP. A loyal friend indeed. A few hundred metres later I drifted into the tent and handed in my time card to the TSO official. More accurately, he removed it from the pouch on my sleeve. I must have looked like a zombie on tranquilizers. It was 8:43 p.m. The sun had set more than two hours earlier. Fourteen hours of nearly continuous riding had wrung me out. I cursed the organizers for throwing such inhuman conditions at me but I swore they wouldn't get the better of me. This, after all, was why I had come to North Africa. If I had wanted a joyride I would have gone to Disney World. If it was a holiday I was after, I could have gone to Club Med. But I wanted to test myself against the worst elements a human being could endure on a motorcycle. When I finished this thing, it would be with the knowledge that I had done something extraordinary, the real deal.

By the time the TSO official gave me back my card, I had a smile on my face, or at least a silly grin. I had even been rejuvenated to some extent. I was no longer the zombie that had just arrived at the end of the special — I was the Paris-Dakar competitor I had told myself I would be. As I restarted the XR, the TSO guy slapped me on the back and said, "Bravo!" I nodded a thank-you and gently eased my bike into gear. I rode the short distance down the narrow road through the village towards the lights of the airport. It turned out I was one of the only motorcyclists to complete the stage that evening. Many were stuck in the desert, out of fuel, broken down or too exhausted to move. They would have to sleep under the stars until they were picked up by the sweep truck. This actually played in my favour. Despite recording a time of 12:31:24 for the special stage, more than five hours behind the first-place finisher, I had earned fifty-fourth for the day, boosting my overall ranking to fifty-eighth. Jordi Arcarons, who won the special, had led a KTM trio which included Fabrizio Meoni in second and Carlo De Gavardo in third, to victory. The Spaniard completed the course in 7:11:16:00. He preceded Meoni, who continued to lead the provisional leaderboard, by just 57 seconds. Arcarons remained in second overall, twenty minutes down from Meoni while De Gavardo held on to third, thirty-eight minutes down. In the car class, Frenchman Jean-Louis Schlesser took his Schlesser/Renault buggy to a win with a time of 7:01:47:00, moving him back into contention in the standings. Although still in fourth overall, he'd made up 21:84:00 minutes on leader Hiroshi Masuoka. He was now trailing Masuoka by just 17:36:00. Masuoka finished the special in sixth place, despite twice getting stuck in the sand. Fellow Mitsubishi driver Carlos Sousa finished second for the day, bumping Mitsubishi Germany's Jutta Kleinschmidt from second overall. With seven stages to go, Sousa and his navigator Jean-Michel Polato found themselves a mere 3:28:00 out of the overall lead. Kleinschmidt stayed in the hunt by finishing fifth for the day, inheriting third overall, 17:36:00 behind Masuoka.

The bivouac at Tidjika, which had the customary military presence around its perimeter, seemed a little desolate. The ambience was different. There weren't many familiar faces, no banter, and the droning generators and heaviness of the cool night were oppressive. The soft glow of fluorescent lights near the Yacco plane were like beacons to me. I rode across the runway straight at it, located my trunk and set out to regroup. It took a bit of time to prioritize what to do next. I needed to put up my tent, have something to eat, work on the bike, find a gas cap, and take on fuel. I decided to set up camp near the edge of the bivouac next to a few other tents. Once my shelter was standing and my gear stowed inside I finally sat down to a meal of spaghetti. I was still reeling from the day's ordeal and the recovery of body and mind was a slow process. But I had no choice. I had to bite the bullet. Before getting some much-needed shut-eye, I had to get the necessary work done on the bike. I walked over to the KTM trucks to seek out a spare gas cap, knowing that the XR's cap was the same as the KTM production bikes. I approached one of the team managers, who was part-Canadian and holder of a Canadian passport. I wasn't sure if being a countryman was going to help my cause, but I figured he'd be my best bet. After some deliberation he agreed to give me a cap, but with a slight condition attached.

"I'll tell you what. You give me your word that you'll help out any KTM riders you may come across who need fuel or whatever other assistance you may be able to lend them," he said as he handed me the cap.

"No problem. That goes without saying." I sauntered back to my campsite: it was between 10:00 and 10:30 p.m., and there were few privateers up at this hour. Most were either already asleep or still out in the desert. Step by step I took care of the minor details needed to prepare the XR for Stage 13. I tried not to think about thirteen being an unlucky number. I needed time to unwind and allow the stress of the day's events to filter out of me. I rode over to the fuel depot and got in line to get tanked up. The fuel guys filled the Honda past the brim, spilling gas all over the place. I was ready to bolt if the place caught fire. The fifty-five-gallon fuel drums were lined up like bombs. One stray spark would light up the dark sky like the Fourth of July. I decided not to start my bike, opting instead to push it away from the depot. Considering how tired I was, it was hard going. I was also experiencing a lot of pain in my left foot, the one that had been broiled out in the desert. It felt soft and mushy and had turned a purplish colour. I hoped it wasn't going to turn really nasty on me. As soon as I was far enough away I started the bike and rode back to my tent. By the time I wiped my face with a wet napkin and crawled into my sleeping bag, it must have been past 10:30. I didn't check the time because I didn't want to know how late it was. I knew morning would come soon enough; even if it had been twenty-four hours away it would come too soon. Stage 12 had been the longest day of riding that the 23rd edition of the Dakar would dish out. I felt a sense of elation that I had put another milestone behind me. I was still upbeat and positive about my chances. I could still picture myself riding on the beach at Dakar and seeing Françoise there waiting for me.

* * *

Stage 13 — Sunday, January 14, 2001
Tidjika, Mauritania to Tidjika, Mauritania
Liaison: 3 km — **Special:** 513 km — **Liaison:** 19 km
Total distance: 535 km

I felt like an eighty-year-old man who belonged in a rocking chair, not someone out in the middle of the desert taking part in the craziest rally in the world. My spirits sank faster than a torpedoed ship. I couldn't muster the courage to pull myself out of the funk I was in. It was my darkest moment. I asked myself if it was prudent to continue in the shape I was in. I had just survived a potentially bad crash. One more of those could spell disaster. I mounted the xR, barely able to throw my leg over the saddle, and sat lifeless and without focus. I tried to get my head together but my brain didn't want to cooperate. I was in denial. Suddenly another competitor flew by at a good clip. I hadn't even heard him approach. The sound of his motorcycle registered after he had already sped by, like the sonic boom of a jet breaking the sound barrier. It snapped me back into the moment. I knew I had to make some kind of decision about what to do, and I had to do it quickly. Sitting on my bike in the desert while the sun slowly fried me was not exactly a smart move. Somewhere in the back of my mind the notion came to me that the rule book could be interpreted in my favour. It was a major revelation, one that gave me renewed hope. I knew that missing control passages carried a hefty time penalty, but it did not spell the end of my rally as long as I was present to at least start the special. I decided that on this day the smart thing to do would be to retreat, so I could live to do battle with myself and the desert another day. I didn't want to become another Paris-

Dakar statistic. I reluctantly chose to make my way back to the bivouac, my tail definitely between my legs.

The noticeable absence of other competitors also influenced my decision. There were very few others at the start of the stage, and I'd seen only one other rider since my fall. Was I alone out here? Was everyone else sitting in Tidjika?

I struck out cross-country towards Tidjika. At one point the landscape took me through some gravel climbs that wound around a wall of rock. I started feeling lost, and panic set in. Nothing looked familiar. Maybe I had ridden farther out than I thought and had struck off in the wrong direction. I felt nauseous and weak. The sun's piercing rays were frying my brain. Self-doubt was welling up inside me. It was a feeling I abhorred, but no matter how much I tried to psych myself up, I couldn't find the optimistic do-or-die person I knew I was. It wasn't until I came across evidence of other human beings that I started to feel slightly more positive. I rode down into a valley, where I was confronted by some barbed wire fences, stone walls and bramble-bush animal enclosures. In the distance I caught sight of the tails of airplanes and helicopter rotors. Or at least I thought that's what they were. The fact that it could be a mirage crossed my mind. As I crept closer, I was relieved that it did not disappear into thin air, but instead grew in size. I rode into the bivouac feeling both defeated and elated at the same time. I headed for my campsite, parked my bike, slipped out of my riding gear, crawled into my tent and instantly fell asleep.

When I woke up some three hours later, I discovered that about half the remaining field of privateer riders, some twenty-two in total, had also decided to forego this stage and opt for sleep instead. We were all in the same boat: totally exhausted and in need of rest. Some had spent the night in the desert, out of fuel or lost. Knowing that I wasn't the only rallyist to choose sleep over the possibility of a Dakar-ending stage made me feel a lot better. I had based my decision on what would give me the best chance to finish the rally. The rule book was written with these kinds of scenarios in mind and was being used by many of the other competitors as well. If you were willing to accept the time penalty as payment for the strategy, it provided a temporary out while still keeping you in the game. Privateers were in a better position to take penalties than factory riders, who had no choice but to perform at all costs. Then again, the pros could rely on others to help get them through the daily ordeals. There was a lot of discussion on this subject, but taking into account the dangers of the rally, everyone agreed it was best to have options available that might help one reach the end. Without these options the number of non-finishers would be even higher.

After I woke up, still tired but at least able to function, I started working on the bike. It was definitely showing some battle scars. One thing that needed immediate attention was the emergency water tank, which dangled off the back above the muffler. The bracket that held it had broken, probably during the crash. I hadn't noticed it in my dazed state. The journalists at the bivouac were making the rounds, talking to the various competitors who were working on their machines. *Motorrad's* Peter Mayer, whom I hadn't seen since the day I wrecked my wheel, was chatting with me when Nelly, a TSO competitor-liaison person, came up to us with a determined look on her face. I had a bad feeling. She exchanged greetings with us both before addressing me.

"I noticed you haven't checked into any CPs today," she said. "I hope you realize you need at least one of three CP stamps of the day or you won't be allowed to start tomorrow." This was news to me.

"When did this rule get put into the book? I haven't seen that one. You're making this up, right?" I said.

She shook her head. "It was announced last night at the briefing. Did you not attend?" *Attend*, I thought to myself. Yeah, right. I didn't even know where I was last night. It was all I could do to struggle back to the bivouac, eat, work on my bike and then fall asleep. Nelly obviously read my mind.

"And I guess you didn't read the posted announcements regarding what was said at the briefing," she said without a hint of sarcasm or judgment in her voice. No doubt she felt bad about having to inform me of the rule change. Although I usually read the bulletin board that recapped the previous night's briefing, that morning I hadn't thought to read anything. It had been enough of a challenge just to get dressed and start the bike.

"I'm sorry, Lawrence. I thought you should know. You're not the only one affected by this," she said. I nodded and thanked her for the heads-up. I knew she had nothing to do with the rules and it would have been unfair to take my frustration out on her. This was a great example of what can happen in an event like the Dakar. The organizers can say and do whatever they want at the drop of a hat. Still, I should have been aware of the rule change and silently cursed myself for being caught with my pants down.

"What are you going to do?" Peter asked me, after Nelly had left. "The only thing I can do," I said. "Try to make the checkpoint."

In a minor panic I threw on my riding gear and sped out to where the special stage started, riding down the same track I had travelled hours earlier. At least I was feeling somewhat rested and handled the bike with much more confidence. It was unnerving, however, to venture off into the desert at such a late hour and face the daunting distance that lay ahead. It was 148 kilometres to the first checkpoint and the same distance back to the bivouac. Who knew what I was in for? It was going to be a long ride in the stifling midday heat. Not far into the course I met up with Elisabete Jacinto and Pedro Machado. They were coming towards me at speed. They slowed and waved, indicating they wanted me to stop. The three of us came to a halt and Elisabete informed me it wasn't possible to reach the first control passage before it closed. Elisabete was obviously very concerned about finishing the rally. Although a privateer, she had major sponsorship from a Portuguese pharmaceutical company. I got the feeling she would have a difficult time facing the media at home if she didn't finish the Dakar. I decided I would hang in with her and Pedro and once again turned around to head back towards Tidjika. We rode to the finish line, 19 kilometres farther out of town along a road that was under major construction. Crews were building up the roadway and constructing submersible bridges. Once at the finish line we were instructed to return to the bivouac where we would be told what to do next. I felt we were being rail-roaded into breaking the rules and that we would be expelled from the rally. The TSO crew at the finish of the special stage asked if we wanted to get checked through and have our cards stamped as having finished. We declined and decided that our lack of information had been beyond our control. At that moment one of the Ford pro trucks came rumbling along the course and into the finish area.

"Explain that, if you will," I said at the TSO official. "How does a truck that supposedly started hours after the bikes finish hours before them?" He shrugged and said "I have no idea, sorry." Someone mentioned that the third control passage was accessible from the main paved road and could be reached in less than a couple of hours. It would be open well into the evening. Riding to the CP and getting my card stamped there seemed like the logical thing to do.

Along the way I was passed by a group of privateer riders from Spain with the same intention: find the third CP and double back over the last 120 kilometres of the special to the finish line. The GPS's needle pointed straight towards the final control passage, which, according to the system, was about 80 kilometres southeast, off the road. After about forty clicks the distance grew farther away from the CP instead of closer. I couldn't believe what was happening. I was heading in the wrong direction. The Spaniards had no more luck finding their way than I did. I had to make a tough decision, continue searching aimlessly and maybe find the CP with the possibility of getting totally lost or head back. I went back and crossed the finish line to have my card stamped.

I was overwhelmed with the feeling that this was going to be the end of the road for me. I recalled Fred Gallagher telling me that if all else failed I could always ride into Dakar via the road. It looked like that was what I was going to have to do. I accepted this sad fact and resigned myself to not finishing the rally. It had slipped out of my grasp despite my best effort. My chest tightened with anxiety. What a disappointing way to end something I had put so much effort into. I had been ready for just about anything, except getting mixed up in some arbitrary rule change that stacked the deck against the competitors. In my mind this was definitely not a fair way of conducting a sporting event. I felt a flush of anger engulf me. I had already discovered the Dakar has many strange twists that affected each competitor's effort in different ways, but a direct deviation from the rule book didn't seem fair.

Back in Tidjika, its squalid collection of bleak concrete houses and huts looking even more hellish than when I first laid eyes on them, I rode into the bivouac and straight towards the organization's planes. I was eager to find out if an official decision had been made regarding the rule change. TSO staff were sitting by one of the planes patiently waiting for competitors to come in. When I asked what the situation was, I was informed there was a meeting underway and there would be an announcement at five o'clock. What really got my goat was that it seemed like TSO just wanted to cut a bunch of privateers because there were still too many in the event. It meant more expense for the organizers the longer we stayed in the race. It was another typical Western bottom-line business scenario: it's always about the money. My emotions ran from one extreme to another. The volunteers must have read the concern on my face and told me not to worry. I was getting the impression, reading between the lines, that they wouldn't eliminate nearly two dozen riders because of a rule they'd changed and supposedly announced while many of said riders were out in the desert or sleeping. It turned out many of the old Dakar hands had calmly stayed in the bivouac the whole day, as if they knew they wouldn't be tossed out of the event. Whatever the case, all I could do was wait for the meeting to end and hear what the powers that be had decided.

To kill some time and take my mind off it I went back to trying to repair the water tank mounting bracket that I had been working on earlier. The most efficient solution was to have the bracket welded. I headed over to one of the BMW trucks, where I knew they had the necessary aluminum welding rods to do the job. Unfortunately, nobody had any spare time on their hands to look after the needs of a privateer, especially one who faced being kicked out of the rally. At the Euromaster truck they had a welder, but no aluminium rods. I went back to the BMW truck and asked if they could spare some rods. They had no problem with that, but to my dismay they weren't the right type of rods for the Euromaster welding machine. Everyone was gracious, apologetic and helpful, but I was no further ahead. I had no choice but to employ a stopgap measure: trying to bolt the bracket back together. When the task was completed the tank was still a bit shaky and it looked like it might not last. But at that particular moment I didn't really care.

For the factory drivers and riders, Stage 13 had been business as usual. Mitsubishi's Hiroshi Masuoka and his navigator Pascal Maimon booked an impressive victory with a time of 6:42:16:00, nearly twenty minutes faster than the duo Schlesser/Magne in the Schlesser/Renault/Megane buggy. Jean-Louis Schlesser leap-frogged from fourth overall on the provisional scoreboard to second. Meanwhile, Masuoka managed to extend his lead over the second-place rider from just a few minutes to over half an hour in his Mitsubishi Pajero/Montero. It looked like the battle for Paris-Dakar 2001 may well be between Masuoka and Schlesser, although it was still possible for Jutta Kleinschmidt, fourth in the standings, or Carlos Sousa, third, to snare a win should the leaders falter. On this day, Sousa and his navigator Jean-Michel Polato drove their Mitsubishi L200 to a third-place finish, while Kleinschmidt and navigator Andreas Schultz grabbed fourth. Finland's Kari Tiainen won the motorcycle division aboard his KTM with a time of 6:53:31:00, which was twenty-five and a half minutes faster than second-place finisher, Isidre Esteve Pujol of Spain. Fabrizio Meoni, who finished fifth, twenty-eight minutes down from Tiainen, kept the overall lead. In fact, the top eight positions on the provisional scoreboard didn't change. All except sixth and eighth place were occupied by KTM riders. Jimmy Lewis, on the factory BMW, held sixth; his countryman Johnny Campbell, riding an Acerbis-supported Honda, was slotted in eighth place. Meoni, who counted a 21:25:00 minutes cushion on second place Arcarons, looked more and more like he was going to be the man to beat.

CHaPTeR 11

The show goes on

▬ ▬ ▬ ▬ ▬ ▬ ▬ ▬ ▬ ▬ ▬ ▬ ▬

Stage 14 — Monday, January 15, 2001
Tidjika, Mauritania to Tichit, Mauritania
Liaison: 4 km — **Special:** 230 km
Total distance: 234 km

185

I woke up feeling rejuvenated and ready to get on with the rally. Yes, I was still doing the Dakar, as were the twenty-two other privateers who had faced ejection just the day before. After weighing the pros and cons of the imposed rule change TSO decided to dish out penalties of eleven hours to each of the riders who had failed to get at least one checkpoint stamp. That's what the existing rule book called for and, in their wisdom, the head honchos decided no new rules would be applied. No doubt the negative publicity they were sure to court if they had stuck to their guns worked in favour of the priva- teers. To me, it didn't matter why they recanted. The only thing that mattered was that I would be allowed to remain in the rally. Despite the heavy penalty, I lost just one position, dropping to fifty-ninth. Just about everyone who was ranked in that range had shared my problem, so not much changed in the scheme of things. As a direct result of this drama, TSO changed the rules the following year to be more fair to all. The new rule states that when a significant group of riders get stuck in the desert overnight, or arrive in the wee hours of the morning, the next day's competitive stage is cancelled for everyone. The entire stage becomes a transit or liaison stage, with the racing portion eliminated. This allows those affected to catch up on sleep and perform whatever repairs to their vehicles that may be required.

***

A fairly short day was in store, and that suited me fine. It meant I would be able to build up my reserves, which I knew I would need to get me through to the end. Only 234 kilometres were on the agenda for Stage 14 — almost all of it a special stage. Nelly and Anne Marie, the other competitor-liaison person, assured me I would like Tichit. Nelly seemed pleased to be giving me some good news. Tichit was a beautiful place, they said — an old village situated in a grand location encircled by white sand dunes and cliffs. I could hardly wait. It would be good to get there early and regroup. The route out of Tidjika to Tichit ran due east and followed an elevation shift in the land that created a *dhar*, or escarpment, across the desert. The land undulated in and around tufts of camel grass. Finding a rhythm through this section was difficult. First gear was too slow; second too fast. Monday, January 15, a solid two weeks into the rally, was another day I rode with KTM-mounted Philippe Bermudes. Two sets of eyes are usually better than one, and together we sought out the best lines around the abundant camel grass. At one point, we strayed from the course and headed directly to the next waypoint following only the GPS arrow. Ultimately, this was not wise. The terrain became rugged, the camel grass grew closer together, and the undulations were more severe. Fortunately, the sand was nice and firm; it had been compacted by recent rainfall. As we rode along, I came to the conclusion it would have been a serious mistake in judgment to ride this course alone. The two of us could support each other to a certain degree if a problem arose. We continued along as cars passed on a tangent about twenty degrees farther north than ours. At one point I stopped and struggled to climb a steep embankment. A hint of panic rushed over me: the water tank bracket had broken off again and the tank was flopping around uncontrollably. Philippe, who was ahead of me and hadn't noticed my predicament, finally realized I wasn't behind him anymore and doubled back.

"Trouble?" he said. I explained the problem I had with the tank bracket the previous day and that it looked like my ad hoc repair job had failed.

"I think I'm going to have to get rid of the tank. There's no way I can fasten it and I can't keep riding around with it like that," I said. "This will only take a minute." I cut the shiny aluminum tank off its second rubber mount and tossed it to the ground, where it glistened like a jewel in the sun. I didn't really want to do this but I had little choice in the matter.

"Maybe someone will find it one day. The three litres of water in it might even be a lifesaver," I said to Philippe.

"You never know, it just might," he replied and restarted his KTM. "Well, let's see if we can get back on course, huh?" I fired up my Honda and we got back into the rally.

We dropped back down onto an open part of the valley floor and came face to face with a small herd of camels. They barely noticed us. They had probably gotten used to the noisy intrusion of rally vehicles into their domain by this point. A while later we caught sight of dust from other vehicles. We changed direction and soon were back on course, heading towards a gap in the escarpment. Except for a stretch of gravel and stony terrain, which comprised about 34 kilometres of the total distance, Stage 14 was sandy. Other than the camel grass at the beginning and towards the end, no great difficulties presented themselves. The temperature, almost endurable the day before, was back in the high thirties. I was glad it was going to be a short day; I just wanted to find some shade and relax. Some four hours after departing Tidjika we arrived at the doorstep of Tichit. A wide passage led us from the edge of the plateau into the small town. The passage was whooped out like a motocross track. Being no stranger to this type of challenge, I felt in my element and rode a bit more aggressively. Philippe didn't follow suit. He probably thought I had succumbed to the Dakar madness. But I had everything under control. I wasn't going to throw away my rally because I suddenly felt like burning some gas. Once past the whoops section, I slowed down and took the time to look around. I may have been taking part in a rally, but the tourist in me also needed to be satisfied. Philippe, on the other hand, headed straight to the bivouac as soon as he had his time card stamped. After getting mine stamped, recording a time of 4:34:19:00, which kept my overall ranking at fifty-nine, I rode around the ancient town for a quick look. Tichit is built in the shadows of an impressive line of cliffs. In actuality, what I saw was just a remnant of what was once a glorious city, founded in the twelfth century. For hundreds of years it was a thriving place, serving as an important salt trading centre along a busy caravan route. What remains of this desert town are a bunch of stone buildings made by piling slate-like flat rocks into sharp, square-edged walls. A tall, square tower, built on the highest hill, dominates the profile of the village. Abundant water produces date-palm groves and the villagers cultivate small plots on the western edge of town. The problem that faces Tichit, like many other desert towns, is the advancing dunes. Huge waves of sand are slowly covering the remaining houses and fertile land. But for an almost abandoned and remote settlement, Tichit felt vibrant; its surroundings were indeed beautiful.

* * *

Meanwhile, KTM's Kari Tiainen registered his second consecutive stage win with a time of 2:53:07:00. Despite his success, his chances of becoming a contender for the overall rally win were very slim as he was well down in the standings, anchored in thirty-second place, more than twenty-two hours behind leader Fabrizio Meoni. Although Meoni had a lukewarm day that saw him finish in sixth, nineteen minutes behind Tiainen, the Italian's hold on the overall lead was still a cushy 20:29:00 over Jordi Arcarons. John Deacon surprised by taking second for the day, giving BMW its best result since Joan Roma's exit from the rally. The Brit followed Tiainen across the finish line with a time of 3:07:39:00. KTM continued to hold down the top five places with Meoni, Arcarons, De Gavardo, Pujol and Cox. Only a fool would bet against the Austrian manufacturer snaring victory in the 2001 Dakar motorcycle division. Jean-Louis Schlesser proved once again why he was defending Paris-Dakar overall car division champion for the second year in a row by grabbing his fifth stage win. He and navigator Henri Magne took their Renault powered buggy across the finish line a scant 24 seconds ahead of Mitsubishi Portugal's Carlos Sousa and Jean-Michel Polato. While the bike division's Tiainen covered the special in 2:53:07:00, Schlesser's buggy took 3 hours, 2 minutes and 11 seconds. Hiroshi Masuoka and his navigator Pascal Maimon finished the stage in their factory Mitsubishi Pajero/Montero in fifth place. The Japanese/French duo continued to hold onto the overall lead, however, besting Schlesser and Magne by almost 34 minutes.

* * *

The bivouac at Tichit was spread out over a great expanse of gravel. A very hot, dry wind twisted tiny dust storms back and forth across the smooth pea gravel runway. The support trucks were well behind the competitors and some of the larger planes weren't able to land on the runway. Except for a temporary shower one enterprising local had set up, everything else, including the fuel depot, was quite a hike from the camping area. The business side of the rally was on the far side of the airport. Here throngs of journalists spent their time tapping away at laptops to send news about the rally's progress to their respective audiences. Representatives of FIA (car) and FIM (motorcycle), those bastions of motorsport sanctioning power, dealt with the problems of the day. Whether few or many, there was always something to address, from protests and appeals, to squabbles and misunderstandings. Mechanics, the worker bees of the rally, slaved away on brutalized machinery in their team paddocks. Many of the cars, trucks and motorcycles looked like they were ready for the scrap heap. It was hard to believe some still ran at all.

As per my routine, I headed for one of the TSO planes to set up camp alongside the other privateers. I always sought out space under a plane's wings as they offered a modicum of protection from the elements. Some of the riders who had arrived ahead of me were struggling to set up their tents in a fierce wind that had been picking up all afternoon. Until enough gear was thrown inside to hold them planted on the gravel, the wind whipped the tents into the air like they were weird kites. With some difficulty I pitched my own tent under the wing of a plane. Before settling down for the evening I did my daily maintenance on the XR, which included the all-important oil and filter change. I had just completed my task and was wiping off my hands when Toby Moody came by with a cameraman in tow.

"Hey, Lawrence, got a few minutes for an interview? Or maybe this is a bad time," he said.

"It's never a bad time for a little coverage," I told him. "Just give me a sec to spruce up a bit."

I quickly wiped my face and pulled on a suitable T-shirt so I looked somewhat presentable. Toby and his cameraman, ever vigilant for the best visuals, used the imposing escarpment that frames Tichit as a backdrop for the footage. It felt good to be the subject of another Speedvision interview. It was a definite boost to my morale. Toby asked me a couple of questions about the wind and how it affected me. I told him that I like to be able to hear when faster cars come up to pass, and quite often the wind hampers that. To wrap things up he said, "Well, you're almost in Dakar, do you see the light at the end of the tunnel?" I replied, "Yes, I can. It's really a matter of holding everything together." The exchange went well and the clip would be aired on Speedvision a few days later. Many people commented on the interview afterwards. I was wearing a Parry Sound Sportbike Rally T-shirt. This drew notice back home in Canada from the crowd that knows or participates in this three-day motorcycling event. Held in northern Ontario cottage country at the summer resort town of Parry Sound, the rally was in its eighteenth year and is quite popular with local motorcycle enthusiasts to this day.

After the interview, I decided to get properly cleaned up

and headed for the makeshift shower I had spotted coming into the bivouac. It was set up in a palm frond enclosure. I was glad to see there was no one else waiting when I got there. At least I wouldn't have to stand in line, something that had become a daily routine since the technical and administrative scrutinizing at Parc Floral in Paris. I was always lining up for something: my departure time for the special stage, getting my card stamped at a checkpoint, waiting for fuel, waiting for breakfast or dinner, getting medical attention. The guy looking after the shower told me it would cost twenty francs to wash up, a small price to pay for such a desert luxury. A garden hose, which provided water for the shower, stretched along the ground off into the distance. It covered so much ground in the blazing sun that the water was warm by the time it squirted out the showerhead in a soft, steady stream. It felt great, and I enjoyed every drop streaming over my body. The water was actually crystal clear, too, a nice change from some of the other slop I had washed with. I emerged from the shower with a renewed positive outlook. I didn't have a towel, but in the desert heat it wasn't a necessity: I was dry before I made it back to my tent. Another TV crewmember came by shortly afterward and asked if I would wear a helmet camera the next day. I was more than happy to oblige, seeing that it meant even more exposure for both my sponsors and me. Of course, if things went sour it would be the kind of exposure I didn't need. I handed the guy my Arai helmet, to which the camera would be fitted. He said he'd return the helmet at breakfast with the camera mounted on it.

At the end of what turned out to be a leisurely afternoon, I headed for a relaxing dinner with the rest of the competitors. Judging by their appearance and body odour, quite a few hadn't taken advantage of the shower. Those who did, looking almost spic and span, were hardly recognizable. It looked like all the locals turned up at the catering tents while the evening meal was served. They scavenged through the garbage and accepted handouts from anyone who was in a giving mood. It was a heartbreaking sight, even though I had more or less become accustomed to this kind of scene. No doubt, for the poor folks along the rally route, especially the bivouac centres, it was a major event when the Dakar came to town. For the lucky ones it meant a feast of bottled water, sugary snacks, cold meats from Europe and freebies like T-shirts. The local tribal militia were on hand to control the crowd, holding two-foot-long sticks on their belts to keep everyone in line. The enforcers also seemed to be self-appointed customs agents, confiscating anything of value from the hapless villagers.

Before turning in for the night, I stopped by the medical tent to see the resident physiotherapist who, like most of the staff, was French. He was a strapping older gentleman who had obviously spent his life around sports people, dealing with sports-related injuries or symptoms. I asked him if he would attend to my shoulders and arms, which were smarting from overuse. He did his magic on my forearms' muscles and tendons to help relieve the tightness. The entire time he was working me over, he talked about one thing or another, asking me about my life in Canada. It was comforting to chat about something other than the rally with someone who was in a relaxed frame of mind. The medical staff recharged my emotional batteries. The doctors and nurses were all in high spirits, constantly laughing and joking around. They were volunteers who saw the rally as a vacation in a series of exotic locales, with people they either had a lot or nothing in common with. In addition to providing the rally with essential medical support, they experienced an unforgettable adventure on the Dakar sidelines. The staff had a satellite telephone that I never once saw unused any time I visited the tent. There was always a competitor, support staff or volunteer using the phone, talking to someone at home. During the evening hours the medical tent was like a coffee shop: a hub of social activity. As the rally wore on, the atmosphere was that of a party, with all kinds of people dropping by to say hello and discuss the day's events. It was a place where you could go to have some pleasant conversation and feel reassured that there was more to life than endless hours in the saddle.

On this particular evening in the medical tent I noticed Carlos Solano lying on a table with an intravenous drip stuck in his arm, looking the worse for wear. The young Spaniard, who had been riding the Boluda Honda from the shop I had visited in Castellon, had obviously bailed off his bike and would soon be on his way home.

Another victim of the Dakar. For someone who was injured he didn't look too glum, however. A flow of fellow Spanish competitors came around to cheer him up. Good old Hosono came into the tent as well. He was there to have the skin on his feet looked at. His fuel tanks had been dripping a constant flow of gas onto his boot, and the skin on the top of his foot was burned from being soaked in gasoline. I could relate, as my right fuel cap had leaked from the first time I filled the tanks. My riding pants would become damp with gas when the right-side tank was full. I learned to use up the first portion of this fuel tank to minimize the irritation of the fumes and gas on my leg. After exchanging a few words with Hosono-san, I finally trundled off to my tent, which was now among a cluster of others. The wind had died down and the night air was warm and soft. Most of the riders in my vicinity were already sound asleep. I figured it was high time I hit the sack, too. I would need all the energy I could muster for the following day. Although Stage 15 was a relatively short 499 kilometres, it was going to be tough. We were scheduled to head north, then east, and finally due south to Nema. To get there we would have to cover a mixed bag of terrain that included sand, stones, a rocky plateau, steep dunes and treacherous camel grass. Before crawling into my tent I glanced up to the night sky, ablaze with a billion stars. I took a deep breath of air at the wonder of it all and entered my fabric home away from home. I popped in a set of foam earplugs to block out the din of the generators and, with nothing but the sleeping bag liner draped over me, drifted off into a serene sleep.

* * *

The unmistakable growl of a twin-mufflered KTM 700cc single brought me back to reality with a start. I had slept in. No worries, I thought, as I poked my head out of the tent to peruse the situation. Waking from a dead sleep, I could be ready in no more than fifteen minutes if necessary. I noticed I wasn't the only one to have slept in. Lots of other riders were just getting up, taking down tents and pulling on riding gear. My gear was laid out ready to be put on. I was dressed in a flash and broke camp in a well-rehearsed fashion with each item quickly stored in its place in the trunk. Once the trunk was closed, I made a last check of the necessary gear and started the Honda. I'd ride it over to the bivouac to save the energy of walking with all my riding gear on. This early in the morning the air was crisp, but by noon, temperatures would be in the mid-thirties. The sun hadn't cleared the cliff's edge yet; its rays streamed high into the pale blue sky. Below the cliff, Tichit was shrouded in shadow. As the sun rose above the towering mountain range a spectacular aura of light blazed across the town and desert floor. Sunlight sparkled off the dust particles floating over the encampment. An airplane roared down the runway and blew its prop blast far behind it. It climbed sharply on its way to the next rally destination, Nema. It would be there hours before the first of the rallyists started to arrive. This day would be another endurance test: almost 500 kilometres of pure desert off-road riding. Stage 15 was the last of the true desert stages, and the last in Mauritania. It would be a tough final desert challenge featuring terrain that combined gravel tracks, deep, soft sand dunes, vast areas of camel grass and rocky areas. Nothing new under the sun — this was getting to be almost old hat. Stage 15 also included something a bit different from what we had encountered so far: a difficult descent down the notorious Enji Pass.

The first bikes started at 7:15 a.m. Just as I headed to breakfast, the KTM of Alfie Cox fired gravel out from behind his 700. He rode down the tarmac to the start line, which was just past the end of the runway. One of the TSO camera crew was waiting for me in the breakfast area. He had my helmet with him and the gear necessary for transmitting audio and video signals. On top of the helmet a pencil camera was taped with wires leading back to a transmitter, and more to a battery. Inside the helmet a small speaker had been placed in the left ear pocket; an equally small microphone was taped into the front jaw protection. Another television guy filled my jacket pockets with the other camera equipment. He explained how the interview was going to work. A helicopter would fly over me, make a circle, and one of the reporters aboard would start asking questions in both French and English. I was now equipped to beam action footage with live commentary to television sets the world over. I felt good about being selected to do the helmet camera interview. It made me confident and pleased that everyone at home would be treated to seeing me in the thick of things. It certainly would be good promotion for my sponsors and the sport of off-road riding in North America.

After receiving instructions from the TV people and wolfing down my breakfast, I rode over to the start area where I waited my turn to depart. Once underway, I didn't feel the weight of the battery packs that were in my pockets, but the wires that were dangling off the back were tugging at my helmet and were a bit of a distraction. The course itself followed a rough two-track road down a dry riverbed; here it was possible to ride fast with virtually no risks. Not five minutes from the start I heard a distorted voice in the earpiece that was fitted into my helmet. It was so difficult to make out what the voice was saying, I stopped to readjust the speaker and then set off again at a quick pace. It was still hard to make out the questions so I winged it. I spoke into the microphone mounted in the front of my helmet, first in English, then in French. I said my plan was to ride safely, conserve energy, and make it to the finish. I also looked over to my left, up at the cliff, so the camera would pick up the spectacular scenery. The reporter asked me to explain what I was seeing. I obliged, trying to sound positive and upbeat. The interview was over almost as soon as it had started and I was faced with carrying the equipment for another 480 kilometres.

After the helicopter disappeared from view, the course took a turn up a gradual slope into the camel grass and sand. The track was well worked-in and the camel grass and sand was difficult to deal with. There was no straight shot through it. I had to constantly work the bars and throttle, and shift my weight back and forth to guide the bike in and around the tall clumps of grass. As the clumps grew closer together the riding demanded more precision and less speed. The going was arduous and slow. Because the Honda was full of fuel, it was a beast to manipulate through the sand. It was like it had a mind of its own. The camera gear, I was beginning to discover, was going to be a problem as well and I wanted to get rid of it. Of course, I couldn't just toss the expensive equipment into the desert. A while later I spotted what could be the solution to my dilemma: a TV No. 5 truck was parked off to one side of an uphill climb. I pulled up beside the truck and asked one of the crewmembers if I could leave the batteries and gear with them. They assured me they would return it to its rightful owners. I was glad to get rid of the stuff and in no time was back underway, heading for the first CP.

I caught up with Philippe Bermudes and together we rode with a small band of other riders who, like us, were just trying to finish the rally. The terrain was sandy with some solid sandstone embedded in the landscape. These conditions were as treacherous as it got. Picking the right lines demanded all of my concentration and riding skill. Fortunately I had a lot of off-road riding experience — I couldn't imagine trying this, or most of the Dakar for that matter, without it. No wonder there was such a high rate of attrition; greenhorns didn't really stand much of a chance their first time out. We passed the crest of a ridge and were rewarded with a magnificent view of a landmark oddity called the *Rocher Perce* or Pierced Rock. This impressive rock formation stands alone on what was once the beach of an ocean millions of years ago. Over eons waves of crashing water eroded holes through the monolithic rock, which towers hundreds of metres above the sand floor. The biggest hole is so large a helicopter could squeeze through it, if the pilot dared. When we arrived, a TV helicopter hovered in front of the hole and watched as we rode past. I broke away from the group and took a small detour around the far side of the rock. I reasoned it was highly unlikely I'd ever get the chance to see this spectacular scene ever again.

The first control passage of the day was hidden in the shade of another huge monolith called the Elephant Rocks, which have been shaped by the passage of endless time to resemble the large beasts. Even the texture of the rocks' surface gives the impression of the epidermis of an elephant. I continued on, lost in my thoughts about what I had just seen. The Dakar really does take you to places no travel agency or tour guide could even imagine. Despite the hardships of the rally, the scenery one encounters along the way often makes the venture worthwhile on that point alone. Another 70 kilometres of hard desert travel took us along a sharp ridge of sand and rocks with no apparent way down. We followed the tracks and GPS arrow along the edge, leaving a wide margin for error. A helicopter flew into my peripheral vision and a few moments later Schlesser's buggy passed me and turned quickly, straight over the edge of the plateau and out of sight. We followed the car over and down a long slide of sand to the bottom. That is how we found the Pass D'Enji. It was like an invisible door leading from one level to the next off this plateau of sand. Essentially the entire route this day followed an elevation change between two gigantic sandboxes: one called Aoukar and the other, much larger, El Djouf. Both are part of the Sahara Desert. Philippe and I rode side by side, in our own separate ruts, urging the other on. Along this twisting track a series of wells are scattered intermittently. Indigenous people have survived for centuries in this wilderness, knowing the whereabouts of these few wells, each of which have specific names and perhaps some tiny settlement attached to them.

We rode into the second CP, just past the halfway mark of

the stage, and had some refreshments. I waited in the shade of a TSO truck while Philippe spoke with Hubert Auriol, who had flown to the remote location by helicopter. I was content to find refuge in the shade for a while. It had been hot, tough, slow going and we still had quite a ways to go. After about ten minutes we set off again, looking forward to the end of the day and settling down for the night in Nema. The course ahead followed a sandy road that was whooped out in a washboard pattern. The narrow passage between the rocks was the only feasible route through the rough terrain. The faster cars now came from behind, looking to pass us. Constantly glancing over my shoulder to see what was behind me took away from my focus. Pulling over to let everyone and his mother pass didn't seem like a good idea either. I was in racing mode and sped up trying to keep a reasonable average speed so fewer cars would catch me. Philippe followed suit and we started making some really good time. Soon we were in an out-of-the-way place called Oualata, a World Heritage Site that served as the location of the final control passage of the day. Oualata is reputed to be among the most beautiful towns in Mauritania, and is one of the oldest settlements in Africa. Like many villages in the desert set along a line of wells, Oualata was originally established as a major centre for trans-Sahara trade. It also became an important centre of Islamic scholarship and remains so to this day, albeit on a much smaller scale than it once was. Many of the older houses in Oualata are decorated well beyond most of what is seen elsewhere in the Arab world, with intricate ornamentation on the walls and doors.

After leaving Oualata the terrain started to change. The sand of the Sahara gave way to more vegetation and the dry grey dirt produced a fine powdered dust: this is where the Sahelien Plain took over. At one point later on in the afternoon we rode up behind a pickup truck occupied by three men wearing turbans. Philippe passed them without drama but as I pulled off the beaten track to accelerate by them, I found myself in loose gravel. I executed a complete 180° spin without wiping out, coming to a stop facing the opposite direction. The passengers in the truck looked at me with wide eyes as they witnessed this pirouette in the sand. *Neat trick, buddy*, they must have thought. One of the guys gave me a thumbs-up sign. Little did they know that I had just scared the living daylights out of myself. The Honda was too top-heavy for these corners. I was surprised it didn't tip over.

Further down the road the scrub vegetation became more dense and the surface of the ground was a dark, finely crushed stone. The ruts in the track were almost ground to fine black dirt. The road wound in and around larger thorny bushes. At one point, Philippe lost concentration and slid into a bush where the two tracks took a sharp turn to the right. It was a shock to both of us, but I was able to negotiate the turn successfully. I turned to make sure Philippe was okay, and fortunately he was. He was a bit shaken and no doubt would show a few telltale bruises later on. But scrapes and bruises are part of the rally life: as long as nothing is broken and there are no internal injuries, it's back on the bike and business as usual. Philippe's KTM was wedged into the spiny tree and it took a bit of effort to yank it free. The bike was none the worse for wear, however, and started with no problem. We continued on into Nema, our destination for the day, arriving just as the sun went down. It had been another long day. It had taken me 10 hours and 20 minutes to complete the 499-kilometre stage, which put my average speed at around 50 km/hr. When taking into account what TSO had put beneath our wheels to get from point A to point B, I was satisfied with my time, and even more happy to have made it through another day.

Nema is about as far east as one can get in Mauritania; from here we would set off for Mali, the second last country on the rally agenda. Nema's architecture is quite pleasing, with stone buildings clad with clay. Lush green vegetable gardens add colour to the desert town. As is the case in most of these backwaters, Nema's airport was a small rundown affair. Crowds of locals were gathered around the entrance to the compound, where they hung around the concrete structure that served as the terminal building. They were chattering away and pointing at us as when we rode into the bivouac. If any of them approached too closely, security guards chased them back. It seemed like a game to the locals, for whom the Dakar stopover was no doubt one of the highlights. The path from the airport ramp to the bivouac, which was spread out over a wide area, was ankle deep with fine dust. The lights of the bivouac were shrouded in a dusty haze that left one's mouth with a constantly gritty taste. After pitching my tent on some rugged tarmac, I hitched a ride on the rack of an ATV, driven by a TSO volunteer. I told him I was going for dinner and he dropped me off at the catering tents. I ate quickly because I had a lot of work to do on the XR. The air filter had allowed so much abrasive dust to pass through, it was essential that I change the engine oil and filter. The Honda's engine still started easily and continued to run strong, but I noticed less compression when kicking it. Changing the oil and oil filter nearly every day since the rest day in Atar ensured the level was correct and the oil fresh. After a long hard day in the saddle, I usually didn't feel like changing anything, but I persevered. It was far better to do the maintenance chores now than to regret later on that you dropped out of the rally because of a preventable mechanical problem — if you treat your machine with respect it is much less likely to let you down.

In addition to grinding down its competitors, the Dakar was really starting to take a toll on the vehicles. The drone of generators sounded well into the night as mechanics toiled on beat-up equipment. The Yacco workstation bustled with activity. Yacco provided oil and other essentials for the amateur bike riders and many were doing what I was doing — changing their oil. The Yacco representatives, like so many of the other company people involved in the rally, were most accommodating. Even though I hadn't signed on with Yacco — I had arranged sponsorship with the French lubricant company Ipone — they let me use whatever materials they had available, including contact cleaner, oil dump pans and grease. Later on in the rally, Yacco ran out of air filter oil, something I had plenty of, so I gave them my extra supply. It was a good feeling to be able to repay their kindness. That evening, I didn't spend any time wandering around the bivouac to socialize. I was dead tired and decided to hit the hay early. Another long day awaited me.

Around 3:00 a.m. I got up to answer a call of nature. The bivouac was like a ghost town. Only one person, Pedro Machado, stirred. He was struggling to unload Elisabete Jacinto's KTM from the back of an old pickup truck. He had spent the night rebuilding the front forks of her bike at a shop in town. Apparently the suspension hadn't been working well and Elisabete's arms had been getting fatigued. Pedro did everything possible to get his charge to Dakar. I had already been amazed by the Portuguese duo. After this encounter I had an even deeper respect for them.

My respect for Kari Tiainen had also been reinforced that day: the Finlander had won his third consecutive stage in the bike class. He led a KTM sweep of the top seven positions, hitting the finish line six hours, seven and a half minutes after setting out from Tichit. This victory moved Tiainen from thirty-second place in the standings to sixteenth, albeit still more than twenty-one hours behind overall leader Fabrizio Meoni, who finished the stage in fifth. In the car division, Hiroshi Masuoka strengthened his grip on the overall lead with yet another stage victory. Masuoka powered his Mitsubishi Pajero/Montero, navigated by Pascal Maimon, through the 499-kilometre competitive section to win by 4:21 over archrival Jean-Louis Schlesser. While the stalwart Frenchman stayed in the mix, holding down second overall, Masuoka's fourth stage win increased his lead over Schlesser to 38 minutes, 20 seconds. It looked like Masuoka and Meoni were on their way to winning Paris-Dakar 2001, although anything could happen in the remaining four stages. But historically, those who led after Stage 15 had a better-than-average chance of winning the rally if they didn't succumb to mechanical problems, or crash out.

* * *

Stage 16 — Wednesday, January 17, 2001
Nema, Mauritania to Bamako, Mali
Liaison: 106 km — **Special:** 214 km — **Liaison:** 456 km
Total distance: 776 km

The 106 kilometres between Nema and the start of the special stage in the village of Timbrega consisted of a smoothly paved road that runs west along the sand dunes that surround Nema. After thousands of kilometres travelling through some of the most brutal off-road conditions I had ever experienced, being on a well-maintained asphalt road seemed almost surreal. Although I had no complaints about having a lengthy paved road shoved under me for a change, riding on it had a trance-like effect. My senses had become so conditioned to deal with sand, rocks, dunes, cliffs, strange vegetation and the like, asphalt had become almost an alien substance. I was hardly aware of my surroundings before I suddenly found myself in Timbrega. Once I turned off the pavement for the start of the 214-kilometre special stage, I quickly learned what the fabled Sahel was. The rally was now deep into the savannah-like countryside I had envisioned this part of Africa to be. Some of the vegetation was magnificent. Tall trees towered above the flat plain, which consisted of high-sprouting dry grasses, scrubby thorn bushes and knotted trees. The Sahel, the boundary zone between the Sahara to the north and the more fertile region to the south, runs horizontally through Africa from the Atlantic Ocean to the Horn of Africa, changing from semi-arid grasslands to thorny savannah. Over the course of Africa's history, the Sahel produced some of the most advanced kingdoms on the continent, all benefiting from the trade across the desert. It is hard to believe such a vibrant region is now home to some of the poorest nations on earth.

The dirt road I was on outside of Timbrega was hard-packed and parched from years of baking in the sun. Oxcart trails twisted in every direction which, with few or no points of reference, presented many navigational challenges. The cartwheel ruts held the bike firmly in the deepest part of the trough. My feet were skimming the sandy edges of the ruts, producing another hazard that required vigilance to avoid. The riding was enjoyable, however, and I could afford to be more aggressive. There were few rocks to contend with, which meant the xr could handle a little extra speed. Finding the right direction was great fun, too. The rally took us into villages on one end and out the other side, with the colourfully dressed local population cheering us on. If there were any questions as to which way to proceed, rallyists could count on hundreds of hands pointing in the right direction. Racing through the villages did pose a major safety hazard. While people could be counted on in most cases to stay clear of the fast-moving cars, trucks and bikes, livestock had no respect for objects approaching at speed. It was something they were totally unaccustomed to, and if not properly corralled or tied up, goats and cows could step in front of a fast-moving vehicle at any time. The results often proved catastrophic.

As the special stage unravelled in front of me the riding offered a new type of challenge, more enjoyable and interesting. The course darted through narrow gaps between trees with a few different options available. It made the ride exhilarating. I was encouraged to press on, using the gearshift lever and brakes to a higher capacity. The gps came in handy when verifying the course, as the grassy plain and the myriad two-track cart paths offered few discernible landmarks. Negotiating the dry creek beds required careful line choice: often steep rises led out of the washouts. The ground looked like it hadn't seen rain for many months. The grasses cracked like kindling as tires rolled over them. Well into the timed special, about 154 kilometres from the start, I came across a classic example of the drama the Dakar offers. Overall car division leader Hiroshi Masuoka's disabled Mitsubishi Pajero/Montero was parked off to the side of the road. The vehicle had suffered a broken rear-wheel bearing. Just as I came upon the scene, Jean-Pierre Fontenay and my old friend Gilles Picard, navigator for Fontenay, stopped to offer assistance. Picard and Fontenay, who is fondly known as the Saint Bernard of the Mitsubishi squad, actually fixed the wheel in just under twelve minutes. But, in total, Masuoka and his navigator Pascal Maimon lost half an hour because of the breakdown. The Mitsubishi duo's archrivals Schlesser and Magne pounced on their misfortune to gain precious time. At the end of the special, a mere 6 minutes and 28 seconds separated the competitors. Although Schlesser had done good business, he still managed to record only a third-place finish in his Renault/Megane buggy. Winner of the stage, with a time of 2:26:13:00, was Mitsubishi Portugal's Carlos Sousa and his navigator Jean-Michel Polato in the L200. Mitsubishi Germany's Jutta Kleinschmidt followed on Sousa's heels, just under three and a half minutes back. The top overall positions remained unchanged, however, other than the fact that Schlesser, Sousa and Kleinschmidt shaved off quite a bit of the deficit.

After crossing the special stage's finish line at the airport near Nioro du Sahel — not too far across the Mauritania-Bali border — we were scheduled to refuel. Hubert Auriol was hanging around the fuel stop watching bikes and cars come in to get gassed up.

"Welcome to Mali. Good to see you're still in the hunt," he said, flashing a big smile.

"Thanks Hubert. It's nice to be here," I said, returning the smile. I waited in line and mulled over the events of my ride so far that day. I had ridden well on this stage and my navigation had worked out almost perfectly. I had made few mistakes and hit my stride without really trying to pick up the pace. It had taken me 3 hours and 29 minutes to get from Nema to Nioro, an hour longer than Alfie Cox's winning time, but an achievement nonetheless and something I could be proud of. In the scheme of things, I recorded the forty-eighth fastest time. Other than the thirty-fifth place I recorded in the opening stage, which was more or less a ride in the park, this would be my personal best for the Paris-Dakar Rally. It was nothing to really write home about, but I was happy with the result just the same. Giovani Sala and P.G. Lundmark capped the top three finishers for the day. The big surprise of the stage was a fourth-place finish by Alain Duclos on the Honda XR650. He followed the KTM of Cox home with a time of 2:40:11:00. As in the car division, the top positions on the overall scoreboard remained unchanged, except for Jordi Arcarons making up 1:28 on overall leader Fabrizio Meoni. Arcarons finished the stage in fifth place; Meoni, no doubt riding mostly in a safe mode to minimize the chances of a Dakar-ending crash, finished seventh, almost eleven minutes behind Cox.

The arrival area at Nioro was a bustling scene of activity. I counted no fewer than seven helicopters parked on the ramp near the runway. Though an impressive sight, seeing those expensive modern flying contraptions parked in a place that is the embodiment of poverty and a virtual throwback to the past was unsettling. The contrast between rich and poor, Third World and the West, was constantly in one's face. I had never really considered that element of the Paris-Dakar Rally when I entered it — now I would never be able to forget it. The geographic barrier we had crossed from north to south became much more evident when observing the indigenous population and their mannerisms. They were dressed differently than the desert dwellers of previous days. Here in Nioro, many wore Western-style shirts and pants. Their feet were mostly shod with worn rubber thongs. The villagers seemed more prone to anti-social behaviour. I wasn't sure what to expect from this crowd. Although I didn't feel threatened, I certainly didn't feel as comfortable as I had around some of the other people I had met thus far. A group of locals jostled around the riders trying to sell soft drinks and bottled water. The heat was dry and oppressive, and I was beginning to dehydrate in the scorching air. I bought a large bottle of water from one of the less-pushy vendors and decided to take a fifteen-minute break before tackling the liaison stage to Bamako.

Many of the other privateers were also taking a rest and I joined a group in the shade of the large TSO six-wheel fuel truck, which had the Total logo emblazoned on the orange canvas cover. We were seated with our backs to the rear tires. I filled my drinking system with the fresh water, then tried to guzzle the rest. I couldn't down it all so I handed the bottle, still about half full, to another rider. I ate some food bars trying to boost my energy level as I got ready to face the 456-kilometre liaison. The crowd of locals was pressing in towards us from all directions. They looked about as friendly as a lynch mob. Their aggressive sales tactics went far beyond what one would consider accepted social behaviour. One of the competitors I had come to know, Stephane Grignac, a young fellow from Dakar, started complaining loudly to an official-looking guy in uniform. From the sound of it, Stephane was urging the official, who had a billy-club strapped to his waist, to do something about the menacing crowd. The atmosphere was tense and getting worse by the second. Finally, the guy drew his club and started waving it around while barking what sounded like threats or commands — probably both. This seemed to have some effect, and everyone started to calm down. I inventoried my riding gear and decided it was time to leave. I was in no mood to get caught up in some sort of melee that might jeopardize my ability to finish the rally. I gave Stephane a nod of approval and proceeded to my bike. Earlier on in the rally I had loaned Stephane a rear wheel for his Honda while he had his own repaired. In exchange for the loan, I asked if he could arrange a place for me to stay in Dakar. His family had visited the bivouac a couple of times during the rally, and his father said he was going to look after my request. In the planning stage of the rally, by the time I had received the information on hotels in Dakar, the rooms had all been booked. As the rally progressed and competitors started to drop out, I figured hotel rooms would become available, and that was in fact the case.

The road away from the airport was made of finely crushed grey gravel called laterite. A *piste laterite* is a wide stretch of road made of this gravel. The base is built up to create a fairly good roadway, save for the potholes that tend to develop during the rainy season. Rain comes down hard in August and September, drenching the concrete-like laterite. The damage it causes has to be seen to be believed. Deep holes are spread across the road the entire distance, so maintaining a good average speed without beating yourself and the bike to a pulp is very difficult. Just as you really get moving you have to slam on the brakes and swerve around a hole. Once in a while I'd lapse into a state of distraction and hit one of these craters, the impact of which sent shock waves through the forks and up into my arms. My entire body would vibrate like a pealing bell, forcing me to quickly refocus my attention on the road and testing every bit of my ability to keep control of the bike. Actually, between Nioro and Diema, every imaginable form of road horror rolled beneath the wheels of my XR: corrugations, huge bunkers full of sand, potholes and lungfuls of grit and dust from other traffic. Completing the package were suicidal livestock and audacious children, who hung around the most difficult sections, where they accosted riders for handouts. In the village of Diema, I entered a traffic circle where bearing to the left spit me out onto a wide, newer gravel road that led to a string of small nondescript towns on the way to Bamako. As the traffic circle came into view, so did hundreds of faces belonging to a crowd of people standing at the side of the road, cheering me on as I rode by. This truly was a day of extremes, from threatening to sublime. The road I now found myself on felt like the lap of luxury: smooth and wide and just begging to be traversed at speed. It might well have been called Easy Street — that's what it was in my mind. I up-shifted through the gears until the XR and I were sailing along at about 120 kilometres per hour. I hoped my Easy Street wasn't going to be a short-lived teaser intended to lull me into a false sense of security.

Of course, there's a downside to everything — the road was almost too good. With the engine throbbing away and no obstacles to keep me focused I slipped into a dream-like state: my consciousness drifted from the here and now to elsewhere and fatigue was slowly setting in. The distance passed beneath the wheels like thread unwinding from a spool. The landscape provided little mental stimulation. The forest I found myself in looked the same kilometre after kilometre. The dirt and dust turned black and thick. Finally, a few hundred kilometres later, the terrain changed and I was snapped back into the moment. I wondered how I suddenly got there — I felt like I had been subjected to a period of "missing time," like that talked about by UFO abductees.

The watershed of the Niger River irrigates this part of Africa. Here, the river sustains life. Roads, villages and people were becoming more frequent. The way past Torodo turned into a poorly maintained three-track dirt road. Dust billowed high up into the air behind each vehicle and hung there for what seemed like eons. I rode nearly the entire distance dealing with some degree of dust: through the village of Dioumara, and the *Vallée du Serpent* — Snake Valley — where the Baoule River and its tributaries wound around on itself on the flat-bottomed land. Past Metanbougou the road left the valley floor and followed the undulations to Didjeni, where it joined another main artery running north to south towards Bamako. In Didjeni, I stopped briefly to get my card stamped at the second checkpoint. The one-day flow of rally traffic on this particular road was no doubt more than it had seen in the past ten years combined. The dust clouds were unbelievable as each set of wheels kicked up an opaque curtain of powder that hung in the air like a blanket of smog. At one point along the way a large race-team truck bore down on me. I rode as hard as I dared to maintain as much distance between myself and my pursuer, trying to hold onto a clean-air window for as long as possible. Suddenly the road took a sharp drop down towards two concrete bridges: one old, the other new. While trying to stay ahead of the race truck I rapidly approached an ancient, slow-moving truck that was obviously a local vehicle. It looked like it was going to block my way and I would have to brake hard to avoid slamming into the back of it. I quickly manoeuvred my bike towards the steeper, older bridge that ran parallel to the new one. The concrete ramps on either side were steep and narrow and I was wondering if I had made the right choice. But I was already committed. The Honda launched off the entry ramp and flew into the air. I hung on for dear life with my heart just about in my throat. I had done plenty of jumps as a motocrosser, but this was a bit unnerving — crashing coming off this jump would almost certainly finish me off. Like an airplane coming in for a landing, I managed to settle the bike back down onto the ground as it cleared the incline on the far side. The feeling one gets from successfully negotiating a jump like this is indescribable. The fact that you know how ugly it could have been if you blew it only adds to the high.

The rush of adrenaline that pumped through me slowly subsided as I motored on towards Bamako. The XR continued to run strong and its exhaust note sounded defiant — it was as if the bike was enjoying all this. The Honda was my lifeline in this adventure. I unequivocally put my trust in this marvel of twenty-first century technology. So far it had truly been a reliable machine: a tribute to the technical acumen and work put into it by its manufacturer. The bond between me and my motorcycle was complete. It had been good to me and, in turn, I lavished as much care on it as circumstance allowed — I only hoped that it would be enough. So far the bike wasn't showing any sign of quitting. With just four days left to go I felt certain it was going to take me to the end. At this point I was feeling increasingly confident. I felt I had paid my dues and earned a spot alongside the other rallyists, whether they were rookies, like me, or seasoned vets. Although I had been cutting my rally teeth for the past seventeen days, I was just beginning to realize what the Dakar was really about, what it demanded of each competitor.

As the day wore on, I arrived in Kolokani, where a second fuel stop was in place to see the rallyists through the remaining 139 kilometres to Bamako. Kolokani appeared larger than the previous towns I had been through. The main road, which ran right through its centre, was lined with towering trees and stone curbs. Painted concrete buildings and stone huts were placed haphazardly between trees, suggesting there were no obvious zoning or building plans in place. This seemed to be the case in many of these towns, often no more than villages that had expanded haphazardly as the population grew. Clusters of mud buildings served as homes for these people as well as lodging for their animals. Cows, chewing their cuds, were everywhere, and dogs and kids ran freely in the streets as if they were in a playground. Shops displayed odd wares such as coal oil lanterns, food staples and cigarettes. Bizzaroville would have been a most appropriate name for this town. Then again, it would have suited a lot of places I'd been through on this bizarre rally.

The designated fuel stop was easy enough to find and was at an actual Total gas station. Two fellows dressed in brand-new orange Total T-shirts and caps — no doubt given to them for the occasion of the rally's pass-through — dispensed gas under the watchful eye of another man holding a clipboard. He recorded each bike's competition number as it pulled up to the pumps. Throngs of people pressed towards the competitors, waving and cheering as two uniformed policemen swished long bamboo staffs in front of their faces to hold them at bay. Bright and smiling faces stuck out from the crush of people. The shining eyes of a young boy wearing a wide grin spanned the language barrier. I wondered what excitement and dreams had been created by the rally for these impressionable children, so far removed from the modern world. KTM-mounted Pascal Heitz hooked up with me after taking on fuel. Before we took off for our final destination of the day, I bought us each a Coke from one of the street vendors. Stephane Grignac joined us and asked how much I paid for the drinks. He laughed when I told him the amount, so I knew right away I'd been fleeced, which came as no surprise. He complained to the vendor that he'd overcharged me and negotiated a Coke for himself at no further charge. Later on, Steph reciprocated by buying a pop for me further down the road at a spot where a TSO truck had stopped and officials were verifying the passage of the competitors. The sugary concoction was probably not the best thing to drink but it's a rally tradition to have a soft drink in the villages.

Out of Kolokani the road was wider but still lined with trees and shrubs. It was perched high up on a deep bed, flanked by wide ditches designed to keep the risk of washouts during the rainy seasons to a minimum. I rode down the centre of the road in case an animal darted out from the brush. The road, one of the few links to the desert from the south, wound its way through the rolling countryside. Sometimes it opened up to reveal a view of an immense forest.

The scenery from my vantage point was awe-inspiring. It was as if a green carpet was suspended high above the ground by trees more than fifty feet high. Numerous types of birds, from the exotic to the mundane, soared in a magnificent blue sky. Here and there, parked off to the side on an access road, I spotted team support trucks waiting for their respective race cars to appear. It was a strange scene, somehow out of sync with the surroundings. I settled into a trance-like rhythm letting the Honda wiggle back and forth over the loose gravel surface. Under acceleration it pulled straight. When it reached a comfortable speed the front sank a bit — the front wheel followed the deflections of the stones. I had a few hours of riding left before the road took us deeper into the greenbelt watershed of the Niger River. Villages and farmland appeared. Tan, grey and off-white coloured humpbacked Brahma cattle wandered loose on the grasslands with their tails swishing. Their long curved horns curled skyward. These cows, like in most other places when the rally intrudes upon an otherwise peaceful existence, posed a danger to passing vehicles. Fortunately, the wide road and ditches that flanked it offered good visibility. With the increase of population centres taking up space in this lush, river-supported area, traffic became more frequent now. As I got closer to Bamako the outlying villages were more crowded and commercially oriented. Lines of repair shops for mopeds, bicycles and cars bordered the edge of the broken tarmac. Cows and donkeys stood motionless next to stone buildings with corrugated tin roofs. Trash lay where it was dropped. Stacks of burlap bags containing grain lay in front of stores that were little more than cubby-holes. Spices were displayed in open bags with the edges rolled down, showing bright yellow or orange powders. Flies were thick in these open-air markets. I rode through at a quick but safe pace — the last thing I wanted to do was take out some local. The day was slowly drawing to a close and there was a lot left to do before crawling into my sleeping bag for a well-deserved rest.

Bamako, situated on the banks of the Niger River, came into view below me. The sight of this large city — the capital city of Mali — standing in the broad expanses of red earth was a little overwhelming. Although shrouded in a haze of smog, and at first glance looking like a rather uninviting place, I was happy to see it because it meant one more Dakar day was coming to an end. The paved road into town led down a steep hillside via a number of switchbacks. The pavement was a tarry surface that had decades of sump oil squeezed into it. Labouring trucks ground up the incline belching out clouds of thick black smoke. I was surprised to see quite a few joggers plodding up the hill sucking in some of the worst diesel fumes I've ever had the misfortune of encountering. Bamako, with a teeming population of around 1.5 million, was in the midst of its day-end rush hour. The streets were jammed with cars, motorcycles, bicycles and pedestrians. Traffic cops stood in the centre of intersections waving the rally competitors past in the right direction. No lanes were visible. It was a traffic free-for-all. I did not hesitate to accelerate through the melee. The streets narrowed into two lanes where parked or stalled vehicles blocked the way. I rode through gaps between cars, vans, mopeds, scooters, bicycles and donkey carts. The mayhem continued all the way to the Niger River, which was spanned by a long, four-lane bridge with a low concrete curb that divided the opposing traffic. At the end of town I found another Total gas station, which had also been designated as a rally refuelling depot. I had decided to head there right away so I wouldn't have to go and fill up first thing in the morning. I tanked up and had the attendant wash my bike in a modern-looking car wash. Across the road the Niger River coasted by, the current hemmed in by the tall grass lining the banks. Some hand-hewn canoes were beached along the shore. There was no sign of motorboats, only dugout canoes, and definitely no personal watercraft skimming the water. Women were hand-washing clothes in the murky water by slamming the clothes onto flat rocks and scrubbing them vigorously, then rinsing them in the river. I wondered how Françoise would feel if we had to do our laundry like that.

Thick dust coated my clothes and face and my nostrils

were clogged with crud. I must have looked like one of the undead in a zombie movie. I asked the attendant if they had a shower and he pointed towards one of the orange doors on the side of the building.

"There's a shower room in there," he said. "I'll bring you some shampoo and soap if you like." Considering I didn't carry soap and shampoo around with me I was grateful for the offer. I decided to get cleaned up at the gas station rather than wait in line at the bivouac.

The shower was in an adequate cubicle that appeared clean enough. There was no mildew or insects crawling around, but then, this was a Total gas station, after all. As soon as the attendant delivered the promised soap and shampoo I undressed and lathered up, enjoying the feeling of the refreshing water on my body. I'd left my gear on the grass outside and kept the door open so I could keep an eye on it. I thought about the women doing their laundry by the river and realized what a luxury showers had to be in this part of the world. I would never take my shower at home for granted again. I got dressed, unfortunately in my sweaty and smelly dust-covered riding gear, paid the attendant, and with my bike full of fuel, rode towards the airport outside of town. Again, it was hell on wheels, doing battle with a stream of cars that looked like they had been in a demolition derby. In some cases, I put my feet on their fenders to keep them from sandwiching me against another vehicle. I had initially presumed that riding on the roads in Europe would have been the most dangerous part of the rally. I was mistaken: it was riding in the streets of Bamako! This was anarchy at its worst, and if road rage is your affliction, in Bamako you could spend your entire day, every day, freaking out or punching out other drivers. That comfortable arm's-length cushion we enjoy in North America between one another is non-existent in the teeming African cities like Bamako. But there was no malice or threatening behaviour in the midst of this chaos. Everyone was friendly and sported a warm smile that made me feel at ease and welcome in their city.

After struggling through downtown Bamako, the airport

was a welcome sight. It had a relatively modern feel to it: wide boulevards with concrete curbs and tall concrete lampposts ushered the way in. Well-dressed and educated people visited the bivouac and the mood was more relaxed than prior evenings. Brightly coloured muumuus were worn by some of the female visitors; matching turbans accessorized their outfits. The remaining competitors streamed in all evening. I set up camp and serviced the bike, which included another oil and filter change. The other riders kept busy around the bivouac, repairing, cleaning and generally minding their own business. Not much time was left for socializing once the chores were done. I went over to sit down with the TSO guys, had a snack and some laughs. One of the volunteers let me make a quick satellite telephone call to Françoise to let her know I was okay and things were going well.

"In four days I'll be in Dakar and this will all be over," I told her before hanging up. "I'll see you then and don't forget to bring clothes for me to change into and some maple syrup and Canadian souvenirs for people who helped me along the way."

When I was finished talking to Françoise, I said goodnight to the TSO people and headed back to my tent. Here, in Bamako, the bivouac had regained its circus-like atmosphere and many onlookers milled about, including a number of people who'd made the trip from Europe. Planeloads of family and friends sought out their competitors and reunions were frequent. I noticed a nervous spouse pacing back and forth, waiting to surprise her husband who had yet to arrive from the day's long ride. This was also the third and final rotation of mechanics, which added to the number of people in the bivouac. I spoke with a few of the visitors, young guys who were having a look at the bikes and race cars. When they realized I was one of the competitors, they gazed at me with a certain awe and asked me all kinds of questions about what it was like to do the rally. Just as I was ready to crawl into my tent, a KTM team member stopped by to take a photo of my Honda. I wondered if maybe there was something of interest on it that would appear on the Dakar KTMs the following year. The bike's massive aluminum fuel tanks, looming Baja-style headlight and unusual appearance had attracted considerable attention everywhere it went. When it was new it had looked even more impressive with its gleaming, gold nitride coating on the fork sliders and gold anodized wheels. Now it showed the wear and tear it had been subjected to, but that just added to its character. The scrapes and dents were like battle scars that told the world this machine had earned its stripes.

Chapter 12

The dream almost comes to an end

▬ ▬ ▬ ▬ ▬ ▬ ▬ ▬ ▬ ▬ ▬ ▬

Stage 17 — Thursday, January 18, 2001
Bamako, Mali to Bakel, Senegal
Liaison: 202 km — **Special:** 370 km — **Liaison:** 232 km
Total distance: 804 km

Bivouac departure time for the front-runners was approximately 4:00 a.m. Arrival in Bakel, Senegal, was estimated to be any time after 4:30 p.m. That's a minimum of twelve-and-a-half hours in the saddle for the pros, and anywhere up to eighteen hours or more for the amateurs. Stage 17, with a total distance of 804 clicks, was the longest African leg of the rally. It's a daunting distance to cover in one day, even in the family minivan. Facing an 804-kilometre ride on an off-road bike could easily be filed under the heading "insanity." When considering the conditions, the environment, the variety of problems that may arise before arriving — if one actually arrives — and the number of days already spent in the saddle, the very idea that someone would choose to do this seems beyond reason. But I wasn't questioning myself when I crawled out of my foul-smelling sleeping bag and climbed out of my tent at 4:00 a.m. It was too early for second-guessing and too late to do anything about it. I knew I had to rise to the occasion. The end was near; that was the only thing that mattered. A restless energy pervaded the bivouac, which was already bustling with activity. Riders were packing their trunks and pulling on their riding gear. By the time I met Denis Rozand for breakfast, it was somewhere around 4:30 a.m. Denis sat at a table in freshly washed riding gear. He had stayed with friends that night at their house, did his laundry, and was well rested and refreshed. I kind of envied him, especially his clean gear. Mine was caked with dust and stained with sweat, and had an odour to match. A few other riders were lazily sipping coffee and stuffing jam-covered baguettes into their mouths as if they were automatons. Some local guy was trying to sell Denis a beautifully crafted miniature motorcycle made of brightly coloured scraps of wire. I couldn't believe anybody would be up at this hour pushing his wares. The intricate little motorcycle was really nice, a fine work of Western folk art created by the hands of a black artist in Africa. The irony was not lost on me. I wanted to buy it, but it was sure to get damaged in my overloaded trunk.

I passed on the baguettes and opted for instant oatmeal, something that would stick to my ribs a little longer than bread. After breakfast, I climbed on board my bike and checked out with the TSO people at the gates of the airport.

As soon as I was on my way I forgot about my fatigue and clicked into an adrenaline-fuelled mode. It felt great riding through the dark streets of Bamako. The city was still sound asleep and the streets almost totally abandoned. It couldn't have been more different from the ride into town. I set out feeling ready and comfortable with my surroundings. The countdown to Dakar was in its final stages. I had grown used to the schedule and the system. Most of the big surprises were behind me — or so I thought. My formula had been simple: be prepared for the worst, fill the bike with fuel, carry as much food and water as possible and keep a positive outlook. Perhaps I was being overly optimistic this day. On my way through town, I caught up to Alain Duclos and Jean-Philippe Darnis and I thought of tagging along with them for a while. As we crossed the long bridge over the Niger River they pulled over, so I stopped to see what was going on. They told me they needed fuel so I directed them to the Total station I had filled up the night before. I bid them adieu and continued on my way, ripping up the series of S-bends that had led me into the city less than twelve hours earlier. As Bamako dropped below the hillside behind me I wound the XR tightly up the steep grades. Unlike the trucks labouring their way up the hillside the day before, the 650cc Honda ate up the incline as if it were a molehill. The bike pulled strongly in the much cooler morning air, but the noise it was making was enough to wake up the dead. By this stage of the rally the muffler's packing had blown out and the exhaust note, which rattled off the low stone wall that bordered the road, was loud to the point of being deafening. Although I had ensured my earplugs were well-seated in my ears, the piercing rumble of the exhaust sounded like a gang of gremlins screaming noisily in my head. For nearly three weeks the earplugs had been part of my body just about twenty-four hours a day. Earplugs were one of the most valuable assets in the quest of the Dakar. Without them, wind and exhaust noise made one's head feel like it had spent the day in a drum being pummelled non-stop. At first my plugs had deadened the mechanical cacophony that surrounded me; now they were like an afterthought, and I wished they functioned better. Ironically, the anarchic exhaust noise seemed to epitomize the self-assured and aggressive attitude the Honda had adopted. Like me, it had become toughened by the environment around us. Our edges had been chiselled off. Dents, scrapes and nicks covered us both. The sheen of the bike's bright red paint job and brightly polished aluminum had taken on a dullness; its snappy detailing scarred and weathered by the elements. We weren't pretty, but we were effective.

After I had put the immediate environs of Bamako behind me, I came across Marc Aivazian, another rider who had set out from the bivouac ahead of me. He had stopped his No. 26 Honda beside the road, so I pulled up next to him to see if he needed assistance.

"You won't believe this, but I'm low on gas," he explained rather sheepishly. "I need to find a gas station. You wouldn't know of one around here, would you?" This time I didn't know of a nearby gas station. I could only direct him back to the one in town where I had showered. I couldn't understand why everybody didn't just fuel up at the end of the day. It seemed like the prudent thing to do. Marc, who obviously hadn't taken on gas either at the end of the day or first thing in the morning, was faced with two choices: he'd have to turn back or ride on with me. He chose the latter after I patted my rear fuel tank and told him not to worry. We had a long stretch of liaison ahead of us in the early morning darkness but I had enough fuel on board to get us both to the start of the special stage in Kita. As it turned out, Marc didn't run out of gas, but at least he would have been all right if he had. A while later, we caught up with KTM-mounted Denis Rozand who had also started ahead of me. We continued on together riding three abreast through the darkness. We shifted gears simultaneously as if we had practised the routine beforehand. My powerful Baja Designs headlight provided illumination, Denis navigated, Marc rode shotgun. The route took us back through the grim suburbs of Bamako past the corrugated tin shacks that lined the narrow strip of cracked, irregular tarmac. We hunted around in the dark for the road that would take us out into the Malien countryside. It didn't take long to find and we soon found ourselves in a new dimension: Africa as I had imagined it. We were into real savannah country — strange vegetation, undulating countryside and clusters of tiny round huts with thatched roofs. This was a raw environment: as basic as life gets. My senses reeled as we thundered down a wide dirt road, passing through villages in the wee hours of the morning.

We were now some 130 kilometres west of Bamako. The dark outlines of monolithic Baobab trees towered over the landscape. These colossal trees, which are thought to be the oldest life forms on the African continent, radiate majesty that is all-enveloping. Many of these specimens have been standing since the time of Christ; others, even longer. The silhouettes of squatting humans were discernible in the shadows of the trees, huddled around glowing dung-fuelled campfires. Smoke drifted across our path, wafting into our nostrils. The pungent odour stung my nose. On our right-hand side was Baoule National Park, a destination for tourists from all over the world. This nature reserve, inhabited by lions, giraffes, hippos, antelope and leopards is one of the few remaining regions in Africa that is home to these rare animals. Despite the fact that we were travelling at speed, and everything was registering through my eyes as if from an express train, the idyllic scenery etched itself into my brain. It was a magical morning, not unlike the sunrise I'd encountered going through the mountains in Morocco on the sixth day of the rally. A couple of times we were passed by some front-running cars. One of them, a Mitsubishi/Pajero/Montero piloted by Jutta Kleinschmidt, blew by us in a big hurry. The speeding vehicle left a thick cloud of choking dust in its wake, so we slowed to let it settle a bit. The 202-kilometre ride to Kita, which lies on the eastern slope of Mount Kita, passed fairly easily. The town, known for its caves and rock paintings, was especially humming on this day with the arrival of the rally vehicles. By the time we reached Kita it was broad daylight and most of the motorcycles were already there. Many cars had arrived as well. Marc, Denis and I pulled into a service station to fill up and do some work on the bikes. Denis's KTM needed an oil change. He had one of the station attendants do the work. The fellow, who seemed pleased to be working on a Dakar bike, cleaned the air filter as well. Denis had a big smile on his face. "Anything is possible in Africa," he declared. Well, if anybody knows, Denis certainly does. The amicable Frenchman owns a large truck and construction equipment business in Togo and has lived in Africa for many years. He had attempted the Dakar a couple of times previously with little success. This year he would ride to the finish line . . . very conservatively. While at the station I washed my bike and filled the tanks with fuel. By the time I was called to the start line it was beginning to get hot. Because I had posted the forty-eighth best time the day before I was summoned to start ahead of many riders I was usually behind.

The first segment of the special led us down a road that was without great technical difficulty and lent itself to a fast ride.

The surface was hard-packed red clay and it wound through the overhanging vegetation. In some places it was narrow and difficult to see around the corners. How fast the bike could go or the braveness of its rider was the only thing that limited speed on a road like this. I could tell by the tracks left by riders who had gone ahead of me that some had flown down here at breakneck speed. It evoked images of Alfie Cox blasting down this road, standing on the pegs, hunched over in the attack position. He would be hard on either the gas or the brakes, trying to coax as much speed as possible out of his KTM and shave off every second. I rode with the throttle turned down more than it was turned up: the Honda was heavy under the full load of fuel and the front brake strained to slow the bike down at high speeds. Long skid marks into the corners indicated heavy braking. Some of the marks wandered off into the brush, a stern warning to keep my wits about me. This was no time to jeopardize a finish so I rode with extreme caution and kept my speed in check. The road eventually became paved and we were sent into a left-hand turn at the end of a long straight. It's the kind of corner that automatically makes one want to crank open the throttle, but I slowed down instead. Some people had stationed themselves there, holding up a sign with the word "danger" painted on it. They were waving to each rider, telling them to slow down. When I came upon them I noticed they were westerners. I though this was rather strange and wondered what they were doing there. The answer was around the next bend: the road dropped down a steep hill carved out of the mountainside to reveal a magnificent valley below. The road was narrow, with tight hairpin bends. The controversial Manantali Dam came into view with a large reservoir of water filling the valley behind it. At the bottom of the incline a control passage checked us through. Hubert Auriol was there to see how his children, the riders and drivers of Paris-Dakar 2001, were faring. I spoke briefly with him and crossed the bridge in front of the towering dam.

Just when I thought maybe this was going to be an easy day, the course took a hard right into the underbrush. A rocky, rugged trail sent us through a burned-out scrubland that was as dry as a tinderbox. Most of the trees were razed; the smell of burnt leaves hung in the air. The temperature was akin to a raging blast furnace and I started to feel light-headed. The pace wasn't fast enough to keep me cool. The new terrain required more moving around on the bike, so dehydration was going to be a concern as I drew up the water from my three-litre drinking system. The terrain had changed again and was now much denser. Sharp-edged flat rocks were strewn everywhere. I had already seen enough rock to last a lifetime. The ground undulated radically, dictating a slower enduro-type riding speed. The baked clay was rough and unforgiving: it took forced concentration to guide the bike accurately up the steep climbs and avoid the bigger holes. But there was something to be thankful for: the cars hadn't caught up to me yet, so at least the dust was reasonable.

The track took me over hills and around abrupt rock faces. Sometimes the trail was so narrow and the corners so tight, I couldn't imagine getting a six-wheel-drive truck through. A one point a downhill cliff crossing turned into a virtual trials section. Loose flat rocks were scattered pell-mell making traction and balance a problem. The drop-off to one side was shored up by a wall of hand-placed rocks, gnarled thorny trees and branches acted as a deterrent to pushing towards the edge. This final crossing of the Tambaoura Cliffs, which was considered best suited to those with a motocross background, sent the track onto a hard-baked clay plain shrouded by towering grasses. As the day wore on the terrain flattened. The abomination of a road I was on was dry, dusty and washed out. I knew this was a day to be extra alert. Standing up on the pegs, switching from second to third gear, braking for the big holes and easing around the washouts was a lot of work. This was true enduro riding. It had been a while since suspension had played a major role and now that it was called into service, I noticed the Honda's Ohlins had become battle weary. The bike felt soft and sluggish in the deep holes. I could feel the chassis strain under the weight of almost 45 kilograms (100 lbs) of fuel and all the additional equipment it carried. Early after-noon, about twenty kilometres past the third checkpoint the xr hesitated: a miss . . . *blat, blat, blat!* The bike had run like a Swiss watch every day. Overheating in the dunes hadn't affected it. Sucking in clouds of dust hadn't gotten to it. Aside from the air leak early in the rally — because of the melted vacuum line — it had run flawlessly. Now that Dakar was within reach it started missing a beat or two. I considered that maybe it was a sparkplug wiskering or that the insulation of a wire had worn through. But less than 500 metres down the road the engine sputtered again and then expired. After the initial miss there had been no further warning, but now my rally partner simply quit on me.

For the first few minutes I didn't want to consider that this could be the end of the road. I wanted to believe I'd get the Honda running again. Over the course of many years of riding motorcycles, I have developed a sixth sense about things mechanical. This bike wanted to run and it liked to run. The xr seemed to want to reach Dakar as much as I did, as if it were a proud thoroughbred that loved the attention that comes with being in the winner's circle. Up until now the xr had started easily and sent good feedback to my throttle hand. But when I kicked it over this time it felt dead, totally lifeless. I felt nauseous and panicky. I pushed it off to the side of the dusty dirt road, through the grass and into the shade of a large tree. I stripped off my riding gear and set out to do everything I could to bring my trusty motorcycle back to life. I quickly removed the seat and fuel tank, pulled the spark plug and placed it back into the plug cap, holding the side of the plug against the cylinder head. I kicked over the motor, but there was no spark, which was no surprise. I had a spare cdi box with me and tried that. It made no difference. All the while, cars and bikes were roaring by, kicking up clouds of red dust that drifted into the air, and settled all around me like a blanket. One of the television directors I spoke to frequently during the rally had told me, "Wait until Mali. The red dust is incredible. You can't wash it off for a week." Now I knew what he meant.

I was hardly in an ideal place to be working on a motorcycle. I stopped a TSO truck and asked them to let someone know where I was. They gave me a lunch bag and two small bottles of water and continued on their way. I went back to pulling the bike apart and hoping against hope I'd be able to fix it. I stripped shrink tubing from the wiring harness to check for a broken wire. It was a last ditch attempt, but I had a feeling it wasn't going to be that simple. With the saw blade of my Leatherman multi-tool I cut the aluminum gearshift lever off so I could pull off the stator cover and look for anything askew. I made a mental note to pack an eight-millimetre wrench for this purpose next time. Behind the stator cover I found nothing out of whack. My spirit sank like a rock towards the bottom of a pond. I was three days away from Dakar and it looked like the only way I was going to get there was in the back of a truck with my disabled bike beside me. The optimist in me refused to give up hope completely. I knew Denis Rozand was behind me and I could ask for his help, whatever that might be. After what seemed like hours, but probably no more than twenty minutes, he appeared through the dust. I flagged him down and quickly briefed him as to the state of my bike. He looked at his watch to see how much time we had left to complete the special. It was 1:30 p.m. in the blazing afternoon sun. I explained I had checked everything possible with the limited resources I had on hand.

"There's only one thing to do," he said. "We need to find a truck and driver and get you out of here." Well, that certainly did seem like the only solution. *But get me out of here to go where?* I thought to myself. We checked the roadbook and noticed there was a settlement some fourteen kilometres ahead.

"I'll ride into the village and find somebody with a truck to come and get you," Denis said. "I know it looks bad right now but it's not over until it's over, right? With a bit of luck you'll be back in action before the end of the day." I nodded and tried to give him the most optimistic look I could muster under the circumstance.

"How much should I offer for the lift?" I asked, knowing I was a ripe candidate for a good fleecing.

"Not more than a thousand francs," he replied. "Don't worry Lawrence, I'll find somebody for you and send them back to get you." Denis fired up his KTM 640 and left. I heard him shift into third gear and fade off into the distance until there was nothing but silence. Denis was my last hope to stay ahead of the sweep truck, which would mean the definitive end to my Dakar.

I sat down in the shade of the large tree and sipped one of the bottles of water. What chance would there be for Denis to find a truck out here in no man's land, I wondered. I hadn't seen any real sign of civilization for more than 200 kilometres. This was parched, blackened and desolate country. I needed a miracle. I started to ponder what would happen to me next. How long would I have to wait here and how would I deal with not finishing this rally? I knew that not finishing the Dakar was something I could deal with if necessary. Before you start such an arduous journey, you have to know there's always the chance you won't finish — you know that the odds are against you. But you don't enter a rally thinking about not finishing — you enter it with the conviction that you will. If you don't, well, life goes on and there's a positive side to everything. It ultimately boils down not so much to success or failure, but to another valuable life experience that has the potential to make you a better person. The problem was I didn't want to come back next year and just try to finish. Getting caught up in an obsession to finish the Paris-Dakar Rally is not what rational people do. I considered myself a rational person and I wanted to finish this, my first one, not the second or third. Although I was in the middle of nowhere, I could feel the world watching my progress via the Internet and television. Thanks to satellite uplinks, rally information was flashed around the planet almost as quickly as it occurred. If I didn't pass through the next CP in a reasonable time a flurry of phones calls would be circulating back home. I could hear it in my mind: *Hacking is out of the Dakar!* For some this would come as bad news. For others, it might be welcome. An entire spectrum of emotions ran through me: sadness, disappointment, anger and bitterness mixed with a sense of good fortune that at least I wasn't stranded somewhere in the middle of the desert frying in the hot sun. I was sitting in the shade of a God-sent tree: could I really ask for much more? Then a strange feeling of relief flushed over me, the kind that comes when you accept the reality of your fate. At least I had an answer to the question of whether or not I would finish the Dakar. "No" was not the answer I had hoped for, but it was an answer. The run had been a good one and I'd given it my best shot. I made it almost to the end and farther than any other Canadian before me. That in itself was something. Yet despite all these conflicting emotions there was one overriding thought: I envisioned myself still making it to Dakar. As Denis reminded me, it isn't over until it's over. It was time to stop moping and put everything I had removed from the Honda back into place. Once the bike was back together, I pushed it to the edge of the road. I parked it with the front wheel visible so the *camion ballet* wouldn't leave me behind when it made its sweep at the end of the day. I didn't cherish the thought of spending the night here. I had just sat back down in the tree's precious shade when six villagers, dressed in flowing robes and turbans, approached me from behind some tall grasses at the edge of the road. One of them greeted me in French and each of them shook my hand vigorously. They said they had come to help and had told my compatriot, Denis, where to find a truck. This can't be, I thought at first. I felt like pinching myself to make sure it wasn't a dream. "Come on, we might as well start heading to the village," they said cheerily as if this was the highlight of their day, week, month — maybe their entire year. Their carefree reaction to the situation made me realize I had to lighten up. This wasn't the end of the world.

I gathered up my gear and set off down the road with the good Samaritans in tow. I had some reservations about following their suggestion to head to their village, but I had nothing to lose. They were friendly and genuinely concerned for my well-being. I considered myself fortunate that they showed up. Two guys pushed the bike from behind while I guided it tight to the edge of the road so we wouldn't get run over from behind by the cars and trucks that were still streaming past. We stopped about a kilometre down the road and sat down in the shade of another large tree. I passed the remaining bottle of water around, which afforded each of us at least one sip. I had no idea what would come next, but at least I wasn't alone. I sat quietly with the villagers and watched the race vehicles flash by. My mind wandered and I started thinking that maybe I could live here rather than return home. Well, maybe for a couple of months until the disappointment faded. Then I could face everyone back home. Maybe I could change my name, move to another part of Canada and take up curling or darts. *I'm being totally ridiculous,* I thought. Perhaps I'd been in the desert sun too long.

The elder villager spoke French well and shed some light on what life was like so far from North America. They were from the village of Bou Bou, which had been close to the road until their well dried up. After that happened they moved about 500 metres farther away from the road to another well. The elder told me that the villagers had taken the day off to watch the race, which like everywhere else along the route of the Dakar, was a big deal for the locals. I wondered what they took the day off from. Life here moved at a snail's pace and there didn't seem like much to do except make sure there was enough food in one's belly. I could feel a sense of tranquility around these people: there was no urgency in their lives. Even though they existed in primitive conditions, they seemed carefree and happy. It was just another day on the Sahelian Plain of Mali for them, albeit one filled with the rare excitement of watching a bunch of maniacs roar into and out of their lives in a matter of hours. Another villager showed up with a large silver aluminum bowl of gruel. It was some sort of corn meal that looked like white slop and had the consistency of wallpaper paste. They offered me some but I shook my hands and head, lowering my eyes in a grateful manner. "*Non-non, etomac malade,*" I said and made the international hand sign for "sick to the stomach," pointing an index finger towards my gut and spinning it in a twirling fashion. To underscore that, I offered them the remnants of my lunch bag. I really couldn't eat any more food. Some of my new-found friends were just as wary of my food as I was of theirs. They picked through the contents, then opened a can of carrots and peas and sampled them. They seemed to like the idea of canned food. They each tried a small amount. We laughed together. They squatted on their haunches and each ate with their hands from the common bowl. I asked how many children they had, then how many wives. We all laughed again. I joked with them about having few children and many wives.

Conversation came easy. They were as curious about my life as I was about theirs. I told them I lived in Canada and that the country was covered in snow right now. None of them had ever seen snow. All this talk of snow made me wish at that moment that I was in the middle of a blizzard. The heat was stifling. The dust caked in my nostrils had taken on the consistency of concrete. I asked the elder if it would be possible to have some water to splash on my face. He sent one of the younger villagers, dressed in pants and a button shirt, to get some for me. Just as he returned with an opaque plastic jug strapped to the rear carrier of his bicycle, a large dump truck rumbled out of the dust from the opposite direction the rally was running. It was an old French-built Berliet from the sixties, painted construction yellow. It had a *One Love Bob Marley* sticker on the cracked windshield. A dozen or so youths were crowded in the box, which was about two metres off the ground. I thought, *Hey, there's a truck, maybe I can commandeer this one.* Then *No, it looks like it's on the way somewhere important.*

The villagers of Bou Bou explained this was the truck coming for me. I was struck with disbelief. *Not a chance*, I thought. Denis actually had found a truck . . . a truck that ran . . . a truck that was available, had fuel and a driver that would come and pick me up on the outskirts of nowhere. The driver wheeled around through the tall grass and came to a grinding halt. Everyone jumped down from the box and three men piled out of the cab. They gathered around me as if I was some kind of circus oddity. A few were dressed in pants and shirts, most were barefoot and their filthy clothes were in tatters. Everyone was chattering excitedly in their native tongue. I didn't have a clue what they were saying. When they burst out laughing I wasn't sure if they were laughing at me or just because they were having a great time. I really felt out of my element. One of the men in shirt and pants, and wearing well-worn cowboy boots, addressed me in not-bad French. He was taller than the rest, with piercing eyes and a toothy smile. Yes, they could help he assured me. Yes, they could get me out of here. "No problem, no problem. We'll take care of you," he said. That's all I wanted to hear. What concerned me just a bit, however, was that no price was mentioned. I asked how much the charge would be but Smiley brushed my question aside or didn't quite hear me. It's always smarter to establish what something will cost beforehand, but I didn't want to push the issue, afraid that maybe I would insult him and his crew. I'd deal with it later, hoping it wouldn't be some exorbitant fee I couldn't cover and they would insist on keeping the bike. Maybe, like a typical Westerner, I was being just a bit paranoid. I wanted to believe that these fine people hadn't come all the way out here to rip me off. My main objective was to try and salvage the Dakar. I had come too far to just roll over and die. I was going with the current, wherever it happened to take me.

"Let's load up the bike right now and get moving. Time is ticking away," I told Smiley with a sense of urgency. I pointed to my wristwatch to make sure we were on the same page. Smiley nodded, giving me one of his toothy grins and barked some commands at the group of men. He was obviously in charge. About ten of them leaped into action while he and the driver supervised. The men hoisted the Honda over their heads, turned the bike sideways and eased it into the box of the monstrous truck. A few fragile-looking pieces of twine were used to secure the xr to the front of the box. This sort of alarmed me, but I couldn't very well expect that they would have such luxuries as tie-downs or adjustable straps. I was lucky to get a lift, period. At this stage of the game, I couldn't be too worried about a few more dents and scratches. A green-and-white tso helicopter flew overhead and started circling us shooting video footage of the madcap scene below. I splashed some water on my face, shook hands with the people of Bou Bou — a few embraced me like a brother who was leaving their midst for the great unknown — and proceed to get into the cab of the truck. I felt as if the Dakar had me by the throat but hadn't quite squeezed the life out of me yet. A small glimmer of hope still shone on me, like the sun that was shining on the parched soil through the haze of dust.

The driver of the truck was a younger man, slimmer than the others; like Smiley, who also rode up front, he wore better clothes than the rest of the crew. My prized Arai helmet, Dainese flak jacket, essential tool belt, and Sinisalo outer jacket were tossed into a heap on the filthy floor among cigarette butts, blackened tools and grimy refuse. As I climbed into the cab, which stank of diesel fuel, unwashed humans and burnt oil, I motioned that I was going to sit near the door. Another person attempted to climb in behind me but, after a few words from Smiley, decided it was best not to crowd the cab. A flurry of arms reached down and lifted him up over the dump-box side and into the back of the truck. Smiley assured me they could get me to Kayes — the next major town — from which I could get a ride to Bakel, Senegal.

The driver ground the transmission into low and the truck lurched forward onto the road in the direction it had come from. I crossed my fingers that he didn't pull out into the path of a fast-advancing race truck or car. I closed my eyes just in case. When I didn't hear a grinding collision I opened them again, glad to see we were on our way. Before getting to Kayes I'd have to get to the end of the special test in Sadiola and comply with the rules to remain in the rally. At least I was making forward progress as the truck rumbled down the road at ever-increasing speed. The driver was, no doubt in his own mind, a participant now in the rally by virtue of having me on board his truck, and he drove accordingly. The road was a bombed out, potholed, washed-out disaster. Untold decades of use by all types of vehicles had eroded the surface to uneven hard-packed, baked mud. The driver accelerated through the gears only to have to slam on the brakes every few hundred metres for the really big holes, which resembled small craters. The suspension bottomed out hard and we were tossed around the cab like rag dolls. I was afraid to even think of how the Honda and the guys in the back were faring. The din of mechanical rattles and the straining engine was deafening. I encouraged the driver to slow down, but to no avail. I had to shout to communicate but he either didn't hear me or maybe like all drivers, didn't want a backseat driver telling him how to drive.

"Not to worry, not to worry," shouted Smiley. "He knows the road like the inside of his house." Somehow I wasn't reassured.

In no time at all the truck pulled to a stop in front of their village, a cluster of thatched-roof huts with mud brick walls that sat a short distance from the road. The area surrounding the huts was covered in a layer of mulched animal manure. Goats and zebu cattle wandered loose, chewing at tree branches and fodder. As the truck noisily ground to a halt, the entire village came over to see what the commotion was about. To these people I was a stranger wearing garish clothes from a snow-covered land, and taking part in an event they couldn't begin to comprehend. Tiny round-bellied children ran around naked with runny noses and glossy, weepy eyes. Only a few had shoes and they were clothed in a mixture of traditional dress and western clothes. I spotted a young boy wearing a pale blue T-shirt with the name and logo of a bicycle shop in Burlington, Ontario, on it. The shop was no more than sixty kilometres from my home in Acton. I had to do a double-take to make sure my eyes weren't deceiving me. It was just too weird. To me this was further evidence of just how small our world has become. I surmised that packages of used clothing had made it to Mali from North America, then all the way to this little village in the middle of nowhere. I wished I had my camera to take a picture of the boy wearing the shirt so I could show it to the owner of the shop back in Canada. I'm sure he wouldn't have believed it. I could hardly believe it myself.

The group of helpers in the rear of the truck jumped to the ground and mixed with the surrounding crowd. I sat in the cab holding the door closed with my elbow. I wasn't sure what I was supposed to do. Should I get out of the truck on my own accord or do I wait until I'm invited to disembark? An old man came up and asked me in French how much I was prepared to pay for the service. About one hundred villagers surrounded the truck and stared at me; more seemed to be coming out of the woodwork. The old man kept repeating the question. Over and over again I responded *mille francs* —— a thousand francs —— remembering what Denis had told me. Finally the old man punched some figures into a well-worn hand calculator a couple of times to check and recheck his calculations. A wide grin broke across his face. The amount of money I'd agreed to pay must have been tantamount to winning the lottery for these impoverished folk. He made a grand announcement to the villagers and everyone grew quieter and looked at each other. Their eyes grew wider and smiles spread throughout the crowd. I began to think it might not have been a good idea to let them know I had that kind of money on me. Maybe I was going to be relieved of everything I had. Ah, yes, what an imagination I had. I'd definitely been out in the sun too long: fourteen days too long. I quickly came to realize that these people shared a similar code of ethics as mine: what's mine is mine —— what's yours is yours. If we share, we share, if we don't, we don't. Our word is our honour. The old man nodded agreement to my offer and I nodded back. The gods had sent me into their midst. My broken but shiny "thunder bicycle" had brought good fortune. The equivalent of $200 would go a long way in this village.

The truck driver, who had crawled out of the cab along with Smiley, shook off his rubber sandals and washed his feet by pouring some water over them. He then put on some shoes, which I thought was rather strange. He spoke to a woman who appeared to be his wife, and from her reaction I assumed he was telling her he would be gone for a while. Other than lingering eye contact, he gave her no open sign of affection. I wondered what he said to her, whether it was something to the effect that this was going to be a good payday, that he would be back as soon as he could, or if there was anything he could bring back for her. The amount of money he was about to earn, which was obviously considerable for such a trip, would buy his family some much-needed goods. After some encouragement I convinced the driver to get underway. Smiley shouted some words to the crowd, and some youths, fewer than before, clambered aboard the truck. Smiley and the driver joined me in the cab and we were off. Everyone waved goodbye as we pulled away from the village. A little farther down the road we slowed down and pulled over. I was surprised, considering we just got going. Smiley noticed my concern and said we were stopping to tank up.

"What, here? There's no gas station," I said. Smiley pointed to a small stone structure to which two of the crew were headed. The men retrieved two twenty-litre plastic jugs of diesel fuel, hidden behind the structure.

"Our own secret gas station," Smiley muttered, flashing me one of his grins. One of the support crew appeared with a length of old garden hose, which he planned to use to siphon the fuel. He put one end of the dirty hose into his mouth and drew on it until fuel flooded his mouth. He then quickly shoved the other end of the hose into the truck's tank while emptying his mouth. He gagged a bit, and I'm sure he must have swallowed a mouthful. He gave me a thumbs-up sign as the diesel flowed from the plastic container. Another guy added some water to the radiator from a container that must have been in the box. When this middle-of-nowhere roadside fuel-and-water stop was completed, the ragtag support crew climbed back into the dump box. We were on our way again. The ride in the truck was a drawn-out affair. I alternated between staring at the glove box door, which had the word *relaxe* embossed on it, and the cracked windshield. *Relax*, I thought . . . *yeah, right!* My focus faded; my mind started racing. What the hell had I gotten myself into? I was a million miles away from anything remotely familiar. It was like I was adrift in some big void. My fate was in the hands of a wild-eyed African truck driver whose name I didn't even know; Smiley; their motley crew; and an old wreck of a truck. At the moment, the outcome of my entire Dakar project was perched precariously on such unsure footing it was nerve-racking to think about. All kinds of scenarios were flooding through my mind: what if this happened, or that, or such and such? Boys don't cry, so the saying goes, but some tears started to well up in my eyes, joy and sorrow manifesting themselves simultaneously. I never knew how much I had wanted to finish the rally until that moment. The chances of doing it had looked grim but there was still a chance. I made up my mind not to crumble in the face of adversity. Dust stuck to the tears on my face. Smiley put his hand on my shoulder to comfort me. It was a gesture that spanned cultures and continents.

From start to end, the 370-kilometre special stage was estimated to take a brutal four and a half hours. That would have been around a 12:35 p.m. finish for the bikes, and 1:35 p.m. for the cars, which started later than the bikes. I glanced at my watch and it was just after 5:00 p.m. It had taken nearly four hours to travel just fifty kilometres in the old Berliet. It was painstakingly slow progress. I was just about at the end of my rope when I noticed a couple of pickup trucks parked along the road. People were sitting on the roofs, waving. Then a fence appeared off to the right: an expensive, tall fence. This meant civilization was near. I started reviving; my heart started to beat more rapidly. It was the end of the special stage. I wasn't sure of the exact rules that applied here so I asked the driver to slow down. They waved him into the control zone. I was happy to get that far. *To heck with the rules*, I thought. A group of spectators cheered and waved as we pulled in past the flags indicating the checkpoint. Word had filtered through that I was on my way in. I handed in my time card to the TSO officials. They explained vehicles had to cross the line under their own power. Well, the XR wasn't going to cross the line under its own power because it had no power. It meant unloading the bike, pushing it across the line, and then reloading it. Whether I unloaded the bike and pushed it across the line was of little real consequence. The officials were aware of my predicament and much to my relief, they waived the rule in this case. The *chef de controle* — the man in charge — said "*J'ai rien vu*" and winked an eye. He hadn't seen anything. Well, he probably had never seen a rallyist coming into his control passage aboard a beat-up old truck, his bike in the back. I knew he was doing me a huge favour, but rules in the Dakar get bent, or reinterpreted, all the time. The TSO crew took some time to add up all the time penalties I was going to receive. While they did, I took the time to speak with a small family of three from Quebec who lived in the area and worked at a nearby gold mine. It appeared that the *chef de controle* was staying at their home. They seemed pleased to have him as company. I was pleased he was staying with them, thinking perhaps he'd made some allowance for me in deference to his host, because I also happened to be Canadian. The Quebecers were cordial and pleased to see a fellow countryman make it this far. I was given the maximum time penalty allowed by the rule book, and my card was stamped. My official time for finishing the special was documented as 17:05:30:00. Remarkably — and this is an indication of the trials many of my fellow competitors had faced that day — I finished in seventy-seventh place. This only dropped me two positions from the overall ranking I had held for the past few days, from fifty-ninth to sixty-first. Not only was I still in the rally, I was still in the top half on the scoreboard.

The first of many hurdles on the way to Bakel had been crossed. The TSO volunteers were very helpful and concerned about my well-being. One of the familiar faces pointed to the driver of the truck and told him to drive carefully, and that I was valuable cargo. I posed with the Quebec family for a photo and got back in the cab of the Berliet to continue the journey. The road widened and improved somewhat as we left the Sadiola arrival point of the special stage. There were smiles all round as we chugged along. I was recharged with the prospect of finishing this day on a positive note. We didn't get far before we had to stop at a police checkpoint to get clearance to continue. I soon learned that traffic movement is well controlled in Mali. I assured the police guard — who seemed confused by the situation or at least suspicious of it — that I was indeed in the Paris-Dakar Rally. I explained what had happened and that my disabled bike was in the back of the truck.

"These wonderful people came to my rescue," I said, gesturing around me to the occupants of the truck. "They agreed to take me to Bakel so I could continue in the rally." He took a look to make sure the Honda was really in the back of the truck.

Satisfied that this was a legitimate trip, and not some joyride for the villagers, the guard spoke to another one of the officers on duty. His colleague nodded and radioed for approval. Within a minute we were told to go ahead. "Good luck," the officer shouted as the driver ground the clutch into first gear and we rolled out of the checkpoint. We were on our way, once again. Other than insisting on slowing down once in a while when the driver's foot got a little too heavy on the accelerator, the ride was routine for this part of the world, a blur of lung-clogging dust and bumps that shook one's innards to the point of wanting to throw up. I caught a glimpse of a family of monkeys launching themselves from tree branch to tree branch as we rattled by. I was worried and stressed out. So many unanswered questions surged through my head. Could I actually get to Bakel? Could I fix the bike? Would I have the right parts? Did I have enough time? At that point, I thought it would have been nice to be one of those monkeys — without a care in the world.

We stopped a few more times during the drive to Kayes. Every once in a while a leg would swing across the windshield like a giant wiper to tell the driver to pull over and let a race car or truck by. At dusk, we stopped at a roadside settlement for more fuel and cigarettes for the driver. I bought a small box of cookies and a soft drink. There was nothing else available and I wasn't really hungry anyway. I began to worry about time. The day wasn't even near being over. Our average speed was very low and more than 200 kilometres were left to travel. As darkness began creeping in all around us, the truck pulled over to make yet another stop.

"What's going on? Why are we stopping here?" I inquired.

"We need to turn on the lights," said Smiley. "It's getting dark." Well, I could see it was getting dark but I didn't understand why he would have to stop to turn on the lights. The reason quickly became clear when some of the helpers jumped from the box and went to the front of the truck where they twisted the headlights' wires together to turn them on. Actually, coaxing a modicum of light out of them was more like it. The dim glow the headlights cast made little difference to what was visible ahead. But at least it warned oncoming traffic, of which there was very little, that we were on the road. I dreaded to think about the tail lights, which were, no doubt, not working. A few kilometres later I noticed a wrecked truck similar to the Berliet crashed in the ditch on a downhill corner. Although time was of the essence, I kept asking the driver to slow down and to tell me how much farther Kayes was. I might get there late, but at least I'd get there in one piece. I considered the time spent with the driver and Smiley as a rare exchange of cultures. Fate had brought us together for a reason. There was a lesson to be learned, perhaps. I felt there was little difference between us when things were pared down to basics. We could have been brothers sharing the urgency of the moment and the commitment to resolve it. We spoke of family life, what we did to make ends meet, what our dreams and goals were. And we shared a laugh when I asked them if they'd ever seen snow. I seemed to be asking everybody that question. I realized it didn't really matter where people lived, we all strived for the same fundamental things in life: love, happiness, a roof over our heads, food and drink in our bellies, and a way to make it all come together.

By the time we arrived in Kayes it was pitch black. A cloud of dust hung over the entire town, the particles of which were diffused by the few lights that lit the streets. Junked cars and trucks lay derelict in the streets. Other than mopeds buzzing by us, there wasn't much activity in Kayes, which owed its prosperity, if one could call it that, to the fact it had a railway line running through it. The driver knew of another truck owner who could get me closer to the Senegal border. We drove around the dimly lit residential area of the town, stopping frequently to ask directions in our bid to try and find the other driver. We headed for the main street, where they assured me we would find another truck. We stopped in front of a ramshackle storefront, illuminated by one fluorescent tube, and parked in the middle of the road. Some of the younger guys climbed down from the dump box and sprinted in all directions trying to locate someone with a vehicle to hand me off to. I was astonished by the concern Smiley and his friends showed towards me. Not once did they try to dump me off to fend for myself.

News spread quickly about the white man and his motor-cycle who needed a lift to Senegal. We were first approached by a couple of well-dressed scoundrels who said they would be happy to take me to my destination. They asked for way too much money, however, and I rejected their offer. Besides, they showed up in a decrepit car and I wondered if they even had a truck. Another guy showed up in relatively late-model Mercedes passenger van. The van looked like it was in good condition so I was again encouraged. Smiley explained the predicament I was in and where I needed to go. The driver agreed to take me to the Senegal border for 700 French francs, not a penny less. This, apparently, was as good as it was going to get, so I decided to take my chances. The support crew and a few curious bystanders unloaded the xr, which amazingly had stayed put where it had been secured with the twine. We pushed it over to the van and wedged it into the back. There never seemed to be a shortage of people to help load and unload the heavy Honda. As soon as a task that needed man-power presented itself, people would stop and lend a hand. Once the job was complete, they continued on their way with no expectations of compensation. I paid Smiley the agreed-upon 1,000 francs and said goodbye to my rescuers, some of whom gave me an awkward embrace, others a vice-like hand-shake. Smiley told me I could come back to their village any-time and stay there as long as I wanted as their guest. "Bring your family," he said. "We'll have a big feast." I thanked them all profusely and without further delay jumped into the passenger seat of the Mercedes. I was glad to see the driver's compartment of the van was separated from the rear by a windowed parti-tion. The xr was leaking fuel, and without the partition the fumes would have been insufferable.

On the way out of Kayes we stopped at a gas station to fuel up. I gave him a deposit of 200 francs, even though he hadn't asked for it. He assured me the road was better than the one I had been on and the trip should be easy. On the edge of town we came to a police post and stopped. It was another traffic-control station. An elderly policeman came out of the small station. He dragged his butt over to the van while putting his hat on his head with an officious air. He didn't seem pleased with our intrusion. The driver told him I was a Dakar competitor and he needed to take me to the Senegalese border. The cop gave me a wary glance and asked for my documents. I offered him my passport but he just nodded, not showing any interest in actually examining it. Then he had a look in the back of the van at my bike. Satisfied that everything was on the up and up, he told the driver to wait and wandered back into the station. While we waited for clearance, rally cars and trucks drove through the checkpoint. Most of the vehicles were support trucks as the majority of competitors had already passed through, probably many hours earlier. After some fifteen minutes the guard returned and told us we could continue. The road we travelled was scattered with potholes. If this was a better road than the one I had taken from Bou Bou to Kayes, I failed to see how. Better is another one of those relative terms and what you get is what you get. I don't think we exceeded thirty kilometres per hour for the 100 kilometres to the Kidira Bridge, which spanned the Faleme River into Senegal. The driver wasn't very talkative, something I was grateful for. I was exhausted and in no mood for conversation. I tried to sleep but the road wouldn't allow it. The jarring and rocking motion shook me from side to side. I made do by slouching down and wedging myself so I didn't get tossed onto the floor. I closed my eyes and turned off my brain.

It was well into the night by the time we stopped at the border crossing on the Mali side of the Faleme River, which forms the border between Senegal and Mali over most of its distance. The driver explained he wasn't allowed to enter Senegal. We asked the border guard for permission to have him drop me off on the far side, as the distance across the bridge was too great to push the bike. For the promise of fifty extra francs I was driven across the bridge. Large race support trucks were crossing the bridge and slowing for the narrow paved road that led away from the river valley. We made it just in time. The border was about to shut down to meet the midnight crossing curfew. I felt like I was being smuggled across the Rhine during the Second World War, caught up in espionage or some clandestine operation. I had been awake for the past twenty hours and was feeling the effects of a very long day. Once the bike was unloaded, I paid the remaining amount owed to the driver and we parted company without the fanfare I had experienced with the Bou Bou villagers and the crew of the truck that had taken me to Kayes.

Word was sent out that I needed a ride to Bakel. All I could do was wait until one arrived. From where I stood, Kidira appeared to be a typically seedy border town, the kind of place you just want to put behind you. I was feeling a bit uneasy, hoping I would soon be in the safety of the bivouac. All sorts of unsavoury types lurked in the shadows near the now-closed border post. It was after midnight and cloaked figures huddled around the glowing embers of fires that were burning here and there. Some were sipping tea, others were chattering and laughing. After some twenty minutes, which seemed like an eternity, a Mercedes van similar to the one that had brought me to Kidira approached me and stopped, eyeing the xr.

"Nice machine. Too bad it's not running. You must be the guy who needs a ride to Bakel," he said. Nice guess, I thought, seeing I was the only white man with a disabled motorcycle at the border crossing. "Well, this is your lucky day. I'll take you," he said, getting out of the van. "Come on, we'll put your motorcycle in the back right now and get going."

I considered his words: if this really had been my lucky day I wouldn't be in the predicament I was in. Of course, it was a new day. Maybe I was due for some good luck, if there really is such a thing.

"How much is this lucky day going to cost me?" I asked the driver as he stationed himself on the other side of my bike, ready to start pushing it with me to the back of the van.

"One thousand French francs. A bargain, no?" he said with a straight face. I couldn't believe this. He was asking an exorbitant amount of money to take me roughly fifty-two kilometres, and then he had the nerve to tell me it was a bargain. But I wasn't in a position to haggle. Most likely there wasn't any other transportation around. I just wanted to get out of there and to the bivouac.

"Okay, let's get the bike into your van," I said.

For some strange reason the rear left-side door of the van was welded shut, making it difficult to get the bike inside. We jammed the Honda through the narrow opening, scraping it against the door jams. One exhaust spring got knocked off and went sailing off into the darkness as it ricocheted off the bodywork. Fuel was still dripping from the bike as we leaned it against a bench inside the van. It rapidly started filling the interior with fumes. Once the bike was loaded, a half dozen people emerged from the darkness, a couple of them smoking cigarettes. One of them spoke to the driver and before I knew it they got in for a free ride into Bakel, or better put, on my ticket. I couldn't believe what was happening but then, this was Africa. Anything is possible in Africa! I had to insist no one smoke for fear of setting the van and everybody in it on fire. The two smokers tossed their cigarettes out the back. Fortunately, the smokes didn't land on the patch of ground soaked with gasoline. My uninvited passengers sat upright and stared off into the pitch blackness as we made our way down the road. I was impressed by the smoothness of the pavement and brightly painted road markings. At least it would be a quick trip, I thought. It was apparent Senegal was a country of some means compared to Mali. But then, that wasn't saying much.

As we drove along, two race trucks blasted past us with their bright lights piercing the darkness ahead. I lay down in the front seat, shut my eyes and fell into a troubled sleep. Next thing I knew the driver woke me up. We were entering the airport gates, where the familiar din of the generators that powered the bivouac greeted me. Dew hung in the air like a low cloud — numerous lights created an eerie fluorescent glow over the encampment. Only one guard was stationed at the gate. I glanced over my shoulder expecting to see the guys who had hitched a ride with us, but they were gone.

"They got out back in town," the driver noted. "They said to thank you for letting them come along."

Yeah, right, I'm a generous guy — as if I had any say in the matter. I directed him to take me over to the Tibau team truck, where we struggled to unload the XR from the back of the van. It was like getting it out of a lobster trap and more scratches were added as we pulled, pushed and twisted it. I noticed the bike had taken a beating from having been bashed around in three different trucks. But at least it was still in one piece. After the bike was unloaded, I asked the driver to take me to the privateer camping area so I could pick up my trunk from the Yacco plane. That being done, we headed back to the Tibau encampment. I wanted to get to work on the Honda right away. After handing over the remaining 500 francs I owed the driver we parted company. It had cost 2,500 francs ($500) to get me to Bakel. It had been an expensive day but, considering the alternatives, it was money well spent. I'd finally reached the destination I had set out for the previous morning. It seemed like a really long time ago. So much had been crammed into the past twenty-two hours.

Once everything I needed was in one place, I started to pull the bike apart under the bright lights that blazed all around the Tibau truck. I had the resources now to fix most anything. The bivouac was settling in for the night, except for a couple of car teams whose mechanics were busily wrenching on their drivers' vehicles. Being back in familiar surroundings was the perfect antidote for my sagging spirits. I soon forgot how tired I was and threw myself into getting the XR running again so I could complete the rally. I had just unplugged everything on the bike that was driven by electricity — thinking my problem was electrical — when a TSO volunteer wandered up to me. Without being asked she brought over some bread and cheese, a gesture that was typical of the caring attitude these wonderful people showed for the rally's participants.

"It's not much, but I thought you might like this. You must have had quite a day," she said.

"You can say that again. Thanks a lot. I appreciate this. I think it's just what the doctor ordered," I told her. Not only had I forgotten how tired I was, I had forgotten to eat. Like a starved dog I devoured the food in a matter of minutes. Just as I was about to get back to work, a ghost-like figure walked out of the darkness towards me. It was Masha, the little Japanese mechanic for Honda rider Jun Mitsuhash. He and another mechanic had just finished repairing Jun's bike and he noticed I was still up working on my xr. In monosyllabic English I explained to Masha what had happened. He offered his help at once and I gratefully accepted. This was a reminder of the camaraderie in the motorsport community and why I was happy to be a part of it. Sometimes I felt as if we were one big family. Sure, we were competitors on the track, but off the track the rivalry was put aside. I told Masha I believed I had some kind of electrical problem; he concurred with my diagnosis. I pulled the stator cover from my spare engine that was stored in the Tibau truck and reconnected all the wiring. To my relief, I got a spark. I kicked the starter and the xr roared back to life.

"All right!" I shouted with joy. Masha was equally excited and he high-fived me. The motor sounded good and strong — as healthy as the day it left the factory. I was back in business. I installed a clean air filter and buttoned everything back up. Masha riveted the master link with a special tool to ensure that it wouldn't separate. It was four in the morning when Masha retired to his tent. As he walked away, I reflected on the events of the past twenty-four hours. It had truly been a day that showed how considerate and helpful human beings can be towards one another in times of need. If we interacted like this on all levels of our lives, not just in some motorsport rally, our planet would be a much better place. I set up my tent by the tall chain-link fence that bordered the airport and turned in for a few short hours of sleep. At least I wouldn't have to contend with an early starting hour and a long day in the saddle. With the time penalty I had accrued I was slated to start well at the back of the pack, which wouldn't be until after 9:30 a.m. And with only a total of 290 kilometres on the agenda, the day would be short. Only three more stages, and I'd be in Dakar, I thought, as I crawled into my sleeping bag. And it was the last thought to cross my mind. I was out like a light and slept like a log.

* * *

Stage 18 — Friday, January 19, 2001
Bakel, Senegal to Tambacounda, Senegal
Special: 285 km — **Liaison:** 7 km
Total distance: 292 km

I woke up to bright sunshine but felt anything but bright. It was 8:30 a.m. — I had slept just four hours and felt stupefied. I wasn't even sure where I was. As I sat upright and rubbed the sleep out of my eyes, the reality of my surroundings came back to me. Once I realized that I was still in the rally, I was ready to tackle the world. I had to eat, reorganize myself, and make some last-minute preparations. By now everything was a mess, especially my trunk. Although I'm a stickler for keeping things orderly and clean, I didn't care too much about that at this point. In two days, if all went well, I'd be in Dakar and this would be over. The events of the past twenty-four hours made me feel like I had truly experienced what the Dakar is all about. Although there were still many factors that could prevent me from reaching Dakar, deep inside I felt I was going to make it. I had paid my dues. The rally gods had tested me and they would smile on me the rest of the way. Nothing comes easy in rally races like the Dakar. Overcoming mechanical failure, physical and mental exhaustion, and self-doubt is what puts competitors on the podium when all is said and done.

I poured some water over my head, got dressed and rode over to the Yacco plane, where I found some familiar faces, including my saviour Denis Rozand.

"It's a pleasure to see you, Lawrence," he said.

"Not as happy as I am to see you," I replied. "You're my

guardian angel, Denis. I'm still in the rally because of you." I couldn't thank him enough for the part he played in helping me the day before. I filled him in on what had happened after he left me at the side of the road, promising he would send back a truck for me.

"I knew you'd pull through," he said. "Guys like you always do. I'm glad I was able to help. I know you would have done the same for me."

The rest of the guys congratulated me on my perseverance and told me it was good to still have me aboard. Conversation eventually got around to the latest bivouac gossip, in which Jutta Kleinschmidt and Jean-Louis Schlesser had the starring roles. Schlesser had criticized Kleinschmidt for blocking his way in the tight, winding road across the cliffs of Timbrega during Stage 17. With no room to pass, Schlesser spent almost two hours on Kleinschmidt's bumper as the brash German woman lifted her foot off the accelerator pedal whenever possible. Schlesser was fuming at the end of the day and openly vented his rage. An unfettered Jutta simply stated on camera that she had no idea anyone was behind her, with the dust and all. It seemed like a case of what goes around comes around. Apparently Schlesser and Kleinschmidt used to be an item. With the relationship ending on a sour note, maybe she had taken the opportunity to exact some revenge. Despite the drama, both kept their heads and let reason prevail during the heat of competition. Schlesser finished first with a time of 3:34:10 while Kleinschmidt finished third, just over two minutes behind him. Overall leader Hiroshi Masuoka, who had started the day in twenty-eighth, put on a clinic and snared second place, just 37 seconds behind Schlesser. An amazing feat to say the least. At one point the Mitsubishi ace even had the lead, ultimately losing it to Schlesser as a result of a flat tire. A lesser driver would have succumbed to the odds and forfeited his lead position in the rally. But the Japanese driver managed to extend his overall lead over the Frenchman from 5:51:00 to 6:28:00. Kleinschmidt, meanwhile, displaced fellow Mitsubishi driver Carlos Sousa at third place on the provisional scoreboard, thanks to mechanical problems that saw the Portuguese driver end the day in thirty-sixth place, more than two hours behind the front-runners. In the motorcycle division, KTM's Giovani Sala beat BMW's Cyril Despres to the finish line by just under six and a half minutes. Kari Tiainen put his KTM into third, John Deacon brought his BMW home in fourth, and Fabrizio Meoni kept KTM well placed in the overall competition by capping the top five, nine and a half minutes down from Sala.

* * *

Christian, Steph and the rest of the TSO staff who took care of the privateer riders all breathed a collective sigh of relief when I showed up to get the GPS code and roadbook for Stage 18.

"Hey, good to see you Lawrence. We thought we were going to lose you," Steph said.

"You're not going to get rid of me that easily. Just a little electrical problem, nothing that couldn't be fixed," I replied.

After I got the code and roadbook I also got a hold of some batteries that I installed in the GPS unit. I wasn't taking any chances with my electrical system and had chosen to eliminate everything from it but the ignition. I rode from the bivouac into Bakel for fuel with Marc Aivazian. I didn't know where the gas station was and he showed me the way. I was really tired and once again running on adrenaline — but at least I was functional. The knowledge that Dakar was basically just around the bend acted like a turbocharger. As I waited for the start, a TSO doctor came over to ask me how I was feeling. Everyone knew I'd had a late night and they won't let you start if you aren't medically fit or didn't get enough sleep. "I slept for four hours. I'm up to the task. I'll make sure I get more sleep tonight," I told him. He looked into my eyes as if to make sure I was really awake and said I was cleared to go. I was the last rider to start the special, which left from Bakel for a 285-kilometre journey over narrow tracks and a lot of vegetation, high grass and bushes. The first part included fast-winding tracks through the bush, the second half even faster sections over laterite tracks. I quickly caught up to Denis Rozand, Dominique

Vion and one other rider. Although I was confident the Honda would see me through to the end, I stuck pretty close to these guys in case anything else happened. The countryside we passed through was more populated; villages became more frequent. We rode from one village to another, each one jumped around a well. Livestock with an apparent death wish were, once again, the biggest hazard. Herds of cows crossed the course in all directions. Ox carts and donkeys clogged the tracks in the most inconvenient places. The potential for a serious accident was considerable. The top three car drivers, Masuoka, Schlesser and Kleinschmidt, were locked in a close battle for the overall lead. The remainder of the elite factory riders were equally tight and driving the wheels off their vehicles in a bid to move up their overall rankings. Even though they had been asked to slow down in populated areas, they didn't, and put everyone at risk. The cars jetted by the backmarkers, like me, with little patience or regard for safety. I felt very uneasy at the thought of being taken out by a four-wheeled competitor, especially having already survived what I thought was the worst the Dakar could throw at me.

As we pushed on, we got into a savannah-like plain with deep rutted two-track roads that seemed to head in no particular direction. The ruts were filled with loose sand so deep that dragging the bike's footpegs was a concern. The other was that if you got locked into the rut and, if for any reason escape was necessary, you were a virtual prisoner until you could find a way out. By that time, of course, it might be too late. I chose to ride along the side of the road on cow paths that offered some easier navigating. It was a matter of not getting drawn off in the wrong direction and avoiding the trees and logs that were scattered all over the place. Still, it was a better alternative than the deep sandy ruts. The faster riders could make good time through this type of terrain and I guessed the average speed would be quite high. Every ten or twenty kilometres another settlement would appear, and the best way to figure out which way to go was to look for the crowd of locals, all waving and pointing. A glance at the GPS confirmed the right direction and the roadbook would settle a dispute. To do this, however, I had to take my eyes off the road, which made slamming into a cow a real possibility. Fortunately, it was an incident-free stage and was over for me in just over four hours. I finished the 285-kilometre special in sixtieth place, which also ended up being my overall ranking. Although filled with enough challenges to make it interesting, compared to many of the other stages this day had been more or less a joyride. As I pulled into Tambacounda I knew that reaching my goal was becoming a reality. I could almost taste it. It's the kind of sensation you have when you know you're nearing the completion of a project: you're not quite there yet but you can see the finish line. Only a worst-case scenario could still throw a wrench into the works, but I was going to do my best to keep that wrench securely in the tool box.

Tambacounda was typical of the larger African cities I had passed through on my journey. The area is rich in African culture. The local way of life is set at a relaxed, easygoing pace. The streets are filled with wobbly wheeled donkey carts that block traffic, the stench of rotting sewage and diesel permeates the air. The populace clogged the streets in junked cars with doors hanging off their hinges, barely running on poorly refined fuel and archaic mechanics. The local taxitrucks, overloaded and belching fumes, weaved along the roads with people hanging out the doors. Along the main artery that led to the airport there were concrete buildings — some private residences, some commercial stores and some that did double duty. I stopped in front of one painted concrete building with a sign proclaiming *telecabine*. It was obvious this place was also a residence, with a public pay telephone installed in the living room. I parked the Honda directly in front of the door and pushed through the brightly coloured plastic strips over the entrance. I was anxious to call home and hear Françoise's voice.

Two younger women appeared and without being asked, directed me to the telephone. They knew I could be there for only one reason. I dropped my weary body onto a stool and dialled. In only a few moments I was connected with Françoise.

She sounded like she was next door. I always found it hard to reconcile the clarity of the phone connections with the fact that I was standing thousands of kilometres away in what was basically a primitive backwater. Françoise was busy at work but she had been following the rally live on the Internet whenever she had a free moment. In some cases she'd known where I was before I did. For some reason the phone connection started to suddenly sound like we were on separate planets: this was more in keeping with my expectations. The poor sound quality kept the conversation short.

"I'm coming to Dakar. I'll be there at ten," Françoise said, and the line went dead. That's all I needed to hear. To have her waiting for me in Dakar would make my arrival all the more sweet. Now, I just had to make sure I arrived there on the XR and not by some alternate means. I paid for the phone call in French francs and asked the women if they happened to have a shower available. They glanced at each other, and after some deliberation said they did, but didn't ask if I wanted to use it. I felt that maybe I was intruding, that their shower was not for public use. Although I felt grimy and longed for the feel of water streaming over my body, I chose not to bother them.

I rode into the airport at Tamabacounda, handed over my time card, and picked up the next day's roadbook. The atmosphere in the bivouac was calm and jovial. You could feel the tension winding down. Most of the main drama had been played out. The final act was in progress, and in just two days the overall motorcycle and car division victors would be decided. Tamabacounda had been a stopover for the Paris-Dakar Rally many times. The locals know the rally provides the opportunity to steal valuables within easy reach. The organizers warned us to keep everything close at hand and in your tent. The airport grounds were burned black and scorched from a recent grass fire. Each step raised a dust cloud and the wind blew black ash everywhere. In my riding shorts and sandals I walked over to the wash area that had been set up for the competitors. The lineup for a shower was long. I had second thoughts about not asking to shower at the telephone place. I noticed a long deep sink with a number of taps stationed along its length. Figuring I would bypass the shower I climbed into the sink and crouched underneath the weak stream of water flowing from one of the taps. Just as I got nicely soaped, the water ran out. There was no choice now but to wait for a shower. By the time one became available, the soap had caked onto my body and it took forever to get it rinsed off under the trickle of water running out of the shower head. Once cleaned up, I went to work on the bike. Alain Duclos, Jean-Philippe Darnis, Marc Aivazian, Takao Hosono, riders who were now like brothers to me, were also busy working on their bikes. We all shared the items necessary to get the bikes ready for the penultimate day of the rally. New tires were in order for my XR, as was an oil change. With the daily oil changes I had performed, all the filters I had brought had been used, but I managed to get good old Masha to donate one.

When I was done with the bike it was time to head to the catering tents for the evening meal. Some local dancers and musicians were there entertaining the rally people and a crowd of onlookers. Despite the fact that everybody was exhausted from the past eighteen days, a palpable energy permeated the place. Most of the seats were taken, but I spotted an empty chair at the table where Jutta Kleinschmidt was sitting. I asked if the chair was free and was invited to sit down. When you meet a high-profile person for the first time you never know what to expect, but Jutta was really down-to-earth and friendly. Right away she put me at ease and chatted freely. You never would have guessed the kind of pressure she was under to secure a high overall podium finish. Theoretically, in third position she was still in the running for a victory. She was just under 40 minutes behind overall leader and fellow Mitsubishi driver Hiroshi Masuoka. Between the two was the ever-present Jean-Louis Schlesser, just seven and a half minutes behind Masuoka. These heavyweights were not exactly an easy pair to overtake, but then Jutta wasn't exactly a lightweight. A lot of people were pulling for her — everybody loves an upset. Meanwhile, Masuoka had won his fifth special stage that day, trailed home by Schlesser in second place. Jutta and her navigator Andreas Schultz had finished sixth with a time of 2:52:05:00, which was just over seven minutes slower than Masuoka. Even though the odds of winning were against the German, no doubt she was entertaining the thought of becoming the first woman to win Paris-Dakar. At the moment it was a two-pony race, but anything was still possible. The 2001 edition of the rally was the most closely fought to date, not just for cars but motorcycles as well. Fabrizio Meoni, who had finished Stage 18 in seventh place, still led the field on his factory KTM. He had accumulated a relatively safe cushion of twenty-two minutes over fellow KTM rider Jordi Arcarons, who in turn commanded a twenty-minute gap over KTM's Carlo De Gavardo, in third. The capable hands of Cyril Despres gave BMW its first stage win since Joan Roma's victories in Stages 6 and 8. But the Frenchman, who recorded a time of 2:15:16 to win Stage 18, just fifty-one seconds ahead of KTM's Giovani Sala, was well down on the scoreboard in fifteenth place. He would not factor into the overall podium finish. Neither would BMW's John Deacon and Jimmy Lewis, holding down sixth and seventh respectively, nearly four hours behind Meoni.

By the time I had walked back to my tent, which as usual was set up near the Yacco plane with the other privateers, I wasn't much cleaner than when I had arrived in town. Black soot covered me from head to toe, but I blended in with everybody else. Pascal Heitz was keeping the locals at bay, shouting at them to keep away from our tents. As darkness fell we sat on the lowered cargo bay doors of the plane with Christian and the other TSO volunteers, who had also become friends. The air felt soft as a light breeze wafted the distinct odour of burning dry grass over the airport. The easygoing ambience made the evening pass quickly. Everybody was in high spirits at this point. One of the Euromaster guys banged on a large bongo drum he had purchased somewhere along the way, and the Ricard Pastis flowed freely. This was the last busy day, as the bike and car teams were making final preparations for the push to Dakar. I was taking everything in with the awe of a child.

ChaPTeR 13

To Dakar and back

Stage 19 — Saturday, January 20, 2001
Tambacounda, Senegal to Dakar, Senegal
Liaison: 107 km — **Special:** 127 km — **Liaison:** 240 km
Total distance: 564 km   253

I had probably stayed up too late, because I struggled to rouse myself from a deep sleep. I don't recall what time I finally crawled into my tent because I got caught up in the festive occasion that marked our final night in a Paris-Dakar Rally bivouac. If all went well I would be in Dakar late that afternoon and, like the rest of the survivors, sleep in the comfort of a real bed in a hotel or private home. Most riders were up early and ready to leave for the start of the special stage, a 107-kilometre ride on paved roads to Koumpentoum. Stage 19's special would take us through the Senegalese savannah. According to the roadbook, the first part was to be run over laterite tracks, which were fast and demanded plenty of skill. In the second Saharan desert section, the vegetation would be denser, with a lot of parallel tracks. I was looking forward to this stage. The savannah is fun to ride through — at least I thought so. Navigation adds an important element to any challenge and riding is always treacherous. I knew I wouldn't be able to drop my guard for a moment if I was going to get through the day without incident.

When I finished packing my trunk I needed the help of one of the local uniformed security guards to squash the lid shut so I could insert the locking rod through the hasps. The trunk was a far cry from the orderly affair it was when I first packed it with Françoise in Paris three weeks earlier. I rammed down a quick bowl of porridge, poured some orange juice on top of it, and climbed on the XR. I was one of the last stragglers to ride through the airport gate. It was around 7:00 a.m. and I would have to hit the gas to make sure I made it on time to meet my departure window for the special. It was a 107-kilometre ride on a so-called paved road, but by now I knew that didn't necessarily mean smooth sailing. As usual the bikes would be the first to leave. The front-runners were slated to start at 8:00 a.m., the car drivers at 9:15. The TSO crew at the gate asked me to turn on my lights. I shrugged my shoulders. I tried everything I could to make them work, but to no avail. Too fatigued to concentrate on analyzing a wiring harness, I gave up. If they were going to disqualify me now for not having lights on, let them, I thought. Not exactly rational thinking, but I was hardly able to think at all. Okay, there's no way I was going to see my Dakar go down the drain because I had no lights. If it was going to become an issue I could always tape my Petzl headlamp on the front of my bike. It would be daylight in less than half an hour anyway and it's not like I had to worry about getting ticketed by the local cops for riding without lights. A TSO guy said it was for safety reasons. Marc Aivazian, another straggler, said he'd ride in front of me so I could have the benefit of his headlight on the way out of town. Everybody agreed that would be acceptable and we were on our way. "Just stick to his rear fender until it gets light out," another one of the volunteers yelled after us as we took off.

There was very little traffic to contend with and we made good time, catching up to Philippe Bermudes just as dawn started to break. The air was still and humid. Fog patches hovered in the low areas. The three of us soared through villages and encountered numerous animals along the way. I had been warned to be extra vigilant about the animals on the road in this part of Africa. Usually there was so little traffic in the area there was no reason for animals or humans to be wary of the roadway. We had to constantly slow down for herds of goats, sheep, cows and donkeys that ambled across the tarmac without warning. Very little grass grew around here and animals were constantly on the move looking for something to eat. Not surprisingly, there were numerous potholes in the road, which was die-straight and paved with tarry goo. Marc, Philippe and I rode in formation, leaving enough room to manoeuvre so we wouldn't take each other out if one of us got squirrelly. Avoiding the potholes was a game of percentages, and for every one I missed I seemed to hit two. Every time I struck a hole the Honda shook vigorously, sending wicked vibrations through my arms. I couldn't help thinking of James Bond's famous martini line: shaken, not stirred — I kind of felt like I was both. It took everything I had in me to keep the heavy fuel-laden bike under control.

Not far from Koumpentoum, I noticed something lying on the road. I was accustomed to seeing roadkill in Canada, mostly cats, raccoons, skunks and squirrels. Because of the abundance of these unlucky critters I usually don't give it a second thought, but this one shook me up. It was a young leopard, its sleek, long-tailed body lying lifeless on the roadway. *What a shame*, I thought. A pang of sadness struck. As the three of us rode by the prone animal we gestured to each other our shock at seeing this magnificent creature lying dead.

The start of the special stage in Koumpentoum was a subject of much controversy for the next couple of days. The rally's organizers carefully control the start procedure: everyone was lined up well in advance of their start time based on the results of the day before. It takes about fifteen minutes to make it to the start line. Patrick Zaniroli, the starter, counts down *five, four, three, two, one, go!* One competitor after another, numbering in the hundreds, all receive the start signal the same way. One minute separates the top ten competitors, the rest go every thirty seconds after that. The same sequence of fingers is held up, until finally the starter points down the trail in a well-rehearsed and definitive fashion. I'd said "hello" to this stone-faced man often, and only once, during a social call in the medical tent, did I see him crack a faint smile. Zaniroli was all business. This particular day, I noticed a couple of things out of the ordinary, and some not so unusual. Hosono's XR was dripping gas onto the exhaust header pipe in a steady stream. A quick check of other privateer bikes showed similar fuel tank problems, my XR included. It leaked out of the rear fuel tank because it rubbed against the swingarm.

In my case it wasn't a big deal. In Hosono's case it looked to me like he was going to set this whole parched savannah on fire in the first kilometre. No one seemed too alarmed about the situation, yet spectators were pointing at the dripping gasoline. The riders gathered in an area just on the edge of the village that served as the refuse dump. A number of children gathered around asking for gifts or food. I gave away some candies that were part of the lunch bag competitors received each day. Mangy dogs scratched at the ground and chewed on garbage, fires smouldered nearby and the air smelled like a Texas tire fire. The second unusual thing I noticed was a rider who'd missed his start time. He was made to wait patiently off to the side until there was a spot for him to occupy. Prior to the start there was an easygoing feel among the riders. They were now familiar faces to each other and conversation came easily. Everyone knew once they'd gotten this far the finish was virtually in the bag. I pushed the Honda up a slope towards the start area in stages. I was anxious to have this day complete, the last long day of the rally.

The significance of the day's start area routine would be clear shortly after I had departed. Jean-Louis Schlesser broke rank and pulled his Renault powered buggy in front of the leading Mitsubishi of Hiroshi Masuoka. As if this bold move wasn't enough, Schlesser dragged his teammate Jose Maria Servia into the fold as well. The two buggies would take the start before their predetermined time. How they got there in the first place was beyond me, and why the TSO organizers permitted this action was unfathomable in my opinion. It apparently stemmed from a rule used in FIA rally racing, but not often in "rally raid" competition, as Paris-Dakar is officially designated. The drama unfolded quickly. Hiroshi Masuoka and his navigator Pascal Maimon were enraged — rightly so, as they had won Stage 18 and thus were supposed to start first. Schlesser and his navigator Henri Magne had finished the stage in second place and thus were slated to start behind Masuoka/ Maimon. Although only one minute separates the starters, in rally racing a one-minute advantage or disadvantage can have a profound effect on the final outcome, never mind two minutes, which is what faced Masuoka and Maimon. With the 7:28:00 overall lead they had built up, they simply had to remain calm and finish the day with at least half of that lead as a cushion to go into the final 25-kilometre special stage around Lac Rose in Dakar the next day.

What had happened was an incredible example of poor sportsmanship and spectators worldwide couldn't believe what had happened to an almost guaranteed win for Masuoka. Dust was a factor. Schlesser's interpretation of the rule book was also to blame. Shino tore after the two Schlesser/Renault/Megane buggies. In the first few kilometres, he caught up to the buggy of Servia and his navigator Jean-Marie Lurquin. An on-fire Masuoka whipped past them and then set his sights on Schlesser. Then, in an attempt to pass his archrival, he veered off the beaten track, and while making the pass hit a hidden tree stump. The impact damaged the left wheel of his Mitsubishi/Pajero/Montero and a hapless Masuoka and Maimon were forced to let Schlesser retake the lead while they repaired the car. Schlesser had set out to force an error and he had succeeded. The winner of the rally was to be decided by the FISA jury that evening. No winner could be announced in the car category until all the penalties were assessed, the videotape reviewed, and all sides of the story heard. There may be no shame in the Dakar, but shameful incidents do occur.

For me, the final stage went according to plan. I stayed safe, rode smart and made as few mistakes as possible. The grasslands opened up, and navigation was straightforward if one maintained constant focus on the roadbook and distance. At one point the track followed a dirt road underneath a power line. The 217-kilometre special went quite quickly. I stayed attentive and chose some good lines through the maze of two-track roads that connected each village. The ground became sandy and speeds went higher as the terrain opened up. There were many intersecting tracks and I was in constant doubt whether or not I was on the right course. In fact, there might have been a couple of correct lines — the one I chose worked. The special stage ended in the village of M'Bake, with many spectators and friends of competitors milling around. Franco Acerbis was there, all smiles when he saw me pull up to the finish line.

"I told you I'd see you in Dakar. I knew you'd pull through," he said and shook my hand. Back at his home in Italy, Franco had seen the television coverage of me riding. He wasn't aware of my near-disaster during Stage 17, and I didn't tell him about it until much later. Although there was still a 240-kilometre liaison stage to be completed to get me to Dakar, and a short 95-kilometre stage the next day that would take the survivors onto the podium in Dakar, I really felt like I had finished the rally in M'Bake. With a time of 3:28:42:00, I finished fifty-first for the day — my overall ranking on the provisional scoreboard rising from sixtieth to fifty-eighth.

Not surprisingly, Schlesser won the stage in the car division; Servia followed in second place. Schlesser booked a time of 2:20:39:00 while his teammate followed 5:25:00 later. The Mitsubishis of Carlos Sousa and Jutta Kleinschmidt were next to cross the finish line, both within ten minutes of Schlesser. But nothing was official yet because of the start-line shenanigans. If justice prevailed, Kleinschmidt would find herself the overall winner of the rally. Meanwhile, Masuoka and Maimon got to the end of the line 52:21:00 later in seventeenth place. Any hope of taking the overall victory was now gone. In the bike division, KTM's Giovani Sala took another win with BMW's Cyril Despres and Jimmy Lewis in second and third. Although overall leader Fabrizio Meoni finished well down, in ninth place, just over eight minutes behind the winning time of 2:28:00:00, he remained at the top of the scoreboard. In fact, he had stretched his lead by three minutes over fellow KTM rider Jordi Arcarons, who finished well down, by three minutes.

After a short pause, I rode into town and found a small store to buy some refreshments. I washed my face and hands with bottled water and sat down with some local people who were lounging about. I ate a granola bar and drank a soft drink with a small group of kids and their parents. It felt like a Sunday afternoon in the tropics. Hardly anyone was out in the midday heat. The town had an almost deserted feel to it. A quiet, peaceful, melancholy feeling washed over me. I started to de-compress. My thoughts were on Françoise, who would join me that night, and going home to our daughter a few days later. When I'd finished my drink I got back on the bike and rode another thirty-two kilometres to a Total service station where many privateers had gathered. Everyone was downing soft drinks and chattering away like a bunch of hens. It was here I realized how Hosono's rally was so much more difficult than most. He spoke no French or English, and was at pains trying to get a drink and pay for it. His calm, unwavering demeanour never faltered — no frustration was evident. It was truly remarkable how he, and many others who spoke only their native tongues, deciphered the information necessary to com-plete the rally. With more than 50% of the entrants being non-French, and English being the universal language, the disad-vantage of not speaking either had to be enormous. Of course, there are other means of communicating as well. Having an open mind to communication is far more important than actually conversing in a given language. Hosono-san possessed this quality and it made up for his lack of a common language with anyone but fellow Japanese.

I had a couple of kids wash my bike at the station and then set off down the road alone to Dakar. It was a solitary ride, but I wanted it that way. It was a personal moment and I wanted it to be a private one. A lot of the other guys rode solo too, as if it was the only and best way to savour the moment. The

Honda rumbled down the pavement as I fought to find a comfortable position on the bike. I dangled my legs, shifted back and forth, slumped down and stood up. Nothing worked. Funny enough, pavement was now harder to endure than the stimulating rides I'd taken across rugged desert. I dozed on the bike and was startled when Stephane Peterhansel and his navigator Willy pulled alongside me. Congratulatory thumbs-up flashed all round as we saluted each other's Dakar before they sped off down the road, their Nissan's snarling exhaust note fading in their wake. As my final, hard-won destination came into view, the realization that this was the end of the road truly hit home. A raging brush fire burned behind the row of shacks that lined the roadway on the outskirts of Dakar. Yet no panic by the inhabitants seemed evident. No one tried to combat the blaze. It would burn itself out when it was destined to. The city's slums reached far into the countryside. A mix of modern buildings and shantytowns provided me with the first impressions of the fabled town.

I was both elated and relieved when I finally rode along the main boulevard into the centre of Dakar. Tall, whitewashed colonial-style buildings lined the wide streets. People were everywhere along the route. It felt almost as if a riot was ready to break out. All sorts of confusion combined with no real direction seemed to create the atmosphere of a tinderbox. I stopped at a control passage, where my number was recorded. Shortly afterwards someone with a microphone tugged at my sleeve and asked me to express how I felt. "Great," is all I managed to say. I continued on past the crowds and onto the *corniche* that led to the Pointe de Alimedes and my destination for the night, the Meridian Hotel. The Meridian is located in a more remote area outside of Dakar. Along the way I rode past impeccable sandy beaches, makeshift shacks and rocky hills along the coastline. The road had a separation between the opposing lanes, and the traffic was absolute chaos. Cars were being driven aggressively in my lane. I had to watch every corner and angle: my peripheral vision was kept too busy for me to feel at ease. My mood changed. I was tired and not accustomed to being surrounded by such a throng of humanity. Crowds of people were milling about everywhere. Once past the gates of the Meridian Hotel I felt an instant sense of security. The palatial grounds of the hotel meant Western civilization and comfort. I parked the Honda where the rest of the privateers had gathered, near a large shipping container that TSO had set up to hold the trunks and spare wheels of the rallyists. It was a jubilant atmosphere. Family and friends gathered around, lots of handshaking and picture-taking was going on. The faces of my fellow riders told the story: ear-to-ear smiles abounded. It was a momentous occasion. We had endured and survived something that truly has to be experienced if you're to understand the magnitude of it all. Most riders were working on their bikes, preparing them for the final ride the next day. Other than making small repairs the work was mainly cosmetic: doing touch-ups and replacing sponsors stickers for the inevitable photos at the finish line. Other than changing the Honda's air filter there really wasn't much I had to do.

I changed into the soiled khaki cargo pants I had in my trunk. I had to walk around with one hand holding them up. My waist had dropped a couple of sizes. I scouted around the hotel looking for a place to eat or have a shower. The pool had a decent change room with hot showers so I took the first real shower I'd had in three weeks. It felt good to watch the red dust swirl down the drain as the stream of clean water beat down on my shoulders. *Luxury,* I thought, *absolute luxury!* What a great world I lived in, to have a shower every day with plenty of clean hot water. I had developed a deep appreciation for the simple things I'd often take for granted. Once cleaned up, I checked for a room at the reception desk. At first, none were available until after six o'clock when, as expected, non-finishers weren't there to occupy their rooms. When I finally got my room I spread out my things on the floor. Nothing was clean. I had no presentable shirts, my filthy pants were hanging off me, and my running shoes were Dakar ripe. Another shower confirmed the difficulty in removing the red dust from my pores. I passed in front of the full-length mirror in the room and was shocked to see how lean I was. But I felt strong, flexible and youthful. My body had adapted well to the task it was asked to do and I couldn't remember the last time I felt so full of life, so rejuvenated . . . and so hungry.

Before my scheduled rendezvous with France 2, the television channel, I tried in vain to find something to eat. The restaurant was closed to all but the BMW team people. The way I was dressed, there was no way to wedge my way in. I ate some peanuts at the bar by the pool and waited around to be interviewed. The program was called *Passion Dakar*. The host had checked with TSO to confirm that I was indeed the first Canadian ever to finish the rally. It was my claim to fame, and the end of my fabled fifteen minutes. Françoise was due to arrive at the airport at 10:00 p.m. Sure enough, she showed up in the lobby shortly after eleven. She brought with her some clean clothes and shoes after a marathon twenty-hour sequence of connecting flights to get to Dakar from Toronto. Darry, our friend from Nancy, France, was due in at midnight to join in the celebrations. I didn't get much sleep that night, but it didn't really matter. In a few days I would be home and could catch up.

* * *

Stage 20 — Sunday, January 21, 2001
Dakar, Senegal to Dakar, Senegal
Liaison: 35 km — **Special:** 25 km — **Liaison:** 35 km
Total distance: 95 km

Sleeping in a real bed had been a treat. Waking up in a clean modern hotel room, I felt order slowly creeping back into my life. I had fresh clothes, new riding pants, and I had wiped off the dust from my helmet. I went down to breakfast in the vast dining room on the lower level of the Meridian Hotel. The spread was incredible. I called back up to the room to make sure Darry and Françoise came down to eat with me. I felt overjoyed sitting on an actual chair at a real table with cloth napkins, real silverware, and a choice of food including fresh fruit, cakes, yogurt, granola and toast that left me with too many decisions to make. The freshly squeezed orange juice tasted so much sweeter than I remembered it. After breakfast, I went back upstairs, rounded up my riding gear and headed towards the *parc ferme* to get my bike for the last day.

The scene was jubilant: friendly smiling faces greeted each other. Alain Duclos was worried about his chain breaking on his bike. He had carried a spare the whole distance. For the final day he decided he had had enough and left it behind. I told him not to worry; if anything happened I'd stop and let him use what I carried to fix it. I rode with Alain back towards Dakar. We stopped for fuel and threaded our way in and out of the morning traffic. I kept a wary eye out for the mayhem on the roads. I felt reasonably awake and attentive, but it was no time to become complacent. Alain and I followed the instructions in the roadbook, which took us north out of the city towards Lac Rose, the site of the renowned final stage of a classic Paris-to-Dakar rally. The road led to a deep sand passage that pointed us towards the beach where a TSO truck was stationed. A breakfast table was set up on the beach and we talked to each other, joked around and took photos. I spoke with John Deacon, the British BMW rider, for about twenty minutes. He had salvaged a decent finish after his difficult start to the rally weeks back in Castellon. It had taken him until the eighth stage to crack the top ten on the provisional scoreboard and, once there, he'd clawed his way to sixth.

Normally, the run along the beach and around Rose Lake at Dakar is just a wrap-up show for the thousands of people who come out to watch and celebrate the finish of the legendary event. While the motorcycle division was a lock for Fabrizio Meoni, who had a twenty-five-minute lead over second place, that was not the case in the car class. The last 25 kilometres were going to be critical in deciding the overall victor in the division. Jean-Louis Schlesser, along with his teammate Jose Maria Servia, had been hit with a one-hour time penalty for jumping the start of Stage 19. They were out of the mix for a chance to clinch the overall. It would be a showdown between Jutta Kleinschmidt, who had inherited the lead, and fellow Mitsubishi driver Hiroshi Masuoka, just a few minutes behind in second.

Hubert Auriol made an emotional speech on the beach before the start of the final 25-kilometre special stage. He fought back tears as he went on to congratulate all the bike riders who finished, saying that as the result of good preparation, the finishing rate was higher than usual among the bikes. It was a moment I won't forget. The rally was next to over. Only the formality of riding a short stage remained. The sun beamed down, and we were sitting in the sand as the waves of the Atlantic washed up on shore. At the far side of this ocean lay North America and home. Life couldn't get much better for me than it was at that very moment. I felt close to being giddy. One last short ride and I could go back to the hotel, put away all my riding gear, the tools, fold up the tent and leave with the dream-like memories of the Paris-Dakar Rally etched forever in my mind. I reclined with my back against the wheel of a Tango, staring off into the Atlantic Ocean, the heels of my boots dug into the sand. The horizon faded into the sky in an unclear line. I sat with the feeling that a new beginning was on that horizon, back home on the other side of this ocean. The distance seemed inconsequential. Now, anything was possible. No challenge would be too great.

Two waves of bikes started down the beach five minutes apart for the final run to the finish line. About ten kilometres of hard beach sand took the horde of bikes into the right-hand corner that led into the dunes. I took off and charged hard down the shoreline. The XR sang a raspy note and never missed a beat. We splashed through the waves and launched off small jumps which at that speed, sent both bike and rider into the air. Spray from the waves hovered over the shoreline forming a haze above the riders. The sea air felt fresh, clean and full of oxygen. Once into the dunes, the loose sand was pushed around in waves of its own. The whoops grew larger as the track became narrow and more spectators lined the course.

The bumps tossed me around; I tightened my grip on the bars and held the throttle down. Denis Rozand passed me like I was parked, his KTM leaping across the tops of the bumps tracking straight and true. He was obviously taking out his frustrations after riding so conservatively the entire distance. At that point I backed off. Emotion swept over me. I had never felt so euphoric. I was a bit concerned about the bike, however, fearful that I might blow the motor or break something, so I didn't push. It had brought me this far and this was no time to be a hero. There was nothing left to prove. No one was going to be any more or less impressed by me passing one more guy or letting someone get by me. What I and everyone else would remember from now on was just one thing: I was the first Canadian to finish the Paris-Dakar Rally.

I slowed right down, stretching this small moment for as long as possible. I wish it could have gone on forever, this feeling of elation, joy and bewilderment. The sun was strong, the maritime air felt clean in my nostrils and lungs. Lucidity left me . . . I clouded over. All my emotions were released at once. I couldn't catch my breath, gasping as I watched the crowds that lined the course follow me. My vision blurred with tears. If this feeling could be experienced any other way I wasn't aware of it. This was the reward for my perseverance. I gasped for breath, trying to control my emotions. I slowed down even more, cruising along the side of the track, drinking in the ambience. Throngs of spectators lined the course, standing or sitting on trucks, cheering and waving. *Cherish the moment,* I told myself. It may be a once-in-a-lifetime occasion. I sped up trying to pass a group of three French riders who'd slowed to ride across the line together. I was ecstatic as I rode past the timing crew for the final time.

The American BMW rider Jimmy Lewis was lying in the timing tent being tended to by medical personnel. In a last-ditch attempt to win a stage, he'd crashed 200 metres before the finish line and injured his shoulder. He was as pale as a ghost and had an IV drip poked into his arm. It was a graphic reminder of how cruel and unforgiving the Dakar can be.

Lewis ended up seventh overall for the event. KTM's Fabrizio Meoni, who had been in the lead since Stage 10, grabbed fifth place in the stage, effectively sealing his overall victory in the 2001 Dakar. Kari Tiainen took the honour of winning the final stage. He did the 25-kilometre special in a time of 15 minutes and 48 seconds. For KTM, the 2001 Dakar would go into the history books as a stellar year. The Austrian manufacturer clinched the top five overall positions with Meoni, Jordi Arcarons, Carlo De Gavardo, Isidre Pujol Esteve and Alfie Cox. Deacon and Lewis, with sixth and seventh respectively, took top honours for BMW. The BMW twins used in the Dakar were big, powerful bikes and they had ruled for a number of years. The 2001 Dakar, however, better suited the lighter, more manoeuvrable factory KTM 700s. The rainfall in the desert had been unusually high and the resulting tall camel grass created some obstacles that didn't help the BMW twins. The average speed had been fairly slow, with little opportunity to make up time. BMW was hoping for some long, straight running over relatively smooth terrain. When it didn't materialize their hopes were shattered. Of the 142 motorcycles that left Paris, seventy-seven arrived in Dakar.

Meanwhile, Schlesser and his navigator Henri Magne took the win in the special among cars, which saw them end the rally in third and fourth overall, respectively. Kleinschmidt, the German woman who had cut her teeth in rally racing on motorcycles, crossed the finish line in fifth, 16 seconds behind Masuoka, who was just 17 seconds off the 18-minutes-and-42-second winning time of Schlesser. While Masuoka, second overall in the record books, will be remembered as the moral victor of Dakar 2001, Kleinschmidt will be remembered as the official winner.

* * *

Once past the time control I fought to stay coherent. Françoise was there with Darry. They had climbed the fence to get into the area. A TSO official came over and handed me a small blue case with a Dakar finisher's medal in it. I took it out, gave it a kiss and held it briefly before giving it to Françoise. In a way she deserved it as much as I did, if not more. She had lived the dream with me. She had encouraged me to follow that dream and gave me all the understanding and moral support any man could ask of a woman. Without her confidence in me, I may never have set out on this rally. This was about the only way I could tangibly share my victory with her. I invited her to get on the back of the bike, and we rode up onto the podium together to briefly bask in the glory of the moment. Now my Dakar was truly history. Other than taking the *balise* off of my bike and returning it to TSO, there was nothing left to do. Photographers were pointing their cameras at us from all directions. The photos that were taken of Françoise and me on the podium would appear in many Canadian newspapers and magazines.

When I received the signal that my time on the stage was up, I rode over and parked off to one side, where we were all wedged into a small area. It took hours for every bike, car and truck to drive over the podium. Crowds of people stood behind fences trying to share the feeling the competitors were experiencing. I had a special Canadian pin Françoise had brought over with her, along with some other Canadian keepsakes to give away as tokens of my appreciation. We walked over to the TSO official who'd helped me out back in Sadiola that fateful day when my bike had quit. I handed him the cast-metal pin of a Maple Leaf and said, "*Merci beaucoup.*"

The heat of the day was bearing down. Now, as my metabolism slowed after weeks of being pumped to the limit, I felt like I was beginning to suffocate. I wasn't responding to the breaths I was taking. I sat in the broiling sun sipping water and trying hard to maintain my composure. I became lost in my thoughts and seemed on the verge of delirium. Speedvision's Toby Moody, who had ensured I received plenty of TV exposure during the rally, rushed over and gave me a bear hug. He was in tears. He really took my effort to heart and shared the joy of the finish with me. He interviewed me with Françoise at my side. "I'm over the moon to be here in Dakar," I said.

Once all the competitors had their moment in the limelight,

the parade back to the Meridian Hotel began. All seventy-seven bikes lined up behind a TSO truck and rode en masse through the narrow streets of the village next to Lac Rose. I squeezed to the front to avoid breathing in the exhaust fumes of so many motorcycles. The wait in the hot sun and the excitement of the final ride around the lake had taken its toll. I wanted to get back to the hotel, park the bike and get out of my riding gear. The parade was a unique experience. John Deacon, Cyril Despres and Stephane Grignac rode near me. We did a few burnouts and a couple of small wheelies in our exuberance. When the column of riders reached the main road into Dakar, the speeds picked up and anarchy broke out. The police had each intersection blocked off but normal traffic continued on the roads. I rode on the sidewalk to get by buses and vans that blocked the way at intersections. It was a good ride and smiles a mile wide were on the faces of my fellow competitors. At one point a young scooter-mounted kid, not wearing a helmet, pulled to the front of the pack doing a prolonged wheelie. A couple of police motorcycle cops had joined us and pulled him over. I guess there were some rules in Senegal after all.

We rode through the gates of the Meridian compound and put our bikes on their stands for one of the last times in Africa. The awards presentation that evening was held on the hotel's tennis courts, where they'd set up a stage for the ceremonies. The evening was cool and serene and refreshments flowed liberally. Hundreds of people crowded into the stands to watch the prizes being given out to the various classes of cars, trucks and bikes. Emotional speeches were delivered, and all the applause was well deserved. The controversy surrounding the event was not. The Nissan team neglected to show up for some reason. According to an announcement they'd been given the wrong information about when the ceremonies started. More likely they were protesting something. Hubert Auriol made some unfavourable comments about this during the award ceremony. The unfortunate thing about the final results is that they were decided by the FIA through penalties that were handed out after the controversial incident between Matsuoka and Schlesser. A dark cloud hovered over the car division and, judging by the look on Jutta Kleinschmidt's face, I believe she felt her win was tainted. Still, for Jutta, it was a win. The Paris-Dakar Rally is rarely without controversy and some ill will. Rivalries are created, hard feelings fester, personal lives spill over into the competition and vendettas play out. The details of victory or defeat linger only in the minds of those affected. The record books only concern themselves with listing the winners — in the end, that is all that matters and all that will be remembered.

Once the awards were over Darry, Françoise and I ate with Alain Duclos, Jean Philip Darnis and his parents in the hotel dining room. It was a raucous time. The Mitsubishi team was having a water fight and numerous other teams were celebrating their finishes.

More photos were taken, handshakes were exchanged, and more thank-yous were expressed for the help that had been extended during the three weeks of the rally. The TSO crew were lavished with all sorts of praise and best wishes. The physiotherapist who'd given my arms a massage told Françoise and I that I had entered a "league of gods." Everyone kept asking her if she was proud of me. People's perception of the Dakar differs from individual to individual. I was beginning to feel it wasn't as big a deal as everyone was making it out to be. First comes the anticipation, then the elation, and after, that it gradually seems commonplace. The feelings I had about my accomplishment were personal, yet everyone around me wanted to share those feelings. Everyone wants a piece of you if you've been successful, because your accomplishment gives them a lift as well. I realized then that being part of a mythical experience involves a certain responsibility to others. It is something I had to learn to deal with. Dakar wasn't my first major motorcycling achievement but it was the first to truly capture the imagination of everyone in my orbit.

The next evening we headed to a nearby restaurant at the tip of Point des Alimedes. Rolling waves lapped at the shore, and far off in the distance the last rays of sunlight speared up from beyond the horizon, illuminating the dark billowing cumulus clouds that were hovering over it. The fresh sea air blew softly across the patio. A large gum-rubber tree spread its branches above us as coloured lights dangled overhead. The evening was as magical as our New Year's Eve in Paris, except now the anticipation had been replaced with jubilation and relaxation. To celebrate the end of the rally and my last night in Africa, Darry, Françoise and I ate a sumptuous meal. Now that the rally was behind me I looked forward to going home. Waiting for me there would be bitter cold January weather and blowing snow that most of the people I had met in Africa had never seen.

I considered myself one of the luckiest men alive.

Chapter 14

Life after Dakar

One of the most difficult aspects of the Dakar is resisting the urge to return. To prevent the rally from consuming your life takes strength equal to that of completing the rally itself. There is a powerful spell the rally casts over people, something that even now I haven't come to grips with. For a long time after I had returned home, nearly everyone who crossed my path asked me if I planned to take on the Dakar again. If the question had been posed that final evening in Dakar, I would have answered with an unequivocal no. But as time started to soften the memories of the hardships I faced, and only the positive aspects of the experience remained — such as the sensation of battling the terrain, the heat and sand and overcoming my fear of not finishing — my answer became definitely maybe. To this day, I have not returned for a number of reasons: the main one being that I wanted to take on other challenges. I tried the Dakar, and the first time out I was fortunate enough to be successful. When I set out from Paris on January 1, 2001, I was told that to finish was a victory in itself. At the time the statement held little meaning for me. Now I can attest to the truth of that statement.

What makes the victory so sweet is elusive. The surge of endorphins I felt, the breathtaking joy I experienced, the very clear image of riding across the finish line and realizing a dream I had harboured for years made me who I am. It validated how I have chosen to spend the time that defines my life. Pride doesn't enter the picture. I reserve that term for occasions like watching my daughter excel at something and seeing the expression on her face . . . that's pride. Doing the Dakar and finishing it was something else — something personal.

A bit selfish, sure. But for me the venture was as much a need as a want. I wanted to do the Dakar because of its allure; I needed to do it because taking on challenges that go beyond the norm is what drives me. I must confess, however, that I hope my Dakar legacy will be remembered the way I remember the accomplishments of my ancestors: with respect, admiration and inspiration. Despite the time penalties I incurred, and my conservative approach to the rally, I finished fifty-eighth overall. I would have been just as happy to finish last, because for me it was all about finishing. If I'd actually finished last I would have been honoured with the *lanterne rouge* — Red Lantern — a prize that is given out to the last finisher every year. Dominique Vion, a young adventurous French rider, received that distinction. If anyone had earned good energy or karma during the rally it was Vion. He rode at the back of the field and stopped to help everyone along the way. His self-prepared Honda XR400 went the distance, and sometimes he didn't get in until well past sunset.

When all was said and done I felt a kind of finisher's letdown. The project that had consumed me for so long was now complete. I already started thinking of what I would do next to fill the void that was starting to hover over me, now that my Dakar was history. I had no immediate plans for the future other than to get home and complete the unfinished projects I had put on the back burner for the past year or more. I had my stock XR650 to reassemble and my Yamaha HL500 project that had dragged on for more than ten years. I had to settle all the details surrounding the Dakar project, recover all the equipment, ship the bike back to Canada and thank all the people who'd supported my effort. Those long days in the desert had given me a chance to reflect on what I had back home, what was important and what wasn't.

Although my life slowed dramatically once the rally was over, there was a residual effect that lingered for quite a while. After I had returned home, I was besieged by the Canadian media for months. I did numerous interviews that included press, radio and television. One interview aired on the international feed on television networks such as CNN Worldwide, making it available to 170 countries. Honda Canada took my trusty XR650 to numerous shows, races and other special events. I attended many of these events on behalf of Honda. The number of people who were familiar with the Dakar was surprising, as was their interest in hearing stories of my adventure. I also did quite a number of speaking engagements that were well attended and generally lasted longer than scheduled because of the great number of questions asked by the audience. In fact, five years after the event I still receive invitations to speak at motorcycle functions, and the XR is still featured at various motorcycle-related venues.

Multiple Dakar competitor Gilles Picard warned me during the Dakar of the withdrawal symptoms that finishers experience. Immediately after the event is over there is very little to do. There is no urgency to do anything in particular, but your mind and body are still in a competitive mode. Then, gradually, a certain calm descends, an unprecedented serenity, a sense of arrival and contentment. In some ways that feeling has yet to wane for me.

I have a poster of the 2001 Dakar. On it I have small photos of myself taken during the rally, placed near the location they were taken along the route. Each bivouac is marked; the special stages are indicated; the liaison sections are shown. I think back on what I was going through, of the sheer exhilaration of riding a throbbing 650cc open-exhaust race-prepared Honda XR in such incredible terrain and conditions. I think of the difficult times when I dug deep into my reserves to maintain equilibrium. While in the thick of the rally, I wanted to get each stage over with as quickly as possible and to get to the next bivouac safe and sound. Now I wish it had never ended. I find myself craving for the sensation of leaving the "real" world behind and forging ahead at speed in some mythical place with no concern for what is left in my wake. Dakar was cleansing — a liberation from who I was and where I was. Each kilometre covered led me towards an unknown, where I would discover another part of myself that until then had been alien to me.

I am still withdrawing, and probably will be for the rest of my days.